Browning
Re-viewed

American University Studies

Series IV
English Language & Literature

Vol. 186

PETER LANG
New York • Washington, D.C./Baltimore • Boston
Bern • Frankfurt am Main • Berlin • Vienna • Paris

John Maynard

Browning Re-viewed

Review Essays, 1980-1995

PETER LANG
New York • Washington, D.C./Baltimore • Boston
Bern • Frankfurt am Main • Berlin • Vienna • Paris

Library of Congress Cataloging-in-Publication Data

Maynard, John.
Browning re-viewed: review essays, 1980-1995/ John Maynard.
p. cm. — (American university studies. Series IV,
English language and literature; vol. 186)
Includes bibliographical references (p.) and index.
1. Browning, Robert, 1812-1889—Book reviews. 2. Browning, Robert, 1812-1889—
Criticism and interpretation—History. 3. Poets, English—19th century—Biography—
Book reviews. I. Title. II. Series.
PR4231.M35 821'.8—dc21 97-27271
ISBN 0-8204-3337-3
ISSN 0741-0700

Die Deutsche Bibliothek-CIP-Einheitsaufnahme

Maynard, John:
Browning re-viewed: review essays, 1980-1995/ John Maynard.
–New York; Washington, D.C./Baltimore; Boston; Bern;
Frankfurt am Main; Berlin; Vienna; Paris: Lang.
(American university studies: Ser. 4, English language and literature; Vol. 186)
ISBN 0-8204-3337-3

Publication of this book has been aided by a grant from the Abraham and Rebecca
Stein Faculty Publication Fund of New York University, Department of English.

Cover design by Andy Ruggirello.

The paper in this book meets the guidelines for permanence and durability
of the Committee on Production Guidelines for Book Longevity
of the Council of Library Resources.

© 1998 Peter Lang Publishing, Inc., New York

All rights reserved.
Reprint or reproduction, even partially, in all forms such as microfilm,
xerography, microfiche, microcard, and offset strictly prohibited.

Printed in the United States of America.

Contents

Preface	vii
Review *Browning's Beginnings: The Art of Disclosure,* by Herbert F. Tucker, Jr.	1
Robert Browning: Year's Work, 1981	5
Robert Browning: Year's Work, 1982	15

Review
The Poet Robert Browning and his Kinsfolk by his Cousin
    Cyrus Mason, edited and with an Afterword
    by W. Craig Turner
	27

Robert Browning: Year's Work, 1983	31
How Substantial Was Robert Browning? *Browning and Italy*, by Jacob Korg *Becoming Browning: The Poems and Plays of* *Robert Browning, 1833–1846*, by Clyde de L. Ryals	45

Review
The Browning Collections: A Reconstruction with Other
    Memorabilia, compiled by
    Philip Kelley and Betty A. Coley
	53

Robert Browning: Year's Work, 1984	61
Robert Browning: Year's Work, 1985	77
Robert Browning: Year's Work, 1986	97
Robert Browning: Year's Work, 1987	115

The Decade's Work in Browning Studies	127
Robert Browning: Year's Work, 1989	159
Robert Browning: Year's Work, 1990	169
Robert Browning: Year's Work, 1991–1992	191

Reviews
  Robert Browning, by Joseph Bristow
  Robert Browning's Literary Life:
    From First Work to Masterpiece,
    by Gertrude Reese Hudson
	209

Browning: Living, Hating, Loving; or Uneven
Developments: Theory in the Browning Boondocks
  The Life of Robert Browning, by Clyde de L. Ryals
  Browning's Hatreds, by Daniel Karlin
  The Infinite Passion of Finite Hearts:
    Robert Browning and Failure in Love,
    by Pratul Pathak
	215

Index of Works by Browning	235
Index	241

Preface

Reviewing is by its nature a controversial, often necessarily somewhat polemical art. So I am not counting on my readers' agreement with me on individual works. Because the last fifteen years, the period in which most of the essays in review printed here fall, has also been a period in which Browning has been broadly revisited and re-viewed, I also do not assume that readers will agree with my overall perspective, which has been one of welcoming, with individual reservations where appropriate, work inflected by the new theoretical concerns of the period and by the new thinking about texts. I will hazard one ground of agreement with my readers: on the factual statement that I have done a great deal of reviewing and re-viewing Robert Browning. I have.

In assembling these responses to work in Browning I hope to offer a modest contribution to the history of reception at the grass roots of the cutting edge. The plot of this history, the way I have tended to narrativize our reading of Browning—is clear enough. I will only go so far in giving away the story as to indicate that it is about two re-viewing activities: seeing Browning through the lenses of various new theoretical positions; and the equally disequilibrating process of reconsidering the text of Browning's work through the also new lenses of revisionist ideas of textual legacy and authorial control. These are my abiding tales of a reviewer of 1980–1995 because they are the major figures I kept finding in the carpet of our ever changing view of a major poet. There has been a good deal of significant work—if also some silly attempts—re-viewing Browning from both these new perspectives. The story, which has brought us in some important ways a new Browning, is also not without its importance and interest in the broader history of reception.

When I was in graduate school some time ago—we all find sooner or later—we were advised to learn the text and not worry much about the criticism. Perhaps our academic culture has come of age since then for we now find in the criticism a lively debate over some of the fundamental issues of our time. So now I recommend that my students begin with reviewing as the quickest way to put themselves in a position of confronting major issues and, by stating them, to begin to develop their own positions. I hope some of these essays will lead my readers along my own paths of dialectical education and provoke them, by mastering in their turn my attempts at seizing the moment in our thought, to develop further their own opinions on some of the great issues I have confronted in my reviewing peripatetics. As I read these reviews over, I see that I found the criticism repeatedly involved in larger issues of literary substance, linguistic play, authorial control, textual priority, reader's positions, lyric versus dramatic genres, the nature of nineteenth-century discourses on hermeneutics and anthropology, multiple versions, Bloomian and post-Bloomian, of literary relations, gender and sexual definitions and conflict, imperial appropriations and political repressions, art alienated from its producers, legal discourse and literary discourse, the relations of historical texts, of Browning's time and of our New Historical time, to literary texts—and on and on: a cross section of the literary topics of our time as they played out in Browning criticism. And, after all this knowledge, there is the problem of sheer multiplicity and over-determination of literary discussion. The reader will judge how well I have kept up with and engaged this discussion; that the discussion is central to our discipline today I think is clear enough.

The practical use of bringing together these essays in review—the majority in fact something like essays written for *Review* and for the year's work section of *Victorian poetry*—is that they provide, controversial and personal though their perspective, a pretty comprehensive discussion of work on Browning for the period since 1980. In the absence of any updates of the two earlier volumes of *The Victorian Poets: A Guide to Research*, edited by Frederic E. Faverty in 1956 and 1968, the present volume fills in a chunk of time for the student of Browning looking for an overview of scholarship and criticism (mind, however, the gap!). I also refer such students to the annotated bibliographies by Sandra Donaldson published annually in *Browning Institute Studies* and its successor *Victorian Literature and Culture* and to the useful overview of all Browning scholarship in Philip Drew's *An Annotated Critical Bibliography of Robert Browning* (1990) and of this century's scholarship in Patricia O'Neill's recent *Robert Browning and Twentieth-Century Criticism* (1995), which devotes over twenty pages to the period after 1980 and even reviews my reviews—quite kindly! Full bibliographies, without annotation, are of course available in *Victorian Studies* and in the MLA International Bibliography. Finally, Mary Ellis Gibson's collection of *Critical Essays on Robert Browning* in the G. K. Hall series (1992) offers a selection of rather more recent essays. My own reviews can make no claim to have covered all works; they do offer a point of view on the many works they consider. I extend apologies nonetheless for any works that have dropped through the crevices of this *ad hoc* organization, namely editors' requests to me for review of particular works, though I did attempt reasonably comprehensive coverage in the year's work reviews.

I have presented the reviews as I wrote them, without now attempting revision or patching, except in a few places where, by ceasing to disinform, I hope like the sworn doctor to at least do no harm. I did restore review of one work, as indicated by a note, where there had not been sufficient room for inclusion in the original publication. I have left in my periodic grumps over prices of books, though the earlier figures—$15—now begin to look almost reasonable compared to the later ones—$150. The reviews also appear in the order I wrote them. The reader looking for the quickest overview should turn directly to the ten-year survey in "The Decade's Work in Browning Studies" (1989), pp. 127–157. The regular index includes all authors; it should allow readers to find quickly works by critics and scholars; it lists all authors mentioned in the reviews. A second index lists references to works by Browning by title; the reader can thus easily assemble discussions of individual volumes and individual poems.

Permission to reprint essays and reviews has been graciously extended by the editors of *Analytical & Enumerative Bibliography, Review, Studies in Browning and His Circle, Victorian Poetry,* and *Victorian Studies.* I thank especially successive editors of *Victorian Poetry,* John Stasny and Hayden Ward, for unfailingly genial and effective editorial support over many years.

Abbreviated Journal Titles

AUMLA	*Journal of the Australasian Universities Language and Literature Association*
BIS	*Browning Institute Studies* (later *VLC*)
BSN	*Browning Society Notes*
CI	*Critical Inquiry*
ELH	*English Literary History*
HLQ	*Huntington Library Quarterly*
JNT	*Journal of Narrative Technique*
MLR	*Modern Language Review*
MP	*Modern Philology*
SBHC	*Studies in Browning and His Circle*
SEL	*Studies in English Literature, 1500–1900*
TLS	*Times Literary Supplement*
VLC	*Victorian Literature and Culture* (formerly *BIS*)
VP	*Victorian Poetry*
VS	*Victorian Studies*
YULG	*Yale University Library Gazette*

Review

Browning's Beginnings: The Art of Disclosure, by Herbert F. Tucker, Jr. Minneapolis: University of Minnesota Press, 1980. xii, 257 pp.

Herbert F. Tucker's *Browning's Beginnings: The Art of Disclosure* stands out among books on Browning in recent years. It is not only a fine achievement as a first book but a major study of Browning through *Men and Women* and a significant new critical perspective to be compared, say, to W. David Shaw's *The Dialectical Temper* of thirteen years ago. Tucker draws upon Bloom's conceptions of influence and Derrida's ideas of language, difference, and absence, but his central debt is to Barbara Herrnstein Smith's *Poetic Closure*. His study of beginnings is really one of deferred endings that allow repeated renewals in Browning's poems and vision of experience. What his study discloses in Browning's poetry is a poetics that avoids closure, that puts off definite meanings and conclusive statements to keep open a future devoted to process, not finalities. As this analysis of Tucker's title alone should suggest, this is a subtle study that will defy easy summary here. Tucker's subject, as he freely grants, is really that oldest of Browning subjects, the so-called philosophy of the imperfect. His aim, which he succeeds in remarkably well, is to rescue this notion from its closed formulation as a dead philosophy and show how it lives and moves and has its (self-renewing) being in Browning's poetic practice, quick with life just because it enacts rather than concludes its faith in process in time. It is Andrea del Sarto, Tucker reminds us, who must complete imperfection by turning it into a philosophy of reach and grasp. It is Cleon who wants a poem to complete its meanings as he completes his vision of life with the image of finality, the well-wrought urn of his own dead ashes.

As his play with well-wrought urns and burial urns suggests, Tucker has a deeper critical bone to pick with what he calls formalist approaches to Browning. The result is not only a number of excellent readings of major dramatic monologues up through *Men and Women* with a fine sense of their vital resistance to closing, simplified interpretations; it is also a relative refocusing of the canon of Browning before 1855. A good deal more than half the book is occupied in studies of *Pauline, Paracelsus, Sordello*, and the dramas (with primary, though only exemplary, emphasis on *Strafford*). To give these works such pride of place is, in effect, a flaunting of formalist criticism of their relative importance. Tucker skillfully draws his thesis about Browning's style and poetic process out of the place where all studies of Browning begin, the complicated glorification and rejection of Shelley. Unlike Browning's Shelley, Browning will make an art that puts off the felicity of eternity. Failure for others (if not necessarily for Shelley) will be trying to thrust into time the permanence of eternity, thus forcing premature closure: the fault that Browning explores in *Paracelsus* and *Sordello*. The dramatic monologues are then less a departure from these works than a continuation, cases of speakers more or less committed to renewal and deferred endings ("Fra Lippo Lippi") or to a perverse desire for death-like closure ("Pictor Ignotus," "Andrea del Sarto," "Cleon"). Tucker is at his best with works such as "My Last Duchess" or "A Toccata of Galuppi's" in which he explores conflicting intentions toward openness and closure.

It is intrinsically hard to be fair to a work of such continuously fine critical insight in a brief summary. Tucker comments on poems as different as the beautiful little lyric "Home-Thoughts, From Abroad" and the hermeneutically sealed passage of book six of *Sordello* where the narrator befriends and speaks for his already more than sufficiently complicated subject with equal fineness and subtlety, showing the underlying complexity of the first, providing a useful key to the last. He brings to this deliberately restricted study of Browning's poetics a wide and very well-organized reading of Browning's life, the influences on him, and the critical heritage. Even the notes, with their genealogies of prominent critical positions of Browning, are remarkably clear and useful.

Tucker concludes that it is really the struggle between affirmation of beginnings and a sense of closure that marks Browning's art. From that view it may be that he is too sympathetic to the ever renewing but ever more obscure art of the early works that are not dramatic monologues, especially, of course, *Sordello*. Perhaps the quality of Browning's greatest art is to affirm renewal but also to traffic in some closure, for the sake of avoiding a complete inane of opening possibilities. In any case, Tucker's approach to Browning does not in itself leave enough room for the necessary process of evaluation properly so dear to formalist critics. The immense sense of poetic growth when we move from *Sordello* to *Pippa Passes* gets lost in the interesting analysis of comparative ideas about closure in the two works. There is not enough appreciation of the added "music and painting" that Browning said he was deliberately putting into his men and women, those brief, highly finished masterpieces of poetic art. A parallel problem suggests itself in Tucker's critical discourse. It will not traffic enough with summaries and generalizations; reading is exhilarating but also fatiguing. Sometimes a fine, philosophical point seems to be pursued for its own sake, obscuring rather than elucidating the text at hand. Sometimes clever play with language takes the place of critical insight. Tucker's most valuable insights were often not in the technical language of deferment and difference, of fictive structures and deconstructed signifiers, of temporal and spatial organization, important as these concepts are, but in his shrewd observations in a more common critical discourse. To read Derrida and use some of his insights into language and writing does not require that we should write criticism in his philosophical style, anymore than critics in a Coleridgian tradition could write in Coleridge's style. The studies of the dramatic monologues seem to me to be the best things in the book just because they follow Browning in bringing complicated critical ideas into a language closer to that of the common reader. Still, if it is sometimes difficult to digest, there is critical food here for thought this year and for years to come: a fine beginning to a distinguished critical career and some important beginnings to appreciation of Browning's sophistication as a poet and his centrality in the modern literature of process.

Robert Browning: Year's Work, 1981

The major event in Browning studies this year and, I would hazard, despite the importance of the long-awaited Tennyson letters, the major event in Victorian studies, is the publication of John Pettigrew's edition of Robert Browning's poems, simply titled *The Poems* (1981). Professor Pettigrew died in June 1977 at age forty-seven, tragically, as this enormous work was nearing completion. Although he modestly speaks of himself as seeing it through the press, Thomas Collins deserves to be considered something like coeditor of this edition for supplementing and completing Pettigrew's work and taking the large responsibility for the accuracy of the printed text. The edition appears in the Penguin/Yale English Poets series under the general editorship of Christopher Ricks; it is a companion to Richard Altick's separate edition of *The Ring and the Book*. Perhaps I can give no clearer indication of the quality and usefulness of this work than to say that it very well complements Altick's fine work and bears comparison with Ricks's own splendid edition of Tennyson in the Longmans series. If anything, Pettigrew took on a larger task than Ricks: *The Poems* of Browning require not one but two outsized volumes of about twelve hundred pages each (the Ricks edition is a modest eighteen hundred and thirty-five pages).

Another way of stating the importance of this work is to recall that there has been no major edition of Browning since the Macmillan of 1915 and no major critical text with annotations at all. The Ohio *The Complete Works of Robert Browning* halted with publication of volume four in 1973 (completing seven and one-half of the eight *Bells and Pomegranates*). A fifth volume, which I will discuss below, has only just appeared. Oxford has begun work on a seven-volume *The Poetical Works of Robert Browning* under Ian Jack's supervision in the Oxford English Text series (volumes one and two are announced for this fall). Despite the much debated problems with the Ohio edition, there are reasons, as I will explain, why Browning critics and scholars will wish to see the completion of that project as well as the Oxford edition. For the undergraduate or graduate class, however, or for the lover of Browning's poems who wants more than a selection, or for most scholarly and critical work, the Penguin/Yale edition should be the standard one for years to come. For these purposes I think there is only one aspect of this work that will be generally regretted. This is the exclusion of Browning's dramatic works, *Strafford, King Victor and King Charles, The Return of the Druses, A Blot in the 'Scutcheon, Colombe's Birthday, Luria,* and *A Soul's Tragedy*, as well as the later translation *The Agamemnon of Aeschylus*. The omission is understandable, inasmuch as these works doubtless would have pushed the edition into three volumes. Yet the plays belong with the poetry, far more so than, say, Tennyson's play. Indeed, they are mostly poetry. The important so-called "Essay on Shelley" has been mercifully included, though the rest of Browning's very small canon of prose (excluding letters), *The Trifler* essay on debt, the *Life of Strafford* that he claimed to have written with Forster, and the *Essay on Chatterton*, has also been left out: no great loss, certainly.

There have been no deliberate omissions of any poems by Browning. The final section brings together uncollected poems, fugitives, unpublished poems and fragments into thirty-seven pages, virtually a further volume of Browning's poetry, though of very uneven quality. The rounding up of so many fugitives (by my count thirty-one of the poems were not previously collected) would justify a book in itself. In addition there are three previously unpublished poems. Two are trifles, "Classicality Applied to Tea-Dealing" and "Last Poem," the first a learned pun, the second a social joke. A third beginning "Sipping grog one day at sea" is a fragment, apparently of a serious poem but clearly, as the editors remark, not going anywhere at the end of fourteen lines. I am sorry to report that some unpublished poems at Baylor and possibly at the University of Texas were not made available to this distinguished scholarly undertaking. Although Pettigrew searched major manuscript collections thoroughly, other unpublished work will doubtless come to light (another epigram on the schoolmaster Thomas Ready is already omitted here).

Although the Ohio edition, with its host of editors and complicated organization, stirred up an interesting, and in the long run productive, debate on nineteenth-century editing, its problems, set against the achievement of Pettigrew and Ricks, may suggest that great scholarship doesn't easily thrive on committees and division of labor. Johnson turned out his great dictionary far more efficiently than the entire French Academy did theirs. Like Elvan Kintner, who also sadly did not live to see his monumental editing work on Browning—the Elizabeth-Robert letters—put into print, Pettigrew did a major work with surprisingly little fanfare and surprisingly little capitalization from institutions aimed at promoting scholarship. His succinct and strongly argued Preface, stating his editorial principles, seems to me a persuasive resolution of most of the issues raised by the Ohio edition. Drawing on some of the information about Browning's control of the Smith, Elder 1888–1889 *The Poetical Works* elicited by the discussion of the Ohio edition, Pettigrew argues that Browning clearly exerted control over this final collected edition in his lifetime and accepts it as his copy text. Browning made corrections in the first ten of the 1888–1889 volumes when they were reissued in 1889. Pettigrew follows two separate records Browning left of his emendations for this reissue in editing the 1888–1889 *The Poetical Works*. (It is still a somewhat unclear point as to whether the amended 1888–1889 edition, as Pettigrew argues, or the 1889 reissue, as the Ohio editors argue, is the best copy text for the first ten volumes. Browning may have made other emendations in volumes 1–10 of the 1889 edition than those in his lists; on the other hand, the printers may have introduced new errors that Browning didn't catch. Neither list entirely agrees with the actual changes in the 1889 text. For the last six volumes, which Browning didn't correct before his death, both Pettigrew and the Ohio editors rightly use the 1888–1889 edition.)

Although he accepts Browning's intent to control his final text, Pettigrew does not endow him with superhuman powers to do so. He therefore, conservatively, accepts readings from earlier editions when they seem to indicate that a printer's error has crept into the later text. He also corrects a few spelling mistakes and obvious typos, standardizes spelling of words differing in England and America, regularizes the use of hyphens in adjectival combinations, adds punctuation that seems necessary for sense in a few cases, and eliminates running quotation marks. This produces a text very close to Browning's own but not slavishly following his last text against good sense or modern usage. Like the Ohio text, the Penguin/Yale rightly rejects Browning's redistribution of his earlier dramatic monologues into a number of new headings.

Two points may be made about this generally sensible editing procedure. First, there is reason to believe that *The Poetical Works*, and even the 1868 edition, may carry on printer's errors that Browning missed or even incorporate mistakes that the older Browning made in editing his earlier works. Morse Peckham makes a persuasive case for about thirty-eight emendations of *Sordello* in his *Robert Browning's Sordello: A Marginally Emended Edition* (1977). Of these, Pettigrew had already adopted ten. The point is that Pettigrew perhaps should have been less conservative in scrutinizing changes from earlier editions that could have been errors rather than deliberate changes by Browning. Even in following only the major variants Pettigrew gives, I had the impression that he was taking some printer's errors for author's emendations. One case I could check, a *Pauline* change in line 238—"won by a word again/Into my own life"—only confirms my suspicions. In 1833 "own" was "old," which indeed makes far more sense. Although the change was made in 1868 and followed in *The Poetical Works*, it is not entered in the Locker-Lampson copy of *Pauline* (Houghton) in which Browning made his revisions. Browning himself was aware that there had been many "vile misprints" in the 1868 edition and blamed them on the "printer's laziness." Especially in matters of punctuation, modern editors have every reason to be not conservative but attentive and suspicious about changes. Second, I think there is a case for following the first edition text for some works, as Altick does for *The Ring and the Book*, on historical grounds: that we are most interested in seeing Browning's art as it was produced at the time of inspiration and first publication. I believe there is a rather strong case for this with *Pauline*, indeed quite a special case because in 1888 Browning resolved to correct the "eyesore" that had bothered him for twenty years in the modestly emended 1868 text. The very changed older man seems often to wage war on his early, decidedly different sensibility in that poem. Honest lovers of Browning may disagree on this issue as on issues of which last text to use; but the Penguin/Yale text is a highly justified and reliable one, trustworthy in its general system and, with my reservations about their conservatism on emendations, in the good sense of the editorial judgments in individual cases. From a number of checks I have made against the copy text, I have found the text also very low in those human things, errors (the first ten pages of that proofreader's nightmare, *Aristophanes' Apology*, has only one error [punctuation, line 36]; I found no errors at all in the first eight pages of *Sordello*).

Pettigrew modestly offers the annotations, unlike the text, as far from definitive. In one sense this is especially true. He has collated his copy text against the first editions and the earlier collected editions of 1849, 1863, and 1868, where applicable (but not the reissue of 1865). Although he has considered all variants from these editions in editing, he offers us only the more interesting selections, as Ricks does in his Tennyson edition. This should be enough for most study of the development of a poem, but it is not, by any means, the full record of the many changes in details, both punctuation and even word choice, that the full textual apparatus of the Ohio edition offers the scholar who wants all Browning's versions of a particular poem before him. On the other hand, Pettigrew corrects a major problem of the first volumes of the Ohio text: the failure to bring in the entire manuscript and proof material available in public collections in England and America. With one exception (the Locker-Lampson *Pauline* at Harvard mentioned above) he has made full use of all the manuscripts, proofs, and emended copies of published works that I know of in the United States and England. Because Browning worked on his printer's page proofs, often called revises, as we would typed drafts, they have an importance similar to that of manuscripts for editing and for studying Browning at work. It was a major limitation of the Ohio text, until the new fifth volume, that not all such materials were collected and brought into their editing process and listed as variants. As with published variants, Pettigrew gives interesting cases of manuscript, revises, or emendation variants, not a full record. The later Ohio volumes will have the advantage of giving us full variants of these materials, too; for the student of Browning's art, the generous examples in the Penguin/Yale edition are extremely useful and interesting.

Pettigrew's explanatory annotations are extraordinarily good, a reason in itself for every serious reader of Browning to want to have this edition. The Ohio editors often did interesting spade work in history or sources in their first four volumes, but Pettigrew's annotations are more accurate, more concise, and usually cover more words that need commentary. (One exception is his somewhat understandable decision not to annotate Browning's own notes to *Paracelsus*.) But he has not shied away from other difficult problems; the notes on *Sordello* (29 pages) and *Aristophanes' Apology* (31 pages), those two Iliums of an annotator's woe, are exceptionally complete. Pettigrew is especially good at calling our attention to Browning's large and highly specialized vocabulary (his recognition of Scotticisms in Browning, for instance). He is excellent on Italian people and places and on Greek language and allusions, but also does as well on the current events of *Prince Hohenstiel-Schwangau* or the music of "Master Hugues of Saxe-Gotha." His condensed presentation and learned good humor make tracking down Browning's wide world of language part of the fun of the reading, as it should be. He tells us the Latin name for parsley *(petroselinum)* as well as swine's snout *(rostrum porcinum)*, confirms Greek methods for cooking eels, gives a pithy definition of one of the high points of British cooking—"*bubble and squeak* a mixture of meat and cabbage which, in England, masquerades as food"—and fully discusses Browning's howler over nun's attire in *Pippa Passes*. He shows how often Browning's erudition on special subjects doesn't go very deeply; yet he also leaves a tremendous tribute to Browning's education and wealth of reading in major writers and thinkers as well as curious authors.

Pettigrew's (and I would imagine also Collins') remarkably well-packed headnotes to volumes and individual poems show how fully the editors have digested the scholarship on each poem. The repeated corrections to DeVane are only one indication that we finally have an authority, poem by poem, to replace *A Browning Handbook* as the first thing we reach for in reading Browning. In an equally well-informed discussion of annotating Browning, "'Commented it Must Be': Browning Annotating Browning," (*BIS* 9:59–77), Ian Jack has shown how useful Browning's letters often are in explaining his meaning. Pettigrew has drawn on such sources in published letters. He did not use the great mass of as yet unpublished letters, doubtless a quarry for further investigation. Jack also makes the point that annotation should befriend the reader on difficult passages, especially where Browning himself has offered explanations of his meaning. This the Penguin/Yale does not often do, leaving us indeed with no editorial friend at all when we face the notoriously difficult passage in book six of *Sordello* (11.590–603) where the narrator befriends his hero to get to the metaphysical heart of the matter. Or, in the splendidly learned and concise notes to "A Death in the Desert," the beginning reader of Browning will find almost no help in trying to understand the basic strategy of the poem.

As Pettigrew so well shows, there is a great deal known and to be known about Browning and his poems. Many readers will find a few points they can correct, as I did (the authorship of the Marot epigram to *Pauline*, the term "York Street Chapel" and implication that there was a similarity between Browning's church and the Zion Chapel of "Christmas-Eve," the failure to list Harold Bloom's provocative work on "Childe Roland" in the criticism on that poem, the statement that Pound was the only person who "ever seriously claimed to have understood *Sordello*"). But these are minor issues in some three hundred and forty pages of concise notes. We have here a very trustworthy, very competent edition that will serve readers and students of Browning remarkably well for years to come.

I wish I could report as favorably on the price and format of the volumes themselves. The price, even for the paperback version, is high, about $15.00 a volume; yet there are obvious economies in the format. Margins are cramped; type for the poems is relatively small; type for the notes is so small that few will want to test their eyes reading them through—which is a shame. I would much prefer the notes on the page with the poems; good as the text is, most readers will read Browning in this edition just because of the notes. A single index of all Browning's poems in both volumes would be more helpful, if more costly. I should note that there are no double columns and few poems printed with split lines; even the paperback is stitched together rather than glued—a real plus. The editors provide a useful guide to further reading and a table of dates in Browning's life.

It is a pleasure, after Browning's many difficulties with texts in the last fifteen years, to be able to report that the fifth volume of the Ohio edition has also appeared this year and is a decided improvement on most of the first four volumes. It includes *A Soul's Tragedy* and the first volume of *Men and Women*, edited by Allan C. Dooley; *Christmas-Eve and Easter-Day*, edited by Harry Krynicky; and the Shelley essay, edited by Donald Smalley. Available manuscript and proof materials have here been included in the full variants, making this a useful record of Browning at work, especially for *Men and Women*, where we have the interesting proofs from Huntington. Changes in the 1865 *The Poetical Works* have been added to the lists of variants following Dooley's evidence that Browning corrected the 1863 edition for that reissue. Unfortunately, the editors persist in putting off to a later volume certain material, such as Elizabeth Barrett's comments on *A Soul's Tragedy*, that, as Pettigrew notes, really give us transcripts of Browning's manuscript in an early state. The editors have also become, I believe, more suspicious about the possibility of printer's and poet's errors in their copy text. They find the need for thirteen emendations in *Christmas-Eve and Easter-Day* and eighteen in *Men and Women*. Of these, Pettigrew made eleven and fifteen respectively. The Ohio changes, like those of Peckham in *Sordello*, are persuasive. Only three errors were discovered in *A Soul's Tragedy*. Again, I would hope the editors will adopt a critical stance toward all changes not *known* to be made by Browning.

I found the general introduction both better informed about the complexities of Browning's various manuscripts and texts and more tightly argued. Detailed information about the manuscript of *Paracelsus* or about the way in which the 1889 reissue was made up from the 1888–1889 *The Poetical Works* suggests that the editors are coming to know more exactly what happened in various versions of Browning's works. Editorial changes, other than emendations for errors, are still held to a minimum, without even the regularized spelling of the Penguin/Yale. The texts themselves, to judge from the samples I took for comparison with copy text, are quite commendably free from the copying errors complained of in early Ohio volumes (my samples were from *Easter-Day,* "Fra Lippo Lippi," and *Bishop Blougram's Apology;* I found no errors in twenty-six pages).

Annotation is on the whole better than that in prior volumes, generally as full as Pettigrew's and sometimes even providing explanations he misses (Heine's change of religious attitude after a fever and the "Hepzibah Tune" of rejoicing from Isaiah, *Christmas-Eve,* ll. 1115, 1356), though the opposite is also true. Pettigrew is much better on the odd word use of "Childe Roland" and generally better on literary echoes. As in earlier editions, the Ohio notes tend to a pedantic fullness of information that gives us more than we need. Dooley, for instance, tells us all of Verdi's major works in identifying Bishop Blougram's reference to *Macbeth* and he gives us a history of all the religious orders mentioned in "Fra Lippo Lippi." The hard digging apparent is commendable and pays off in Biblical identifications or full information about the figures in Lippo's *Coronation of the Virgin,* as well as in the excellent notes on spiritualism; but the Ohio editors could learn from Pettigrew's conciseness in directing his notes specifically to the points the reader needs clarified. Serious students of *Christmas-Eve and Easter-Day* and *Men and Women* will probably want to have both sets of annotations before them. They will also look forward to the Oxford edition to decide whether the Lady's palace in "The Statue and the Bust" is the Budini-Gattai (Pettigrew) or the Palazzo Grifoni (Dooley) or whether these are, like Tennyson's Hesper-Phosphor, a double name for what is one. For *A Soul's Tragedy* (not in Pettigrew) and the Shelley essay (not annotated by Pettigrew) we will have to rely on the Ohio edition alone.

As a library text beyond the resources of most scholars, the Ohio has certain comfortable features not in the Penguin/Yale. It uses large print and generous spacing. Except for the system for recording variants, which requires study to use, its apparatus is convenient. Variants, if not annotations, appear on the page with the text. There are also useful lists of Browning's redistribution of the dramatic monologues and a cumulative index of poems.

This year's bumper crop of Browning editions has squeezed out the other interesting work to which I would like to give some attention, especially Mark Siegchrist's *Rough in Brutal Print: The Legal Sources of Browning's* Red Cotton Night-Cap Country. Even with the Oxford edition expected hard on the heels of the Penguin/Yale and the Ohio editions, I hope to find room next year to give this work the favorable notice it deserves, along with some interesting articles on Browning's poetry. Finally, I would like here to second my predecessor's accolades for Herbert F. Tucker, Jr.'s *Browning's Beginnings: The Art of Disclosure* (1980), certainly one of the better critical books on Browning in the last twenty years.

Robert Browning: Year's Work, 1982

Last year, Browning studies were dominated by the appearance of the Pettigrew-Collins edition of Browning's poems in the Penguin/Yale edition. We are just now seeing the appearance of another major edition of Browning's complete works, the seven-volume Oxford edition under the competent general editorship of Ian Jack and Margaret Smith. As only one of the first two volumes announced for the year is out at the date of this review (and Oxford has not succeeded in getting the first one to me despite my pleas), I am going to defer examination of this new edition until next year—which is just as well because I have some important work from last year to mention and two biographies and two new significant critical approaches to Browning to look at.

These last two are books prepared quite independently, one by E. Warwick Slinn, in New Zealand, another by Constance Hassett in New York City. But the books have remarkable similarities. Both are essentially studies of the ways in which Browning's poems could be said to create individual identities for their speakers. Both focus essentially on the traditional major Browning: the monologues of his early and middle periods. And the two works have quite remarkable moments of congruity in the poems they discuss and even in the issues they stress in the poems. All of which is not to say that the two authors agree in their conclusions or in their readings of individual poems: only that they take on the same general problem—basic to Browning yet not confronted in a full work since Honan's study of Browning's techniques of characterization—and that they define it in terms similar enough to lead them to some of the same examples.

The distance between them is really greater than New Zealand and New York, as great in fact as New Haven and Cambridge, Massachusetts. Slinn is a professed deconstructionist for whom a signifier points only to another signifier and language exists as an abstract system quite apart from any non-symbolic reality. Criticism is thus a process of exposing the fictive quality of all discourse. Literature, indeed all language, strictly speaking means nothing but itself. The critic cuts through the sloppy or sentimental notions of the genesis of the work or its relevance as meaning or value. His business is to decode such apparent meanings back into the essential artificial structure of language that they are.

In *Browning and the Fictions of Identity* (1980), as his title suggests, Slinn approaches the issue of character in the monologues from a "dramatically based model of man as verbal artifice": that is, Browning's creations act out their quest for identity by verbal constructions and the critic displays their histrionic artifice. Personality becomes not the integrity of a single identity but a "shifting series of dramatic hypotheses, unified only by a self-perpetuating consciousness."

This view of the dis-integrity of character, troubling as it is to most of us, has quite a pedigree in the fragmented personalities offered us by most postwar literature. It has been forcefully put forward by Leo Bersani's interesting *A Future for Astyanax* (1976) and, as Hassett notes, suggested for Browning's work as early as Peckham's *Victorian Revolutionaries* (1970). That deconstruction may find an apparently comfortable home in Browning is suggested by the reviews we can find in the latest *Browning Society Notes* (12:21-27), where Slinn himself criticizes Tucker's excellent *Browning's Beginnings* (1980) for mixing Bloom with its Derrida. In turn, Angela Leighton takes Slinn to task for not sticking rigidly to his premises about linguistic self-reference (pp. 27-28).

The lesson to be learned here is really the opposite. Tucker's is the finer work, indeed one of the better works on Browning in the last decade, because it so ably combines the abstract and skeptical approach to language and meaning of a Derrida or Foucault with other new and traditional critical approaches, most notably that of Barbara Herrnstein Smith, as well as Bloom. By contrast, Slinn's work seems continuously hampered by his extra-literary premises about language and discourse. Slinn has a subtle dialectical mind, in this respect much like his author, and he illuminates rather neglected works like "Mr. Sludge," "Evelyn Hope," "Cristina," and "The Last Ride Together" by communicating the excitement of their pyrotechnic discourses. Problems emerge when he attempts to submit Browning's best-known characters to deconstructive analysis. Fra Lippo Lippi's obvious passion for the color, texture, and beautiful line of life seems hard to force into a black box labeled self-reflexive subjective fiction of identity. Our minds can follow this view: Lippi is of course, as we used to say in our New Critical courses, only so many words on a page. But our imagination runs off with them and makes a character that we call vivid, that is lifelike, and lifelike especially because it seems to make sense as a self-definition that speaks of wholeness of personality. When Slinn comes to *The Ring and the Book*, he is faced with a comparison between Caponsacchi and Guido that would equate the identity-making of the redeemed priest with the verbal inanity of the murderer—a character clearly intended by Browning to exist as an amalgam of incoherent language and fictions, who takes apart everyone else's myths as he fabricates a kaleidoscopic series of his own: a deconstructionist with a vengeance.

Leighton complains of Slinn's inconsistency, but I think it should rather be applauded, even as we note the weakness it reveals in his overall approach; he faces such problems by admitting there are fictions and fictions, some more potent than others. Eventually there emerges a debate in his own argument between a humanism that would endow certain characters with belief—whether expressed as sincerity, authenticity, integrity, or vividness—and an anti-humanism that insists on the word as distinct from the flesh.

I recommend Slinn's work for what I'm afraid it will not be appreciated, a number of fine and subtle readings of argument in the monologues. The weakness of his readings follows the weakness of his general single, excessively philosophical approach: diminution of attention to Browning's art other than in its dialectical argumentation, lack of relation to Browning's opinions on this topic, and failure to distinguish great dramatic monologues from weaker ones or to develop any system of evaluation.

Hassett does not exercise the powers of dialectical analysis of Slinn, or of the finer works by Tucker or W. David Shaw behind his. And some of her readings of much-read poems did not stay with me. But overall I think her study, *The Elusive Self in the Poetry of Robert Browning* (1982), does the better job. She begins with, or at least certainly manifests, a far firmer sense of Browning's life, intellectual and artistic context, and artistic aims. Her opening chapter is filled with good ideas about Browning's relation to the Western mode of confession and self-confrontation since Augustine, especially the comparisons between moments of epiphanic self-revelation in Browning and Meyer Abrams' definition of the Christian "right-angled event" or Wesley's "instantaneous conversions." She also has a firm sense of that most difficult issue in Browning, his own swerve away from a self-expressive art after *Sordello* toward (not necessarily to) an art that "looks hard" at an objective outside thing, even that most subjective of things outside us, others' talk about themselves—a crucial distinction that Slinn's theory of universal subjective fictions rides right over.

Hassett writes as a critic and literary historian, not as a philosopher, and she writes well. She never falls into simplistic confusions between fictions and real life, Browning and his characters, or source and work. But she does reach for the traditional vocabulary of the self of our literary humanism: sincerity, authenticity, conversion, integrity, unified identity, self-knowledge, self-awareness, "ontological certainty" expressed in "metaphors of center, core, and depth." And she has an alternative traditional vocabulary for characters' failures to inspire their fictions with potency, grace, life, or imaginative credibility: excessive subjectivity, solipsism, failed myths, failed confessions, psychic chaos, indeterminacy: all those qualities that Slinn would hold are naturally owing to the linguistic, fictive nature of all attempts at self-definition. With these critical vocabularies—words doubtless that slip, slide, "strain, crack and sometimes break under the burden" but have done duty in the ordinary universe of literature and our talk about literature—Hassett can make the meaningful distinctions that elucidate Browning's varied work rather than merely test out a philosophical theory. Far from arguing, à la Browning societies of yore, the rubicund and rosy exuberance of Browning's host of vital characters, Hassett displays Browning's work already tortuously split along the lines that divide our own critical establishment into anti-humanist and humanist camps. She shows how, on the one hand, Browning masterfully adapts a traditional religious notion of conversion and apocalypse to an inner reorientation of the self at moments of religious, amorous, or artistic epiphany. Her splendid work on Caponsacchi's monologue nicely details Browning's use of a language of last things to give credibility to the priest's conversion by Pompilia. And there are fine points about the theophanic quality of Browning's imagination as it communicates through metaphor a sense of the grace that seems to inspire his characters' moments of self-revelation. On the other hand, she seizes on just the poems, such as *Fifine at the Fair*, that best work for Slinn's philosophy of fictions, to show the other, modernist, deconstructive Browning, who easily imagines characters who are nothing but words. In between are those who quest after legitimate self-knowledge but swerve from the goal, whether through deliberation, weakness, or folly.

Hassett's broad vision is thus of a world of Browning characters who display our Western crisis over personal identity: poems that approach an area of sacredness and mythic reification by their imaginative and metaphorical force set cheek to jowl with poems that present human identity as a fun house of self-deceitful or plainly lying fictions. For a small book (about 160 pages) this is a very broad re-vision of Browning's central work that is impressively catholic in its ability to adopt the deconstructionist's idea of the elusive (or totally ineluctable) self without throwing out other perspectives on the historical place and imaginative center of Browning's art. Perhaps it is worth remarking, however, how much Browning is, in a balanced assessment like Hassett's, preoccupied with the nihilistic devil's party: *most* of his monologues show characters at war with themselves, striving with less than total success to affirm integrated coherent selves. If part of him looks backward to a world of stable selves, much of him is closer than we perhaps usually think to the extreme skepticism about personality of a Conrad or a Gide (not to mention a Beckett or a Pynchon).

Other purely critical studies of note have been few since Tucker's work. Both Slinn and Hassett could have benefited from the parallel speculations about author and character in W. David Shaw's "Projection and Empathy in Victorian Poetry" (*VP* 19:315–336). Using the ideas of Victorian theorists—Arthur Hallam, W. J. Fox, and E. S. Dallas—as starting points, W. David Shaw plays deft and interesting variations on important critical themes—especially those of empathy and projection in poetic impersonation and what Shaw calls the question of plenitude or emptiness: whether behind the masks by which he approaches the universe the impersonating poet finds God's fullness or only an empty tabula rasa. As a friend of Fox and chief dramatic poet of his age, Browning is obviously central here and Shaw offers interesting approaches to a number of his poems. Shaw's approach through nineteenth-century theorists leads him to the opposite of our contemporary mode of reader response criticism: author intention criticism. His use of it raises, however, old problems of this kind of criticism, especially those of how we can know the author's position in the text (when Browning shows through in a monologue) or how we can be sure of his position outside the text (Shaw is drawn into biographical speculations on Browning's feelings or reading that are really outside the scope of his enterprise).

George Bornstein has been moving his broad studies of the modern romantic tradition from Yeats and Eliot to Browning, with first fruits in an interesting study of "Pictor Ignotus" (*VP* 19:65–72) that reads its form by the formula of Abrams' greater romantic lyric. In "Last Romantic or Last Victorian: Yeats, Tennyson, and Browning" (*Yeats Annual* 1:114–132), he comprehensively surveys Yeats's complicated relation to Tennyson and Browning, their parallel reactions to romanticism in early and later careers, and Yeats's attempts in this to avoid merely imitating them.

We still need a new biography of Browning, at least one that covers the period up to 1860 when Honan's scholarly account takes over from Irvine's more leisurely, more critically oriented study. Perhaps no one will have the resources, time, and energy to do this until the huge amount of Browning manuscript material for which Philip Kelley has claimed responsibility for so many years is properly edited. And who would say when that will be or whether the result will serve Browning with the kind of distinguished, scholarly, definitive editorial work and commentary we associate with the letters of, say, Keats, Byron, or, now, Tennyson? Before we could have our splendid selection of great biographies of Keats we had Hyder Rollins' equally splendid editorial work. How much is still to be done on Browning's letters is indicated by Ian Jack's exemplary editing of six letters of Browning to his American publisher: "Browning on *Sordello* and *Men and Women:* Unpublished Letters to James T. Fields" (*HLQ* 45:185–199). As Jack observes, it is remarkable—but it is in fact typical of the state of Browning's correspondence—that such central letters have remained unpublished (one was previously published in part). They show Browning's (eventually abortive) plans for revising *Sordello*, his continued estimation of that poem in 1855–1856 as his best performance, his bargaining over the American edition of *Men and Women*, and his concern with correcting errors in his text of that volume.

Donald Thomas' *Robert Browning: A Life Within Life* (1983) is the first full biography since Honan and Irvine's. Based almost exclusively on previously published work, Thomas' life is not the comprehensive new biography we need. Indeed, it does not even make use of the major scholarly work on Browning's letters in the past twenty years, Elvan Kintner's excellent re-edition of the love letters. Although he cites my own study of Browning's origins and youth in his bibliography, he nowhere responds to my critiques of various biographical myths. Like a good medieval scribe he sets his various authors together and melds them. He is diplomatic, but diplomacy can easily get in the way of truth. For any matter of fact I would avoid this life as plague-stricken. As an interpretation of Browning's life and work it is, however, interesting.

It is well written, lively, and sensible within its limits of knowledge: the work of a competent professional writer. Thomas consistently highlights the morbid interest of Browning, as his previous work on Swinburne and the Marquis de Sade might lead us to expect. Here I was pleasantly surprised to find that he was not so much interested in shrinking Browning—proclaiming him sick and digging for its causes—as in doing justice to a major aspect of his genius and work. We still need to see Browning not as the Pippa of the Victorian world but as something far closer to an English Balzac or a nineteenth-century Jacobean, much preoccupied with crime and other aberrations of the heart and mind. Thomas' account at least brings this side of Browning vividly before us.

A much more important work of biography—a thorough, reliable, and very readable study—is Roy Gridley's *The Brownings and France* (1982). Gridley's graceful earlier brief biography of Browning had already called attention to the importance of French reading and thinking in Browning's work. This quite original new biography of Robert and Elizabeth's French lives—both in the literature and culture of France and in Paris and the French countryside and seaside—makes graphically clear how important this world was to their experience and art. Although Gridley has not gone to the unpublished manuscripts, his is a competent and scholarly knowledge of the Brownings' lives and works and he gives a splendid sense of the contemporary French intellectual, cultural, and political scene in which he places the Brownings. If the Brownings weren't always bored in Italy, forced "exiles from Balzac," they certainly came alive in Paris. Gridley gives students of Robert an excellent account of his reading, stressing his devotion to his favorite writer Balzac, as well as his interest in Stendhal and Flaubert. Browning's work is intelligently placed in relation to French ideas of realism and even naturalism. At a time when we all seem hell-bent on jumping back into the view that all nineteenth-century critical ideas came from Germany (though all twentieth-century from France) it is pleasant to note Gridley's good case for a French context to many of the ideas in the "Essay on Shelley." This is an important book that finely combines scholarship, wide reading, and critical good sense to give a new map of Browning's cultural and intellectual location.

To add to Thomas' stress on Browning's study of the dark passages of human nature and Gridley's focus on the French Browning's realism and even naturalism there is Dorothy Mermin's well-written and well-informed "Browning and the Primitive" (*VS* 25:211–237). Mermin performs a new reading of Browning's later poems that convincingly shows Browning's fascination with, as well as frequent revulsion from, an idea of man's primitive nature. She relates Browning's interest in primitive survivals in France, Druid ruins, and in the very un-Victorian parts of Greek culture to the development of anthropological ideas of primitive cultures as the origins, not the degradations, of civilized culture, especially the work of Edward Tyler. She shows Browning's preoccupation with primitive urges, sexuality, religion, and violence, and his location of these qualities not only in earlier primitive societies and their survivals but also in modern man's unconscious (or dreaming) self. Yet she resists the tendency to read Browning forward a few years to *Heart of Darkness*. She shows how Browning not only has a Conradian sense of the necessity/danger of acknowledging man's primitive origins but also tries hard to see in the spectacle of man's cultural evolution an argument for the need of Christian religion. I think this is quite a new and exciting approach to those late poems for which many critics have been trying to find an unlocking key. Mermin even offers interesting general comments on the redirection of Browning's art caused by this new, non-dramatic interest in myth, the unconscious, and the essential nature of man. (Unfortunately her study was completed before Frank Turner's comprehensive account of Victorian visions of Greece was available to provide a broader context for the interest in ancient Greeks as primitives.)

Finally, for those who entirely share Browning's interest in dark and morbid psychology there is Mark Siegchrist's study in cold blood (and careful scholarship) of the second-best poem of Browning's that claims to be based only on "fanciless fact, the documents indeed,/Primary lawyer pleadings for, against": *Rough in Brutal Print: The Legal Sources of Browning's*

Red Cotton Night-Cap Country (1981). Siegchrist has diligently assembled news reports and documents on the Mellerio case (changed to Miranda in the poem to avoid a libel suit), the prolonged battle in various French courts between Antonio Mellerio's jeweler cousins and his designated heirs, and his mistress and the convent of la Delivrande (la Ravissante) as to whether Mellerio was incompetent to make a will and unduly influenced by his mistress. In his introduction and summary chapter Siegchrist shows that there was no simple fact of the case, as Browning alleges, but three interpretations of the situation: that of the cousins, who wanted the estate to revert to them, that of the mistress and convent, who wished to keep their inheritance, and that of the poet, who wanted to read a universal point about the need for firmness of belief in what one does believe. All claim to deal only in facts but the poet exceeds even the greedy cousins in the amount of distortion he makes in the interests of interpreting the story by his light. Siegchrist not only presents with great clarity and charm this exposé of poet's preference for imaginative unity over the mere gold of fact that he pretends so to value; he also avoids pedantic moralizing over Browning's lapse from truth to Truth and instead makes some interesting speculations on Browning's subsequent hesitancy to write poems reading a meaning from raw newspaper or courtroom facts. (The French courts, by the way, beautifully lucid and logical, refused to leave us any decision on the main point: did Mellerio fall? or, as Browning has it, did he jump? Wrong about the nature of the convent or the mistress, the poet may still have seen, with the angels who didn't catch Mellerio, into his soul.)

I'll end with a cheer and a sour note. The cheer is for Thomas Collins' plans to bring out a new concordance to Browning's work: another great service to Browning scholarship. The sour note is a complaint about the nature of periodical publications on Browning—though perhaps it is true of work on most authors. On the whole there is obviously too much rushing into print brief articles and notes perhaps inspired by love of sharing knowledge but certainly inspired by pressures of tenure and salary review. Perhaps it is also a result of editors' desires to include many authors in publications of limited size. But the result is a general lack of weight and seasoned reflection in our publications. I hope every student of Browning who has something important to say will find a place in print. But no one who reads through the year's work (two years' work this year) can help but wish authors and editors alike would work toward chunkier items, such as Mermin's article, that may take up more than the usual ten pages for a contributor but that really are contributions to our knowledge and understanding of Browning.

Review

The Poet Robert Browning and his Kinsfolk by his Cousin Cyrus Mason, edited and with an Afterword by W. Craig Turner. Waco: Baylor University Press, 1983, xxv, 240 pp.

The Poet Robert Browning and his Kinsfolk by his Cousin Cyrus Mason has the marks of authenticity everywhere. It is so filled with ill will of a peculiarly family sort; it is so often and so confidently wrong; it is inspired by such pride in trivia as buoys up the disgruntled spirits of those who would find their personal significance in mere family qualities; it is so strongly directed by outrage at slurs at family origins and becomes so hopelessly enmired in the mythical prehistory of family genealogy; above all, it moves with so entirely little irony from envious deprecation of cousin Robert, the poet, to boastful self-congratulation at being part of the family to which that luminary (of course) owed all his shine. An authentic family document! We understand entirely why the poet said so little about this particular branch of his family—the son of his half-aunt who eventually emigrated to Australia—and why Mason should return so constantly to charges that the poet neglected and brushed aside such kinsfolk in his maturity.

Browning was no Maggie Tulliver to let himself be calcined in the crucible of family origins. These people, with their concern for their filbert fingernails and the derivation of their surname (misty signs both of aristocratic origins), with their black widow's caps and their heavy (no-veneering-there) furniture, Browning knew well enough (and was abetted sufficiently by his semi-Bohemian, Pied Piper of a father) to warn away. Cyrus recalls with indignation how the young poet, riding madly at midnight on uncle Reuben's horse York, nearly ran him down, then almost whipped him when he got into his way. Such romantic gestures weren't entirely sufficient in the age of society and prose on which the ambivalent follower of the romantics had fallen. This Puritan family disapproved of the young poet's long and unsuccessful flirtation with the theater. Yet at the production of *A Blot in the 'Scutcheon* the family was there to laugh in its Forsytean sleeve at the drama's various embarrassments. More serious, the family gathered to try to make head or tail of *Sordello* and ended up with a standing family joke. Not surprisingly, the only really striking remark in the memoir is one by the poet himself which remained, in its gist, in Cyrus's mind over the many years between his childhood knowledge of the poet and his decision to write up a history of the poet's relationship to kinsfolk after the former's death. The conventional old widow of the poet's stern and successful grandfather dared one day bring up the painful subject: "Robert, why don't you write something we ordinary folk can understand?" Quick as a Stephen Dedalus the poet silenced her: "'I must tell you' he answered petulantly 'that what I do write, is not intended to be understood by this generation.'" It is a moment that fascinates in an otherwise insipid chronicle: Mason, the naive evangelist, ignorantly leaves us this sign to interpret the young Browning's program as a poet in the light of *A Portrait of the Artist* and the poetics of the high modernist movement: a poetry that creates the sensibility of the future while it must alienate itself from the present language of the tribe: a confirmation of Pound's intuitive understanding of the modernity and centrality of *Sordello*.

The tribe of the time, in the form of widow Jane Smith Browning, shook its cap strings at the family poet's "exhibition of superiority." And these little epiphanies of the poet's relatively unrecorded early life and milieu are also precious. As a first-hand observer of the life and world of his genius cousin, Cyrus might have left us a wonderful document. There *are* some important moments and new perspectives, especially into a scholarly side of the family that, Mason claims, nurtured the artistic and bookish propensities of Browning's father and led, in turn, to what Mason defines as the family plan to make a poet. There are family rivalries here, centered on a sense that a Robert Browning would be the leader of each generation and focused on a division in this Puritan temper between worldly success (the grandfather) or scholarly and artistic values (the father). The dialectic of course ends with the artistic success story, the poet—a poet who does write for the next generation in contempt of his own yet ends up somehow married into the upper classes (as Mason notes with envy), the holder of thousands of pounds in consols, favorite dinner companion of the best (and richest) company of his generation. Well may Mason center his complaints on the odd but poignant one of the lost (family) leader: not that he sold out family values but that having fulfilled them *all* so well, he should not bring along his poorer relations with him.

In trying to generate his own limelight in the shadow of his cousin Mason misses his chance at immortality. Mostly, instead of revelation about Browning, we have Mason's own unattractive personal and class interests: A large part of a work of just over a hundred pages is devoted to Mason's compulsive attempts to establish the family on a better footing than Furnivall's footman ancestor. And much of the rest is occupied by his ego needs to make his (now) odd-seeming case of Browning's disloyalty to relatives—a poor one in any event, as Craig Turner very competently shows, because Browning had very close relations with his immediate family and very good intellectual and supportive relations with many in his large family of half-brothers and sisters near his age, especially the cultivated Rothschild bankers, Reuben and William Shergold Browning. The work is also not the wonderful window into a hidden period that we would wish it to be for two other reasons. Mason was a good deal younger than the poet and thus presents a good amount of his material secondhand. Except for the interesting family books he cites, most of his material on the origins of the Browning family before and in London is bound to be both vague and suspect. He cannot take us back into Browning's childhood or origins because he wasn't there. Even his story of the making of the family poet has a precoded, family-myth quality about it. Second, he seems not to have had too good a memory. Except for a few prominent points, most of what he tells us, as Turner's notes well reveal, could have been remembered out of published materials on Browning he might have been reading. He is perhaps four-fifths biographer (and a very naive and amateur researcher and biographer he is) and one-fifth memoirist.

And what part inventor through imaginative memory? even as a biographer who has used him very skeptically, I shudder to think. Craig Turner most kindly and with great professional courtesy made his earlier version of this edition available to me when I was studying Browning's family and early milieu. He has now, with similar generosity, given all Browning scholars a meticulously edited version of Mason's long unpublished manuscript, with full listing of changes and corrections and with full annotations. He conveniently republishes the newspaper accounts of the widow Von Müller vs. Browning case that Mason leans on to make a case about the poet's mishandling of his father's affairs. His notes and competent, scholarly, and interesting "Afterword" should forewarn any future student of Browning who uses this document of its biases and inaccuracy. I have only to disagree with him on one point, the relative value of what is left when one has taken out Mason's myth-making and his crotchets. I am afraid his own careful scholarship shows how little firsthand material Mason was able to bring out of the madeleine of envy dipped in a tea of family pride. But a little overestimation of the work on which Craig Turner has put in such a labor of scholarly accuracy is easily understandable. All those interested in this byway of Browning studies can be grateful that he insists on the highest regard for editorial clarity and biographical judgment even in this poor history by a poor relation.

Robert Browning: Year's Work, 1983

The last two years, like 1981, have seen the appearance of basic scholarship on Robert Browning that tends to overshadow the competent critical studies that have also appeared. In 1981 we had the fine Pettigrew-Collins edition of Browning's poems in the Penguin/Yale series as well as the fifth volume in the ill-fated Ohio edition, much improved over the earlier four volumes. In the succeeding two years Ian Jack and Margaret Smith have brought out the first two volumes of their *The Poetical Works of Robert Browning* in the handsome Oxford English Texts series. Fundamental as the long-delayed, much exacerbated creation of an adequate text for Browning is, the work of Philip Kelley and Betty Coley in *The Browning Collections: A Reconstruction with Other Memorabilia* (1984) is even more basic. Indeed, it is work that in logic should have preceded the attempt to create a text. The first criticism I must make of it is really a major compliment. Casual readers may, as I did originally, mistake this work for a reprint of the Sotheby Browning sale catalogue or a compilation—which would be a good deal in itself—of the various sales catalogues developed by the dealers, such as Maggs or Dobell, who bought heavily at the Browning sale. It is this, but it is a great deal more. In their desire to symbolize by their title and book cover (stamped with the cover of the Sotheby catalogue) the reconstitution of the great Browning-Barrett family collection dispersed "to the four winds" (as a contemporary news account put it) at Sotheby's auction, May, 1913, they risk readers' mistaking a major research tool for merely another curiosity of Browning enthusiasm, another Browning interest published in an odd format by Baylor.

As the interesting Introduction and second appendix tell us in detail, the Barrett-Browning family holdings—books, manuscripts, furniture, bric-a-brac, locks of hair, and literary detritus of two of the finest and most lionized poets of the nineteenth century, themselves both from literary and literate families who threw up a great deal of collectible materials—hit the cuisinart at Sotheby's because no one cared enough to cede his interests to the poets' son's (Pen's) plans for a memorial center at Casa Guidi. Either someone stole Pen's will or he neglected to make one. With pious protestations on all parts, the poet's beloved daughter-in-law and the distinguished first cousins in the family of the Barrett sent everything to the block. Pen had considerable Italian real estate holdings and it appears that his creditors could easily have been satisfied without this expedient. Kelley and Coley have thoroughly traced the sale and pursued the destination of items sold through other dealers' catalogues into public and private holdings. They have created an ongoing research file at Baylor on the sale to continue this effort. Nonetheless, two points must be made: first, the items sold at Sotheby's will probably never be fully traced and located. A large part of this list of Browning books, manuscripts, and other items is homeless waifs—Sotheby and other dealers' descriptions of items that have not surfaced and may, alas, have long since been used to wrap fish and chips or corndogs. Second, like most bibliographers, Kelley and Coley have been most important as dogged compilers rather than as collectors. There are important new items, especially from Kelley's contacts in the Barrett family and a major collection located in the Brighton Public Library (the bequest of a major purchaser at Sotheby's). But the real importance of this monumental work is that it finally identifies and catalogs an exhausting list of public and private collections. And to this there is added a survey of an astonishing number of booksellers' catalogues for sale descriptions. This is a wonderful aid to Browning students—even those who care little about book and Browningiana collecting and less about the history of the Barrett and Browning families and their real property since Robert's death.

In its seven hundred generously printed pages, *The Browning Collections* presents remarkably clearly about seven thousand items, roughly half identified from the Sotheby sale catalogue and its children and half apparently of independent provenance. Best of all, a thorough index of close to sixty pages plus sortings of entry numbers by date and by location make this huge amount of primary information on Robert and Elizabeth readily accessible. Most students will turn first and most often to the stunning lists of manuscripts, arranged by individual poems, where we finally have a comprehensive list of all the proofs, revises, and corrected copies of Browning's many editions that have kept turning up here and there to discombobulate the efforts of editors to follow the poet's intentions. With this key we can finally unlock the poet's word processor, if not his heart, and display the fine craftsman at work reprogramming and reforming his works throughout their gestation and throughout his life. There are no great surprises in new manuscripts (a re-attribution of the Theocritus translations at Harvard as copies in Robert's hand of Elizabeth's work); but there is cumulative significance in the large number of minor verses and fugitives finally corraled. There are over five pages of lists of various notebooks, two brief diaries of Robert's early Italian journeys, and assorted personal writings, address books, and memoranda. A separate section lists all the known copies of the so rare *Pauline* (along with Elizabeth's *The Battle of Marathon*).

Almost as valuable to critics will be the reconstruction of books owned by the Brownings and their families, 2519 in all. Impressive as this is, it compares poorly with the 6000 said to be in Robert's father's library alone. It is predominantly made up from bookseller's advertisements so the critic cannot necessarily expect to be able to call up the family's edition of Wordsworth's *Prelude* (which they had from its original owner Charles Eliot Norton) and find out whether the lost leader was thereby reinstated in their esteem. Still, the compilers record all that is known of such volumes and this can be a help in letting us see clearly how wide and catholic was Robert's reading. Be warned that the Browning Library contains works that Pen or Sarianna may have added after the poets' deaths. And, of course, who reads all the books they have? Still, I would love to see the copy of Donne's *Poetical Works* (1779) with Robert's signature (1834) and annotations (Aug. 6, 1837) or Arthur Jonston's *Psalmi Davidici cum Argumentis et Notis*, also with Robert's signature. Another useful section gives us 642 presentation copies of both poets, largely of course of their own works: an excellent way of tracing literary relations. A final section, clearly less exhaustive than the others, gives other books, again mostly by the Brownings, that suggest literary or personal relations: Carlyle, Swinburne, or even Faulkner's copy of Browning works. A list of 284 association manuscripts has necessarily the character of a miscellany or grab bag of items about the Brownings but not by them; yet here are items of importance to Browning's literary relations as well as his biography and personal relations.

The other sections will be of more interest to the Browning biographer or collector: likenesses and photos of the Brownings and families, works of art, household and personal effects, including thirty-seven locks of hair. Vulgar material details, these, and of no interest to the critic whose interest lies only in the history of the soul: unless, like Browning, he cares about the externals by which alone we know the soul. Even locks of hair—hideous things—tell us something of the culture of the nineteenth century. The poor corpse of Robert must have gone virtually scalped into the Abbey to satisfy the needs of friends who had to have something more physical than his immortal art by which to remember him. Especially by the aid of the excellent index, critics as well as biographers may find here suggestive associations. Students of Browning's association with the fine arts, as well as those interested in his relations with father and son, will welcome the careful work put into further authoritative lists of drawings and manuscripts by Browning's father and paintings, sculpture, and drawings by Pen—the latter consisting of works that failed at Sotheby's in 1913 and have not staged a comeback there since.

I know I am not the only student of Robert Browning's to have wished at times that Philip Kelley had confined his abundant energies to his chosen work of bringing out the letters of one of Victorian England's two greatest poetic geniuses. We have seen writer after writer, many much more recently deceased than Browning, achieve a fairly good collected letters while Kelley has been compiling these endless lists of manuscripts and collector's items. But with the appearance of such comprehensive and careful work in this volume and in the earlier companion *The Brownings' Correspondence: A Checklist* I begin to believe that our generation's belatedness may yield to leadership in the next. We now know where the primary documents are and what they are. Other items will doubtless appear, but we have a machinery to fill them into the mosaic. We now need letters and editions that bring a perspective from this large, fully assembled picture to bear on each detail. I hope this is what we will be given in the edition of the Brownings' correspondence for which two volumes have recently been announced.

As far as texts go, had this large picture been available back when the Ohio edition began, the first four volumes of that work would have been less unsatisfactory. Their fifth volume and the Pettigrew-Collins edition of *The Poems* have drawn more fully on Browning's manuscript corrections and corrected copies, manuscripts, and revises. It is one of the special strengths of the new Ian Jack–Margaret Smith *The Poetical Works*, of which two volumes comprising *Pauline, Paracelsus, Strafford*, and *Sordello* have appeared (1983, 1984), that it brings these primary materials, including the marginalia of Browning and his close friends and family and Browning's explanations from letters and memoirs, into the text and annotations. It is altogether to be deplored that the full record of manuscripts and special copies was not available even to them for these first two volumes. They give full accounts and citations not only from the well-known copy of *Pauline* that Mill read but also from the Widener (Locker-Lampson) copy corrected by Browning for the 1868 *Poetical Works* and from another corrected copy identified for them by Kelley in the John Rylands Library. For *Paracelsus* they not only print the 1835 manuscript as one of their two parallel texts but also provide Domett's annotations from his copy (Turnbull Library copy). They also cite variants from corrected copies at Berg and Yale and take note of three other copies (Harvard, Yale, and Sterling libraries) with fewer corrections. For *Strafford* they cite corrections in the Pritchard/Locker copy at Berg. In the case of *Sordello* they, like Pettigrew and Collins, cite Browning's revisions and comments in the 1840 proof copy at Boston Public Library. They also cite the comments by Domett and responses by Browning in the British Library (Ashley) copy and the extensive revisions in a copy now at Syracuse.

This is a great deal. Yet Kelley and Coley have located other special copies that should have been brought in, especially the corrected proof of the first edition of *Paracelsus* owned by A. W. Yates of Beaumont, Texas, as well as a corrected copy presented to Anna Jameson and corrections for the 1865 *Selection* and the 1872 *Poetical Works*. Similarly, they identify a very interesting transcript of *Strafford* in the Lord Chamberlain's licensing records in the British Library and the Woolner copy of *Sordello* in which D. G. Rossetti wrote "Sonnet on a first reading of 'Sordello.'" I cite these not as a criticism of the editors who, like the rest of us, had no way of knowing of these copies. It is rather a failure of the Browning scholarly world, where there has not always been the spirit of cooperation in the common aim of serving knowledge of Browning and his work that becomes disinterested literary study. The *Browning Collections* and the ongoing data bank at Baylor ensure that future Oxford volumes will provide an even fuller record of Browning's revisions and comments and the comments of friends and relations.

With regard to the actual text presented, Jack and Smith (Smith as textual editor) have, like Pettigrew and Collins, made an adequate solution to one of the major problems presented by the history of Browning's publication and found a unique, if uneconomical, solution to the other. The first problem has been that presented in a conventional attempt to establish the poet's last will on his text by the many reprints and revisions through which his earlier works went. The problem is that as Browning kept polishing and correcting (sometimes revising) his text in successive editions he kept opening the way to new errors. Word processing and computer printing would stop much of that but Browning had to correct the next edition on the last and the printers, of whom Browning was uniformly critical ("Errors of the press—past calculation!" he wrote in a copy of *Paracelsus* he presented to a friend), kept slipping in new errors he didn't always catch. On top of this, as Thomas J. Collins pointed out ("Browning's Text: A Question of Marks," *The Library* 4:70–75), there are errors, such as misplaced question marks with quotations, that go back to the first edition and perhaps even were the poet's in manuscript. Jack and Smith have adopted the same copy text as Collins and Pettigrew (the 1888–1889 *The Poetical Works*) and, like them, they include the corrections Browning made in volumes 1–10 in the Dykes Campbell copy and in a list now at Brown. A bit more than Collins and Pettigrew, they have approached this text, with the aid of various manuscripts and corrected copies—and they have used more of these than both Ohio and Penguin—on the lookout for those uncalculated errors of the press. Inasmuch as their own level of new errors is very low (I found none in an eight-page check against the copy text of *Sordello* as I also found none in the Penguin/Yale text for a similar sample), it would seem the most authoritative text. Yet I was left with the sense, as it turns out I was rightly so with the Penguin/Yale text when I reviewed it, that there are probably still cases where more skeptical treatment of changes as printer's errors rather than poet's emendations is still in order. Rather than cite a number of cases I found in reading through the variants where I might have wished to doctor the copy text, I will only note that I preferred Morse Peckham's corrections to the 1888 *Sordello* (*Robert Browning's Sordello: A Marginally Emended Edition* [1977]) in seven of the nine cases where Oxford didn't follow him. (I should add that Oxford catches a few Peckham missed.) I would also not have been as conservative in not following the somewhat authorized edition of *Strafford* (1884) where it differs from Browning's final text.

The second problem in editing Browning's text that has become increasingly clear in all the controversy since the Ohio edition hit the reviews is that of the poet murdering to correct. Nothing in Browning matches the revisions of *The Prelude* but his changes in some of his earlier works are considerable enough to give scholars and critics reason on occasion to prefer the original text to that of the septuagenarian editor of his own work (or, if you prefer, the accretions of a "continuously innovating medium"—if I recall the original Ohio phrase correctly). The Ohio edition, with its variorum readings of virtually every edition during the poet's lifetime, gives the reader the option to make his own text—which can be useful, though the inaccuracy of the first four volumes makes this hazardous.

Jack and Smith take a more decisive approach, choosing those texts where the reader would like the original and giving it fully in parallel texts with the 1888 version. We are given the 1833 *Pauline* and also the manuscript of *Paracelsus* in the Victoria and Albert. As Jack himself interestingly points out, Browning's revisions in *Pauline* were not as decisive as DeVane asserted; yet the 1833 text puts us much closer to the early Browning we normally wish to study historically when we read that work. With *Paracelsus* Browning actually reversed some of the revisions made for the 1849 *Poems*. One could even argue for a third text to show that interesting variant. Jack and Smith assume the manuscript of 1835 is closer to Browning's intention at the time because the manuscript was subject to house styling. Mr. Yates's copy of the proof sheets might complicate this story, though the manuscript, showing Browning's original punctuation, will most interest readers who want to see what Browning wrote at the time. For *Sordello*, the editors have taken the liberty of including Browning's running commentary (added in 1863 but not in the 1888–1889 copy text)—certainly a reasonable service to the reader who is then able to focus his attention on the significance of the poetry rather than the confusions of the plot.

Like the Penguin/Yale edition, this is not a variorum edition, but it offers significant variants and the more important accidentals. On this issue Professor Jack had a rather unpleasant encounter with Professor Honan in *Browning Society Notes* 13, with Honan accusing Jack of gentility, amiability, and a concern for literary tradition and Jack, more moderately, calling attention to Honan's connection with the Ohio edition and to the Oxford system for indicating significant variants in pointing. It comes down to this: that the Oxford edition doesn't offer the complete variorum apparatus of the Ohio but does provide all significant variations as judged by very well-informed and intelligent editors. For most scholarly and critical purposes it displays Browning's changes clearly and succinctly.

One problem not solved by the Oxford editors is that presented by the slow accumulation of new manuscript poems and fugitives by Browning. The juvenile "The First-Born of Egypt" and "The Dance of Death" are included, along with "Lines to the Memory of James Dow" and "A Forest Thought" as a kind of afterthought in an appendix to Volume One. Others are excluded as inappropriate to this edition. A final volume of such works would have been preferable (Penguin/Yale has them). It will be too bad not to have the Essay on Shelley somewhere in the edition, as well.

Annotation (provided by Jack) is excellent. That in the Ohio edition tended to essaylike treatment of historical points, sometimes pedantically full without adding a great deal to our understanding of the poem. Pettigrew's notes in the Penguin/Yale are models of brevity and intelligent selection. The Oxford are only slightly less concise and to the point. They are a good deal more comprehensive than the Ohio or Penguin/Yale, with usually many more items covered (for example, Oxford annotates 199 lines of *Pauline* to Ohio's 25 and Penguin/Yale's 59, and 301 lines of *Sordello*, Book V, to Ohio's 77 and Penguin/Yale's 122). Oxford is especially strong in citing parallels with other poets (particularly Shelley and other Romantics) and in Browning's own work and in identifying unusual words or phrases (also a strength of Pettigrew's annotation, which also occasionally makes identifications that Jack misses; a thorough student would be wise to consult both sets of annotations). I think Jack renders an important service to readers in befriending them when the syntactic going gets rough, as it so often does in *Sordello*. If this is what the amiable tradition does in editing—share its hard-won and sensible readings of semantic cruxes with readers less steeped in Browning—I'm all in favor of it. As a further aid to winning readers to *Sordello*, Jack has provided a kind of opera-plot summary in only fifteen pages. It should be required reading for new readers of *Sordello*. Veterans of many battles with the text—such as the present writer—may be embarrassed to find how many skirmishes with Browning's simple plot they had decisively lost without even knowing it. Collins and Pettigrew provided useful headnotes to each poem summarizing recent scholarship. Jack's edition brings what we have learned about Browning's work briefly into the notes, where it can aid directly in reading the work. An especial strength is his use of comments provided by Browning himself, in editions, in letters, and in memoirs and other records of his talk. As Jack has argued, we should obviously not ignore the large amount of Browning annotating Browning, even if we reserve the right to trust the work and not the author. Jack draws upon unpublished as well as published materials by Browning so that the notes not only summarize scholarship on a poem but often add to it. Finally, the annotation is especially strong in properly translating and identifying Browning's use of foreign quotations and phrases (another strong point in the amiable tradition). Overall it gives us a sense of the wide range of Browning's reading, especially in the classics of Greece, Rome, France, Italy, and England. It shows, as I have argued at length, how much Browning knew what he was doing when he chose to go his own way as a poet and how often his work comments, most often by differing, on the major works behind him. This is not to offer a "rather bland" Browning, as Honan has charged. It is to rescue him from charges of naivete and being a mere sport in English poetry. Like Pound, he can be radically new just because he knows the past so comprehensively.

Jack's prefaces to each of the four works in these two volumes are, like his annotations, thorough summaries of scholarship on the works with significant new contributions of his own. Although I had a few reservations about certain points (for instance, the emphasis on *Epipsychidion* as the principal Shelley poem behind *Pauline*, which is not really supported by the annotation, or the failure to be entirely clear about the difference between Browning's evolutionary view in *Paracelsus* and Darwin's), I would now turn to these well-written, concise digests of available information on the poems rather than to DeVane. Jack is thorough, accurate, and has dug hard in published (an *Edinburgh Review* article of 1829 on Paracelsus that Browning may have seen) and unpublished sources (including some of Professor Purdy's Ripert-Monclar letters). Jack tells the biographical story behind *Strafford*, with the complicated personal relations among Browning, Forster, and Macready, with accuracy and skill. Many may find it a more interesting drama than the work it precedes. The preface to *Sordello* throws new light on its composition (mostly through a sheet of paper, printed in an appendix, on which Browning seems to have collected quotations to shore up his courage to complete *Sordello* and gives a fine brief survey of Browning's sources and a translation of the full article on Sordello that Browning read in the *Biographie Universelle*.

I can join with other reviewers, and the editors themselves, in deploring the high price of these volumes ($69 and $74). They are lovely books, in the Oxford tradition, with large type, ample space, and the luxury of parallel texts for *Pauline* and *Paracelsus*. Notes are, gloriously, all on the bottom of the page, textual notes clearly separated from annotation. I am sorry half lines couldn't have been more often avoided.

Where are we now in Browning editions? Doing quite well, finally, thank you. We have a very practical two-volume Penguin/Yale edition with a reliable text and intelligent, useful annotation and good summaries of scholarship. We have two volumes toward an authoritative Oxford English Text that has a most competent text based on study of almost all known manuscripts and corrections by Browning and providing virtually all variant readings that any critic could use. Its prefaces and notes offer a fully mature biographical and critical context to Browning's work which Browning scholars may proudly set beside any other standard text. There is, finally, always the Ohio for a full variorum account of Browning's revisions, much better in its fifth volume. We could regret so much parallel effort, but should we? We have learned a great deal about Browning's publishing history since the Ohio project first began; we have now a fine text to use in the classroom and study and an authoritative text for the library and the thorough student. And the most thorough student will pick good points out of a collation of annotations in all three. Certainly our experience so far does not lead to a call for a cooperative effort in completing Ohio and Oxford. The Ohio group have made more noise about their collaborative work, but Pettigrew and his completer, Collins, and the team of Jack and Smith, have worked more effectively under the old amiable scholarly rules of individual responsibility.

Giving these major new research sources on Browning the attention they deserve forces me to give shorter space than they merit to three other books on Browning that have appeared this year. (My brief comments here will be elaborated in reviews elsewhere.) The first work is also a primary document, but not finally of major significance: Craig Turner's edition of *The Poet Robert Browning and his Kinsfolk by his Cousin Cyrus Mason* (1983). Turner does a highly professional job in editing a rather untrustworthy account of Browning and his family written by a cousin on his father's side. Turner's editing and Afterword is useful just because it points out how Mason's distance from his subject (half a century and half a globe) and his harping concern with family origins and the poet's slights to kinsfolk distort his judgment and weaken its value as a firsthand account. We have two interesting full-length critical studies of Browning this year by two well-known critics: Jacob Korg, *Browning and Italy* (1983) and Clyde de L. Ryals, *Becoming Browning: The Poems and Plays of Robert Browning, 1833–1846* (1983). Both are competent, interesting works that effectively cover major subjects in Browning. Korg's study adequately summarizes the scholarship on Browning's interests in Italian life, history, and art, though it is somewhat weaker on Italian literature. Although it adds little new to studies of Browning's life in or work on Italy, it does offer an interesting vision of the importance of Italy in encouraging Browning's mature objective style after *Sordello*. It presents his sympathetic and interested outsider's vision of the variety of human nature in Italy as a paradigm for the structure of author/speaker in the dramatic monologue. I found his views of history in Browning less persuasive.

Ryals' work seems to me finally the more interesting, despite its less promising subject. *Becoming Browning* complements Herbert Tucker's important *Browning's Beginnings* by explaining Browning's essential mode as one of irony, especially a Romantic Irony that stations the poet at increasingly higher levels of consciousness where he is aware of the limitedness of everyday life and matters but also of the insufficiency and mythic fabrication of one's becomings into higher intellectual and spiritual states. Such a vision of Browning as essentially an ironist allows Ryals, better than Korg, to suggest a model for Browning's work which unites the aims of Browning's subjective and objective poets. Browning is a humanist, as Korg would have him, focused on the human scene, yet always with a consciousness that strives to place that scene in the biggest picture to which he can aspire. The strength of Ryals' work as a new critical and theoretical approach to Browning's art is somewhat obscured by his determination to make this also a full study of the entire early Browning, which it is, and a competent one. Ryals is best on *Paracelsus, Sordello,* and *Pippa Passes,* often very good on works he doesn't like but feels obliged to cover (mostly the plays), somewhat disappointing on many of the great early dramatic monologues, even though his critical approach through irony remains persuasive there as well.

Of briefer studies this year I liked Ashton Nichols' look at the grotesque in Browning (*VP* 21:157–170, John Coates's note on Cervantes as background to "How It Strikes a Contemporary" (*SBHC* 11:41–46), and John Hunter Lammers' free-wheeling "Free Association Versus Unity: Browning's Imagination and Philosophy of Composition, 1833–1864" (*SBHC* 11:9–28). There were two other good studies of Italian backgrounds to complement Korg's: Mary Louise Albrecht on "The Statue and the Bust" (*SBHC* 11:47–60) and Allan C. Dooley on "Andrea del Sarto" (*MP* 81:38–46); Lawrence Poston's "Counter and Coin: Form as Meaning in 'The Statue and the Bust'" (*VP* 21:379–391) makes a thorough analysis of local and general form in the poem as an analogue to the themes of Browning's fable.

Anne Williams (*VP* 21:27–42) proposes facing death as the essential subject of "Childe Roland"—a good idea a bit over-argued. Rita Maria Verbrugge's attempt to show that Browning plays with "Molinist" in both its senses, the quietism of Miguel de Molinos (explicitly referred to in *The Ring and the Book*) and the quite different theology of Louis de Molina (*VP* 21:229–240) seems to me to overlook Browning's own heretical Protestant bias and gives Browning and his reader too much credit for knowledge of Catholic theological history, knowledgeable as the article is itself. Finally, I enjoyed Margaret

Belcher's thorough trouncing of the bard on one point, his unfair allusion to Pugin in "Bishop Blougram's Apology" (*VP* 21:171–183). It brings home a point about Browning's art and its appearance of realistic detail that both Korg and Albrecht make well about Browning's Italian allusions, that Browning liked to give the appearance of real toads in his imaginary gardens, but insisted upon his poet's right to lie. As Korg well puts it, Browning "was entirely capable of going to much trouble to learn small facts . . . and then altering them to suit the needs of his poem." Source hunters and literalists take warning! Artist at work.

How Substantial Was Robert Browning?

Browning and Italy, by Jacob Korg. Athens: Ohio University Press, 1983. ix, 246 pp.

Becoming Browning: The Poems and Plays of Robert Browning, 1833–1846, by Clyde de L. Ryals. Columbus: Ohio State University Press, 1983. x, 292 pp.

Over the years discussion of Robert Browning has tended to be dominated by biographical issues. As with the very different life of Keats, Browning's life seems to stand in a special kind of symbolic relation to his work. Coming from a sheltered, very self-involved family, he moves out, in both life and work, to embrace a rich world of men and women. He leads Elizabeth Barrett out of her far more sheltered, invalided, life; they find a brilliant life of love, high art, political engagement, and literary society in Italy. The loss of Elizabeth brings Robert to the dark tower but, from there, back to a more profound involvement with human life, in which he confronts, most magnificently in *The Ring and the Book*, the depths of depravity, the heights of selflessness and love, of humanity. Were there two Robert Brownings? Henry James initiated the question grandly and it has echoed ever since in biographies. Yet the diner-out and man of the world isn't so far as many would like to think from the central biographical-critical idea: the poet involved with his world, student of men and women, fierce metallurgist intent on smelting in his poems no less than the truth of human life.

The conception of Browning, man and poet, that emerges has attractive mass in our days when even nuclear particles wink and disappear into quarks and photons, and signifiers point only to other signifiers in the endless recessions of aesthetic theory. It is not surprising that while most attention in Browning studies recently has been turned to controversy over the substantiality of the various editions—Ohio, Penguin/Yale, and now Oxford English Text—there has been emerging a very real debate—sometimes explicit, sometimes only implicit—over the traditional vision of the substantiality of the poet and his works. Back in the sixties, W. David Shaw's *The Dialectical Temper* focused brilliantly on the process of argumentation in Browning that created not so much a solid vision of human life as Kierkegaardian levels of being in his characters. Hillis Miller's *The Disappearance of God* saw all Browning's characters confronting an essentially identical existential condition, swimming for very life in the rough waves of phenomena, yet driven by a spark of divinity within to find a way to transcend reality in its very apprehension. In biography, Park Honan uncovered the restless, disturbed side of the older Browning, showing lumps and faults, threatening to crack entirely under the pressure of the great potter's shaping blows. My own study of the young Browning disassembled simple fictions of the biographical Browning into a fluid diversity of family and cultural streams and personal potentialities. Following Betty Miller's excessive account of Browning's guilty abandonment of his subjective heritage in Shelley, critics such as Harold Bloom have seen Browning's work not so much as an engagement with real life as a prolonged encounter with his Romantic forebears.

More recently. Herbert Tucker produced *Browning's Beginnings* (1980), an excellent first book with an eclectic theoretical background in Bloom, Derrida, and Barbara Herrnstein Smith that formulates the issue explicitly in terms of Post-Structuralist ideas. In Tucker's view, Browning creates a poetic discourse that avoids finality, whether of life or art. Browning puts off closure, avoids definitive meanings and conclusive dramatic statements. He is always beginning again, avoiding artistic closure and finality by a process of differing from his predecessors and from his own earlier work. It is modern poetry precisely because the mind must always act, again and again, in an endless process of finding what will suffice—and of course nothing really will, or the process would have ended long ago. Two even more recent studies, by Constance Hassett (*The Elusive Self in the Poetry of Robert Browning*, 1982) and E. Warwick Slinn (*Browning and the Fictions of Identity*, 1980) come even closer to the issue of substantiality, though neither is as impressive an approach to Browning as Tucker's fine work. Slinn subjects Browning to a rigorous reading on a "dramatically based model of man as verbal artifice." Personality, substantial character, the Browningesque world of so many critics and biographers is dissolved into a "shifting series of dramatic hypotheses, unified only by a self-perpetuating consciousness (pp. 154, 156)." The center of human character will not hold. *Uberhaupt* this Post-Structuralist vision of character *stammt aus Browning*. Hassett's work, very much on the same track, seems to me better in subjecting this ideology to an historical vision of Browning's works within her special subject of conversion. Earlier Browning tends to work to a vision of conversion that creates a coherent personality for its subject; later Browning begins to deconstruct its own sense of stable, substantial character. Perhaps there is a moment in which the idea of coherent, stable character is created and another when it is destroyed: Browning presents those crises.

In the context of this larger discussion, two new full-length studies of Browning by senior scholars, Jacob Korg's *Browning and Italy* and Clyde de L. Ryals's *Becoming Browning: The Poems and Plays of Robert Browning, 1833–1846*, make rather opposing statements. Korg ignores the discussion itself, yet the premises and structure of his inquiry make a very decisive statement. He finds in Italy the essential real object on which Browning cuts his personal and poetic teeth. Browning's two trips to Italy as a young poet, in 1838 and 1844, and then his long life in Italy in his middle years until Elizabeth's death are crucial in his development into the objective dramatic poet that Korg admires. It is a settling, attractive idea which affords an irresistable research project for anyone who shares the Brownings' interest in Italy. Korg has been and seen, and he shows us how the real became the poetry. He accounts for Browning's swerve away from the intricacies of *Sordello*. Browning's own Italian research for that perplexed, inward-turned account of the way of a poet's soul brought him to a very different vision from that of the poem. In Venice, Browning—later the narrator Browning of *Sordello*—sees and realizes the plight of poor suffering humanity; he adopts his muse from the poor women he observes there, thus making manifest the objective side of his poetic genius. "Direct experience of Italy and Italian life" rescues Browning from the abstractions of his excessively subjective heritage and lets him focus his art on the human scene. The varied human theater of Italian life opens Browning's eyes to the potentialities in a full display of the variety of human nature—men and women—as the great subject of his art. And, more interestingly, Browning's position in Italy—the keenly interested and sympathetic observer who nonetheless retains his critical stance as a representative of a different nation and set of values—sets up the characteristic relation of sympathy/judgment of the dramatic monologist to his subject.

Writing a book around a single theme is difficult. Browning doesn't in fact write all that much about human life in contemporary Italy as he would have experienced it however much the realist-fantasy melodrama of *Pippa Passes* (following immediately on *Sordello*) suggests that Italy was a gateway to Browning's turn to the dramatic monologue as his central poetic form. Korg stresses that his is a critical study, but the organization is determined mostly by the connecting story of Browning's encounters with Italy—a pleasant story that Korg retells well. (He has consulted the Hall Griffin papers in the British Library and has seen Browning's brief records of his Italian journeys, but most of his account repeats previous biographies, with some new first-hand impressions of places Browning visited and art Browning saw.) On top of this account, the past Italy, which is the major use of Italy in Browning's work, comes in somewhat awkwardly. Korg wishes to move from the present Italy that Browning saw to the past Italy that Browning more often writes about as if they were both substantial realities confronted by the poet. But the past, especially for a poet so concerned with art history, is not so much reality as fictions of history (like the documents in *The Old Yellow Book*) and works of art. Korg's paradigm of poet-confronts-reality-creates-art is undermined by the more common one of poet-confronts-art-creates-art. Korg summarizes Browning's sources in history and art without adding much that is new, though he draws together conveniently a great deal of Browning scholars' collective digging among old pictures and places. His ideas of history in Browning, poetry as resuscitation of the past, seem somewhat naive as historiography and don't relate Browning sufficiently well to the many complicated strands of historical thinking in his time. The third subject implicit in the topic, that of Browning's relation to Italian literature, is dealt with least adequately. Korg's work is a convenient and generally reliable summary of what we know of Browning's poems of Italian life and art. Perhaps the most important critical point he raises comes up incidentally as the result of repeatedly comparing Browning's art to its sources in Italian artifacts or history: that Browning was always exercising his poet's right to lie. As Korg well puts it, Browning "was entirely capable of going to much trouble to learn small facts . . . and then altering them to suit the needs of his poem" (p. 187). The point is not highlighted, perhaps because it is somewhat subversive of Korg's general thesis. Browning put real toads in his imaginary gardens, as Marianne Moore might say, to make them even more powerful fictions.[1] Italy does not so much do the grinding as provide more grist for his imagination's mill.

Browning wrote, "Florence looks to us more beautiful than ever after Rome. I love the very stones of it, to say nothing of the cypresses and river" (p. 95). So spoke *Mrs.* Browning. Mr. Browning, despite the testimony of "De Gustibus," generally rather preferred France, especially as a contemporary social and intellectual reality with which he and his mind could interact. That was the subject of a fine study by Roy Gridley of two years ago (*The Brownings and France*, 1982), to which Korg's seems almost planned as a companion piece: tours with Browning—in France, in Italy. Browning's love for France, and the major influence of French literature and culture on his work,

---

[1] I borrow the nice application of Moore's conceit from Mary Louise Albrecht, "The Palace and Art Objects in 'The Statue and the Bust,' " *SBHC* 11:47–60, in a study that stresses Browning's high-handedness in reassembling history for his poetic aim. Allan C. Dooley, "Andrea, Raphael, and the Moment of 'Andrea del Sarto,' " *MP* 81:38–46, supplements Korg on another Italian old favorite.

was to some extent news, especially in the accumulation of detail that Gridley presented. Browning's interest in Italy is, of course, not. Indeed both Gridley *and* Korg contribute to our overall vision of Browning by reminding the Italo-phile in most of us of the limits to Browning's immersion in Italy, especially in contrast to his enthusiasm for contemporary French culture. Korg correctly stresses how little contact Browning sought with contemporary Italians and Italian culture.

The bulk of Korg's work is a very competent job of compilation and collection. But its strength, the clear vision of what influence confrontation with Italian realities had on Browning, is also its weakness in the larger critical debate it ignores. We are essentially given a finely tuned version of the traditional Chestertonian vision of a hearty art made from the assured and manifest realities of the sunny South. That Chesterton built his own old ale and small human community vision as a bulwark against his more than Conradian fears of unreality and disintegration should give critics in his tradition at least some pause.

Clyde de L. Ryals, who has already published a good study of the late Browning, might seem a glutton for punishment. In *Becoming Browning,* he has moved back from the hard and unread late Browning to the hard and little read early Browning. Unlike Korg's, his work is very much aware of the broad critical controversies that have been developing around the definition of Browning and his art. In many ways his work attempts a broad mediation and conciliation of disparate views, much as Browning himself in his essay on Shelley sought to balance and credit both poetics from which he could see himself derived, the subjective (or Shelleyan), the objective (or Shakespearean). Although Ryals's book fills in the context for Browning's early poems, it is a work essentially of criticism as Korg's is one essentially of biography. Because it puts forward a general theoretical definition of Browning's art rather than a genetic account of source-into-work, it is bound to be more controversial and likely to be more influential.

If Korg's study of Browning and Italy has to undergo comparison with Gridley's of Browning and France, Ryals's more critically focused and theoretical work will necessarily have to withstand comparison with Tucker's fine and innovative *Browning's Beginnings*. It says a good deal for Ryals's *Becoming Browning* that it can withstand the comparison, even though it is neither quite so exciting in its readings nor so strong in its critical apparatus. Both critics cover essentially the same material, as their similar titles suggest. Whereas Tucker looked at the dynamics of Browning's art as an attempt to avoid artistic closure and finality, Ryals is more concerned with rhetoric than poetics, especially the way in which Browning creates as ironic structure in most of his work. Ryals identifies this with Romantic irony, especially as it was defined in German critical writing of the Romantic period. His aim is not to make a dubious point about Browning's debt to German culture (a third companion travel guide on Browning and Germany should not be written), but to define the peculiar art Browning develops most fully in *Sordello* and uses as a structure for his best monologues. If Browning, in Tucker's view of him, is always beginning over again, in Ryals's he is always becoming, moving to position himself at a higher level of being or consciousness but always aware of the ironic crosslights this creates: of the limitedness of everyday life and matters; of the insufficiency and mythic fabrication of one's becomings into higher intellectual and spiritual states. Ryals offers this as an approach that simultaneously constructs and deconstructs Browning along with Browning's own movements. As such, his view is close to Constance Hassett's vision of conversion and deconversion.

The critical conception of Browning as a master of a complicated double irony is a bold and quite convincing new framework for understanding Browning's achievement. Taking the young Browning through *Bells and Pomegranates*, Ryals offers impressive readings of Browning's ironic patterns, from the opening *Pauline* and *Paracelsus*, with the increasing self-division of the first and the full dramatic irony of aspiration, attainment, failure, aspiration in failure of *Paracelsus* to the complicated ironic relations of speaker and implied author in the famous early dramatic monologues. As with Tucker (to whose book, by the way, Ryals acknowledges some debt, though his thinking was essentially complete before Tucker's book came out), his finest work is on *Sordello*. Where Tucker dazzles, Ryals makes solid headway in rendering this poem comprehensible, especially by focusing on the radically shifting and strangely humorous motions of the narrator in his ironic presentation of Sordello's possibilities and failure. Such a critical strategy is sufficiently successful to help take even the least patient readers into the work: "Only believe me," as the narrator of *Sordello* futilely commanded.

Ryals's study, also like Tucker's, is weaker where it ought to be strongest: on the glories of early Browning in *Dramatic Lyrics and Dramatic Romances and Lyrics* (however, again like Tucker, his study of *Pippa Passes* is excellent). The book also suffers, as Korg's does, from DeVane-ism: a disease that drives Browning critics to cover *every* work by Browning in their purview and to retell all the well-known facts of publication and appearance. Inasmuch as Ryals covers early plays that he likes and dislikes alike, I would also recommend this as a good general study of the early works, though that is not its essential virtue.

Ryals fashions a new approach to Browning by borrowing equally from the insights of those who argue for the substantial, objective Browning and those who see his art as a fabric, or maze, of dialectic and fictive structures that unravels itself. Occasionally he seems to attempt to wash away controversy in compromise. But on the whole his study illuminates Browning precisely because it allows these diverse views of Browning's art to play their conflicting and often ironic patterns over his puzzling yet so manifest art. The quite conflicting visions of Browning presented by Korg and Ryals suggest that the broad issue of substantiality will continue to be a subject for debate in a variety of new arguments and critical structures. After all, what is more basic than the issue of substance: our own, our world's, our creations'?

Review[1]

The Browning Collections: A Reconstruction with Other Memorabilia: The Library, First Works, Presentation Volumes, Manuscripts, Likenesses, Works of Art, Household and Personal Effects, and Other Association Items of Robert and Elizabeth Barrett Browning, compiled by Philip Kelley and Betty A. Coley. Winfield, Kansas: Wedgestone Press, 1984. lvi, pp. 708.

Although scholars hoard and treasure and massage every rare scrap of contemporary information about Aeschylus, Chaucer, or Shakespeare, few have known what to do with the different problem of many Victorian or modern authors: the great mass of records, manuscripts, books, memorabilia, and bric-a-brac of all sorts that is often scattered everywhere behind him when the writer parts in glory. There is no better example than the Brownings, whose case doubles the complications by the presence of not one but two major writers and by the unusual thoroughness with which history scattered their remains about the world. For scholars they have presented an especially acute problem of locating major items, manuscripts of poems, letters centrally important to the biographical record, evidence in books or association items of the poets' interests, culture, or friends. The troubled history in the past twenty years of the quest for the true grail of the proper copy-text for Browning's works (we now have three major editions competing for recognition, one complete, two still in process, and a long history of acrimony) has been in good measure due to editors' initial ignorance of the large manuscript record in letters, manuscripts and proofsheets that could supplement

---

[1] This review repeats parts of the brief notice in the 1983 Year's Work review, but seemed sufficiently different to appear separately—1997 note.

abstract editing theory with knowledge of the actual publishing practice in this poet's case. Even the importance of proofsheets and revises—used in effect as typed copies for author's revision in a way no author would dare today—as records of the author at work has only slowly become evident as the proofs themselves have come to light, scattered in collections in both hemispheres and three or four continents. For librarians of special collections there has been the problem not only of how to find space to store materials that range from conventional manuscripts to rings, paintings, or even furniture, but also of how to catalog and identify such varied and disparate materials.

Initially, the development of an entire large library at Baylor University in Waco, Texas, devoted to Browning materials, seemed somehow droll: a whole library for the Brownings? Yet slowly, it has been filling up with the seemingly unfailing flow of manuscripts and memorabilia that keep hitting the market. Indeed, special collections begin to look something like auction houses, and their catalogues like those of auctioneers. Doubtless Betty Coley and Philip Kelley, in their *The Browning Collections: A Reconstruction*, offer the correct solution to this problem of increasingly unwieldy accumulations of miscellaneous remains of genius: in effect, to make a worldwide catalog, not so different from that of an expert auctioneer's, of physical objects—of writings and other matter of all kinds organized by appropriate classes—owned by the poets or significantly related to them. As with good auctioneers, Coley and Kelley have also rightly chosen to list everything of value and, better than most auctioneers, they have not yielded to the temptation to vague descriptions of general lots (e.g., a large collection of books, formerly in the possession of Robert and Elizabeth Browning, some with interesting inscriptions) that would leave researchers and catalogers groping in the dark for important sources of information. Their rather unprecedented and successful attempt to provide a full world list of Browning items runs the risk of not obtaining the recognition it deserves, both by students of the Brownings and by scholars and librarians dealing with similar embarrassments of riches, rather ironically, just because the authors have accepted and played with the comparisons to an auctioneer's catalogue. They have taken their title from an actual Sotheby auction, a rather famous—or notorious—one in 1913 and they have stamped their cover and end pages with replicas of the Sotheby catalogue.

Casual readers may, as I did originally, thus mistake this work for a reprint of the Sotheby Browning sale catalogue or a compilation—which would be a good deal in itself—of the various sales catalogues developed by the dealers, such as Maggs or Dobell, who bought heavily at the Browning sale. The work is this, but it is a great deal more. In their desire to symbolize by their title and book cover the reconstitution of the great Browning-Barrett family collection dispersed "to the four winds" (as a contemporary news account put it) at Sotheby's auction, they risk readers' mistaking a major and rather innovative research tool for merely another curiosity of Browning enthusiasm, another Browning interest published in an odd format by Baylor.

As the interesting introduction (a kind of biography of the poet's real property) and second appendix tell us in detail, the Barrett-Browning family holdings—books, manuscripts, furniture, bric-a-brac, locks of hair, and literary detritus of two of the finest and most lionized poets of the nineteenth century, themselves both from literary and literate families who threw up a great deal of collectible materials—hit the cuisinart at Sotheby's because no one cared enough to cede their interests to the poets' son's (Pen's) plans for a memorial center at Casa Guidi in Florence. Either someone stole Pen's will or he neglected to make one. With pious protestations on all parts, the poet's beloved daughter-in-law and the distinguished first cousins in the family of the Barretts sent everything to the block. Pen had considerable Italian real estate holdings and it appears that his creditors could easily have been satisfied without this expedient. Kelley and Coley have thoroughly traced the sale and pursued the destination of items sold through other dealers' catalogues into public and private holdings. They have created an ongoing research file at Baylor on the sale to continue this effort. Nonetheless, two points must be made. One: the items sold at Sotheby's will probably never be fully traced and located. A large part of this list of Browning books, manuscripts and other items is homeless waifs—

Sotheby and other dealers' descriptions of items that have not surfaced and may, alas, have long since been used to wrap fish and chips or corndogs. Two: Kelley and Coley have been most important as dogged and thorough compilers rather than as discoverers or collectors. There are important new items, especially from Kelley's contacts in the Barrett family and a major collection located in the Brighton Public Library (the bequest of a major purchaser at Sotheby's). But the real importance of this monumental work is that it finally identifies and catalogs an exhausting list of public and private collections. And to this there is added a survey of an astonishing number of booksellers' catalogues for sale descriptions. This is a wonderful aid to Browning students—even those who care little about book and Browningiana collecting and less about the history of the Barrett and Browning families and their real property since Robert's death. (Those who can resist details such as the identity of the present owner of the Barrett's West Indian estate at Cinnamon Hill—singer Johnny Cash.) For scholars of other authors, it provides a very impressive demonstration of the research value of a universal list of literary holdings throughout the world.

In its seven hundred generously printed pages, *The Browning Collections* presents remarkably clearly about seven thousand items, roughly half identified from the Sotheby sale catalogue and its children and half apparently of independent provenance. Best of all, a thorough index of close to sixty pages plus sortings of entry numbers by date and location makes this huge amount of primary information on Robert and Elizabeth readily accessible. Most students will turn first and most often to the stunning lists of manuscripts, arranged by individual poems, where we finally have a comprehensive list of all the proofs, revises and corrected copies of Browning's many editions that have kept turning up here and there to discombobulate the efforts of editors to follow the poet's intentions. With this key we can finally unlock the poet's word processor, if not his heart, and display the fine craftsman at work reprogramming and reformatting his works throughout their gestation and throughout his life. There are no great surprises in new manuscripts; but there is cumulative significance in the large number of minor verses and fugitives finally corralled. There are over five pages of lists of various notebooks, two brief diaries of Robert's early Italian journeys, and assorted personal writings, address books, and memoranda. Perhaps most interesting are a great number of special annotated editions or manuscripts, corrected proofs of Robert's masterwork, *Men and Women*, a copy of the drama *A Blot in the 'Scutcheon* in Robert's sister's hand, altered for acting by the great actor-director Macready, a copy of Robert's *Colombe's Birthday* prepared by Robert for a stage presentation, corrections by Robert in volumes 3–6 of his 1872 *Poetical Works*. (This last has already led to new conclusions by Michael Meredith about Browning's practice in revising his work; in the aggregate, this kind of information should be of great use to editors.) A separate section lists all the known copies of the so rare, first published poem by Robert, *Pauline*, and that by Elizabeth, *The Battle of Marathon*. The authors limit their descriptions to brief identification; rightly, I believe. The list will be of great aid to future, more formal, bibliographical descriptions but it would have made the survey, which is essentially a checklist of items, impossibly bulky to attempt to include more adequate descriptions.

The reconstruction of books owned by the Brownings and their families, 2519 in all, will be of great use to Browning critics and also sets a standard for compilation of an author's library from libraries, private collections, and sellers' records around the world. Impressive as this is, it still compares poorly with the 6000 said to be in Robert's father's library alone. It is predominantly made up from booksellers' advertisements so the critic cannot necessarily expect to be able to call up the family's edition of Wordsworth's *Prelude* (which they had from its original owner, Charles Eliot Norton) and find out whether the lost leader was thereby reinstated in their esteem. Still, the compilers record all that is known of such volumes, and this can be a help in letting us see clearly how wide and catholic was Robert's reading. Be warned that the Browning Library contains works that Pen or Sarianna may have added after the poets' deaths. And, of course, who reads all the books they have? Still, what Browning student wouldn't love to see the copy of Donne's *Poetical Works* (1779) with Robert's signature (1834) and annotations (August 6, 1837) (as I have through the help of this list and the owner's generosity), Arthur Jonston's *Psalmi Davidici cum Argumentis et Notis*, also with Robert's signature, Elizabeth's copy of Tennyson's *In Memoriam*, or Robert's edition of Shelley's 1818 *Revolt of Islam*? The editors are somewhat inconsistent in recording books known only from references in letters. Useful as this may be, probably these should be left for students to find through indexes to letters. Another useful section gives us 642 presentation copies of both poets, largely of course, of their own works: an excellent way of tracing literary relations. A final section, clearly less exhaustive than the others, gives other books, again, mostly by the Brownings, that suggest literary or personal relations: Carlyle, Swinburne, or even Faulkner's copy of Browning works. A list of 284 association manuscripts has necessarily the character of a miscellany or grab bag of items about the Brownings but not by them. It raises a problem that will arise in any such attempt at a full list of relevant items: where does one cut off? Do you list major writers' but not minor writers' copies of the Brownings? Do you list legal documents, as compilers of Shakespeare have? How far do you go into items from close or more distant relatives? No firm rules can be developed that can be applied to all writers. Different situations will make different kinds of material worth cataloging. Coley and Kelley know the Brownings well. Their decisions are generally sensible; if anything, they are a bit too generous and inclusive. Yet here are items of importance to Browning's literary relations as well as his biography and personal relations.

The other sections will be of more interest to the Browning biographer or collector: likenesses and photos of the Brownings and families, works of art, household and personal effects, including thirty-seven locks of hair. Vulgar material details, these, and of no interest to the critic whose interest lies only in the history of the soul: unless, like Browning, he cares about the externals by which alone we know the soul. Even locks of hair—hideous things—tell us something of the culture of the nineteenth century. The poor corpse of Robert must have gone virtually scalped into the Abbey to satisfy the needs of friends who had to have something more physical than his immortal art by which to remember him. Especially by the aid of the excellent index, critics as well as biographers may find here suggestive associations. Students of Browning's association with the fine arts, as well as those interested in his relations with his father and his son, will welcome the careful work put into further authoritative lists of drawings and manuscripts by Browning's father, and paintings, sculpture, and drawings by Pen—the latter consisting of works that failed at Sotheby's in 1913 and have not staged a comeback there since.

I know I am not the only student of Robert Browning's to have wished at times that Philip Kelley had confined his abundant energies to his chosen work of bringing out the letters of one of Victorian England's two greatest poetic geniuses. We have seen writer after writer, many much more recently deceased than Browning, achieve a fairly good collected letters while Kelley has been compiling these endless lists of manuscripts and collector's items. But with the appearance of such comprehensive and careful work in this volume and in the earlier companion, *The Brownings' Correspondence: A Checklist*, itself a monumental assembly of the Browning letters also scattered throughout the world, it begins to appear that the belatedness of this generation of Browning scholarship may yield to leadership in the next. We now know where the primary documents are and what they are. Other items will doubtless appear, but we have a machinery to fit them into the mosaic. With similar energy and competence, Kelley and his associate Ronald Hudson are now turning out excellent volumes of *The Browning Correspondence* (four have appeared to date) that bring a perspective from this large, fully assembled picture to bear on each detail. When Kelley and his associates have completed their huge work (the letters will run to about forty volumes) we will probably have a fuller, richer picture of every aspect of these two central male and female figures in Victorian poetry than of any other major writer of their generation. Certainly *The Browning Collections* offers a model for scholars and librarians for the ambitious task of making available to scholarship a unified record from the incredibly diverse repositories, private collections, and booksellers' publications in which the earthly remains of a writer lie relatively inaccessible until resurrected by such painstaking and careful compilation.

Robert Browning: Year's Work, 1984

In the last two years we have had three full-length critical studies of Browning, Jacob Korg's *Browning and Italy* (1983) and Clyde de L. Ryals's *Becoming Browning: The Poems and Plays of Robert Browning, 1833–1846* (1983) and now Lee Erickson's *Robert Browning: His Poetry and His Audiences* (1984). Of the three, Ryals's seems to me the most important as well as the least diffuse. The two criteria, importance and focus, probably go together. Korg very competently surveyed the host of poems with an Italian setting or background, told well the long biographical tale of Browning's love relation with Italy, and researched and rehearsed the relations between the Italian poems and their sources or artifacts. He presented a compendium of biographical and critical information but at the cost of any very clear critical focus or point of view except his general vision of Browning moving through experience of Italy to a poetry of real people and things. There was the sense that an attractive broad topic in Browning was being pursued for the sake of the topic, with the result that we had a work usefully containing what there was to know about Browning and Italy but not a study that importantly changed our vision of Browning. Ryals's focus on the early Browning, more importantly his focus on a critical problem—the idea of Romantic Irony by which he defines how Browning moves to ever higher mythic fabrications while at the same time being more and more conscious of their insubstantiality and distance from ordinary realities—made his a more challenging reading. Like Herbert Tucker, Jr.'s even more impressive—and in many ways rather similar study—of a few years before, *Browning's Beginnings* (1980), Ryals's study offered an approach to reading Browning that would be hard for future critics to ignore. Like Tucker, who drew on the approaches of Barbara Herrnstein-Smith, Harold Bloom, and to some extent the philosophical thought of Derrida, Ryals offered quite a model blending of our discipline's recent turn to critical theory with our inheritance in close rhetorical reading of texts.

Those who take up Erickson's work will have every reason to expect another, and quite differently focused, rereading of Browning in the light of recent critical thinking. His ostensible subject, Browning's poetry and its audiences, encourages one to look for a reader response approach to Browning or even a more modish study of Browning's reception. Inside, we find at least a comparison of his own work to Jauss and a good deal of reliance on Bloom for orienting Browning in relation to romanticism. In fact, Erickson has proceeded with a study of Browning's poetry and audience in his own way without critical grounding in the schools of response (Iser, Fish) or reception (Jauss). In carrying no party cards in our increasingly more political critical atmosphere, Erickson succeeds in avoiding the somewhat too determined critical line of a work such as E. Warwick Slinn's resolutely deconstructionist *Browning and the Fictions of Identity* (1982) of a few years ago. Unfortunately, I find he also lets his individual critical approach slip into diffuseness and imprecision. There is an attempt to cover too much of Browning (from *Pauline*, indeed, to *Asolando*) with the consequent absurdity of a section on *The Ring and the Book* that nonetheless attempts comprehensive critical pronouncements. Further, there is that old problem in Browning studies: `. Everyone has to cover as many poems as possible and give, as Erickson often does thoroughly but somewhat tediously, full footnotes on well-known general critical issues, even where they don't relate to the question at hand. Finally, there is the biographical urge, which forces us to tell the Browning (here the Brownings') tale once more (here often with fine feeling). Erickson gives a long apology for this aspect of his criticism, but I found it, as I did Korg's, not entirely convincing. The urge to tell all seems more fundamental than the critical intention.

This is not to say that Erickson has no thesis about Browning's poetry and its audience. But on second look at the subtitle we see those terms were quite deliberately chosen: it is a study of Browning's poetry and also of his audiences—not audience. I have to conclude that we would have been better served by a narrower work focused on the critical subject of the audience in Browning's poetry or another on Browning and his Victorian audience. Erickson gives an intermittent commentary on the latter topic and he has a number of interesting points—especially his emphasis on the significance of the excellent sales of the *Poetical Works* of 1863 as an indication of Browning's having finally arrived as a recognized poet after the years of eclipse following *Sordello*'s public debacle. He often uses contemporary reviews very interestingly to point up earlier recognitions of Browning's difficulties with his contemporary readers or to suggest the critical ambiance by which Browning may have felt himself surrounded.

The study of the audience in the poems as a critical, as opposed to historical, phenomenon is a more constantly pursued theme in Erickson's study but will also, I fear, strike most readers, as it struck me, as less satisfactory. The problem is again one of diffuseness. "Audience" is redefined in such a broad way as to embrace a host of people and beings, fictive, real, theological and to violate its ordinary meaning. Erickson's central theme, and it is a theme more than a critical issue, is really that of Browning's relation, as a poet, to other people. This easily blurs into the broader issue of Browning's relation to people generally, as man and poet. Erickson interestingly charts Browning's movement from an early hope to serve his fellows by his work to a more limited focus on private but effective communication with one individual, Elizabeth Barrett, to ultimate concern, after her death, with reporting, like the poet of "How It Strikes a Contemporary," to God alone. The audience in this sense becomes identical with those the poet professes to hold dear or value, the relations he celebrates in his work.

Even on its own terms this version of Browning's "audience" has its problems: sister Sarianna, far more of a lifetime companion in fact than Elizabeth, isn't even mentioned and the larger, complicated personal and sociological issues of the Browning family audience and milieu are barely explored; the tensions between Robert and Elizabeth, which recent biographies have been exploring, aren't mentioned even when we come to that grand venting of conjugal distress, "Mr. Sludge," far less Browning's Balzacian drive to explore what Erickson calls "sordid" subjects such as the Roman murder story or the French suicide tale (which, incidentally, Erickson badly underrates). More importantly, the central formulation of Browning's relation to other people can be plausibly criticized. Was *Men and Women* written with an eye mostly on Elizabeth or on the public back home whom Browning hoped finally to please with a serious art built on the form of his earlier most popular works, the dramatic monologues? Certainly the letters record Browning's hope for broad attention and his dismay at the mediocre reception accorded his masterwork. Are the later works all vitiated by their singleminded I-thou relation to God or are some preachy and garrulous in the manner of the Victorian sage, the writer who may claim a direct line of communication to God but who very clearly expects to be massively overheard by his contemporaries in his colloquy with the Almighty? Erickson interestingly follows the line of private poems looking to reunion with Elizabeth in the late Browning. But the mass of poems has more relation to the public man Browning of the time than we may like to think: the talkative man of the world *and* poet who *will* pipe up in Browningese rather than in the subtleties of the dramatic monologue on the great subjects of the day.

In his opening comments on *Men and Women* Erickson seems finally to be about to deal with the very interesting critical questions concerning the implied real reader and the (sometimes present, sometimes absent) fictive auditor of the dramatic monologues. Although he begins to uncover some of the theoretical and practical complexity of this critical issue, Erickson's attention soon moves in another direction. He is generally aware of the issues raised, say, by Langbaum's classic formulation of a reader asked to balance impulses of judgment and sympathy; and his own discussions of classic interpretive problems such as the attraction of the Duke of "My Last Duchess" or the possible guilt of Gismond's lady are well articulated and sensibly conservative. But the reader who hopes for a thoughtful study of the triangulation of speaker, auditor, and implied audience in Browning's major monologues will have to await a different study. To what extent does

Browning expect us to follow the fictive auditor's response as that of a stalking horse for the reader—so that we too are impelled to run off to Australia with Gigadibs if we read Bishop Blougram rightly? To what extent is the auditor a straw man to provoke in us a more perceptive response? That envoy may be fooled and even charmed by the Duke, but *we* are no such fools; Lucretia may not be taken in by Andrea's fancy artistic talk, but we are. What is the effect of the apparently more direct address to the reader in poems without a fictive auditor?

Erickson's readings of individual poems are stronger than his various conceptualizations of Browning's career and are often valuable in themselves. His definition of Browning's relation to romanticism in terms of his need for loving relation to others is lucid and helpful as are his studies of some extremely complicated poems such as "A Death in the Desert" or "James Lee's Wife." There is a fine critical intelligence here that often seems hamstrung by the excessively broad range of arguments it has taken on, sometimes somewhat unreflectingly.

Readers interested in pursuing the issue of the auditor in Browning are probably better advised to begin with the much briefer but more formally focused discussion of Browning in Dorothy Mermin's general study of auditor poems in Arnold, Browning, Clough, Meredith, and Tennyson: *The Audience in the Poem: Five Victorian Poets* (1983). Mermin's comparative approach and her narrower focus on the fictive audience in the poem (auditors) centers her study far more on the uses Browning and other Victorians made of the audiences in their poems, especially their attempts to mediate in such poems the conflicting demands of the Victorian age for expressive "sincere" statement and for communication. Looking briefly at a number of poems by Browning as well as, at more length, at *Fifine at the Fair*, she rightly distinguished between different uses of auditors, for instance poems in which auditors empower the speaker with a mastering speech ("Count Gismond"), those in which the auditor's sympathy is not fully engaged, though the reader's may be ("Fra Lippo Lippi"), or those in which the auditor is rhetorically manipulated—though we may resist it ("Bishop Blougram's Apology"). Like Hassett and Slinn in their studies of a few years ago, she sees

Browning's poems, especially the later ones, moving toward radical skepticism about our ability to interpret acts or character by language. Though, like Erickson, also unresponsive to recent critical movements in reader response or reception, Mermin's lively critical mind opens up a major subject that deserves fuller exploration in detail for Browning. Her sense of the fictive speaker-fictive auditor relation in the Victorian poems as a way in which poets could present themselves to be overheard rather than speak directly suggests that future criticism needs to explore further the third corner in the communication system of such speaker-auditor poems: the overhearing audience to which the poem is actually directed.

A number of briefer studies centering on issues of audience or reception suggests how current these critical issues are. Mary Ellis Gibson's "One More Word on Browning's 'One Word More'" (*SBHC* 12:76–86) deserves mention in this context. Using Ralph Rader's useful classifications of dramatic monologue, mask, lyric, dramatic lyric, and expressive lyric, Gibson intelligently displays problems in defining genre in Browning by the "hybrid" case of "One Word More." Rather than pursuing a better taxonomy, Gibson uses her hard case to define more clearly the qualities that distinguish different Browning poems, especially the different relations by which the reader is situated in relation to the poet in different generic configurations. Her sense of the variety of such positions, like Mermin's awareness of varieties of auditors, suggests again the need for further study of Browning's reader *and* auditors.

Browning's relations to the readers of his time are explored in articles by Arnold Cheskin and Ashby Crowder. Cheskin amusingly interprets "Jochanan Hakkadosh" (*SBHC* 12:134–147) as a poem *à clef*, a sly comment by Browning on the contemporaneous founding of the Browning Society and his strained relations with its aggressive leader F. J. Furnivall: Rabbi Jochanan Browning and Tsaddik Furnivall. Tsaddik itself, Hebrew for righteous or just—a proper term for the Rabbi but given by Browning to his presumptuous disciple—suggests Browning's subtle critique of Furnivall and the naive interpretive/interrogative strategies of the Browning Society.

Crowder's more historical study of reception in the case of *The Inn Album* (*SBHC* 12:120–133) documents the chorus of Victorian disapproval for Browning's bold subject and crude language in *The Inn Album*. Walter Kendrick's spirited, more general introduction to the same poem (*BIS* 11:113–125) complements Crowder's study by interpreting Browning's intention as one essentially antagonistic to his audiences, a poem that embodies the language of his time that it also condemns. Kendrick grants the modernity of this strategy while essentially dismissing the poem. Should it be dismissed? or is it still suffering too much from a Victorian condemnation of its vicious subject matter?

Other formal studies this year have tended to center on the complex aesthetic issues of *The Ring and the Book*. C. Stephen Finley's close critical study of "The Other Half-Rome" (*BIS* 11:127–148) persuasively demonstrates that this character's position is far closer to the "author's" position than he gives it credit for in Book I. Finley is also careful to set limits to this reinterpretation: Other Half-Rome, despite his sympathy for Pompilia, has finally a secular eclectic vision that contrasts with the Pope's grand Christian view of Pompilia's strength. William Walker's "*Pompilia* and Pompilia" (*VP* 22:47–63), once again a study focused on issues of auditors, makes a good argument that we should not regard the sainted victim as entirely free of rhetorical strategy. This is a useful corrective to the tendency to read this monologue as a more primitive form, say in fact a saint's life. Unlike Finley, Walker doesn't well set limits to his interpretation so that we begin to have questions raised, in the manner of reinterpretation of "Count Gismond," about the real paternity of Gaetano. Finally, Susan Blalock suggests an attractive new approach to Browning—through Bakhtin—in her restatement of the traditional Jamesian comparison between *The Ring and the Book* and the novel (*BIS* 11:39–50). Her brief but suggestive article sees in the poem, as in the form of the novel according to Bakhtin, a spirit of subversive carnival and parody. Old truths are broken up and discredited in this epic re-written as novel as the author-stage director-fool leads us to his own radical suspicion of all human speech. Blalock's brief account of carnival days in the poem as moments of intersection between mythic order and debasing secular visions deserves full and careful explication—a promising approach that, one hopes, does not merely turn into another claim for an undifferentiated relativism among the speakers of the poem.

The year saw some interesting statements on major thematic topics, some relatively new to Browning, others new roastings of old chestnuts. A persistent lesser interest in Browning, never entirely satisfactorily expressed in his work nor entirely well analyzed by his critics, has been the poet's politics. The difficulty, as two interesting and full studies by John Woolford and Robert Viscusi have suggested in very different ways, is the elusive and essentially self-contradictory implications of Browning's liberalism. Woolford's "The Philosophy and Poetics of Power in Browning's Early Work" (*BSN* 14:1–20) is a thoughtful and intelligent attempt to define Browning's political vision. Browning's idea of power, stemming from what Woolford calls Puritan anarchism, made him reject even the humanistic uses of power of erstwhile progressive mentors such as Goethe or friend Carlyle. (In this regard it is perhaps worth underlining how relatively unaffected Browning was by Carlyle's paternalistic political vision compared to contemporaries who fell as fully under Carlyle's personal spell.) Woolford makes an interesting, if less compelling, attempt to relate the themes of renunciation or abdication of power (clear enough in his look at some of the plays) to the ambivalence expressed in *Pauline* about poetry as a mastery over or a serving of its subject. Viscusi's wide-ranging article approaches Browning's politics through his international relations, in the process providing an important addendum to Korg's study of Browning and Italy. "'The Englishman in Italy': Free Trade as a Principle of Aesthetics" (*BIS* 12:1–28) helpfully and rather beautifully offers a context to Browning's Italy in the Italies of prior English literary generations and even in the very typefaces of writing itself. Roman and Italic, the two Italies that Browning really projected out of himself onto the land, suggest to Viscusi the essence of Browning as a poet and political man of his time: a liberal's ability to hold alternates and even antinomies in suspension. Viscusi's subject is really Browning as a version of English liberal imperialism over Italy: the imperialism of free trade as exemplified by the Englishman grasping the (cheap) delights of the virgin('s) land. Yet Browning's subtle, detached method, exemplified by the strongly distancing title, leaves us wondering: is he the Englishman or has he, like his fine interpreter, captured the essential view of Italy of the Englishman of his time (one of so many voices, not his own)? In light of our current balance of trade difficulties one may also ask the extra-literary question as to whether cheap goods from abroad are a successful imperialist expedient.

Along with the general tendency to expand Victorian feminist issues from female to male writers, Browning's treatment of women has received interesting discussion. Nina Auerbach examines Browning's relations to women by going to the crux, or crucible, the relation between Robert and Elizabeth. "Were the Brownings really married," she asks in "Robert Browning's Last Word" (*VP* 22:161–173) and proceeds to deconstruct or disintegrate that famous achievement of Victorian culture and interpersonal love, the Brownings. In this she has backing from most recent biographical studies that have stressed the tensions and differing viewpoints that were part of the Brownings' marriage. If Erickson's study romanticizes the marriage of Robert and Elizabeth into a restrictive idea of Browning's audience, Auerbach overstates the rivalry between the two. Interestingly, she also connects her vision of this non-marriage of two minds with a specific view of Browning's auditors, which she essentially incorrectly equates with Mermin's. If Elizabeth, as Robert himself said, speaks out, with a bardic female voice personifying the truth, Robert gives only a skeptical, truth-void world of speakers adjusting their truths rhetorically to auditors. Auerbach's reading of *The Ring and the Book*, not merely as a placing of Elizabeth's idealism against the evils of the world but as an appropriation and, in effect, murdering of Elizabeth by her husband, ignores (certainly misstates) Pompilia's central position in the poem, parallel to the Pope, if without his range of moral reference, as a voice of relatively great truth. Doubtless *The Ring and the Book* answers Elizabeth and locates her direct "white light" approach to truth within Robert's broader indirect approach—as another, if especially powerful, testimony. But in overstating Robert's wish to appropriate and silence Elizabeth, Auerbach, like the male speaker in *Fifine* as Mermin well interprets him, falsifies by leaving out the love that, in Roberts's vision, alone gives truth to human speech. Published as a pendant to Auerbach's article, U. C. Knoepflmacher's wittily wide-ranging "Projection and the Female Other: Romanticism, Browning, and the Victorian Dramatic Monologue" (*VP* 22:139–159), perhaps gives Browning too much credit for enabling an authentic female voice to speak. Knoepflmacher attempts a great deal in an article: essentially a reading of Browning's rereading of the romantic appropriation of the female other. Leaning on its opaque statements rather heavily, he finds in "James Lee's Wife" (Shelley's wife) Browning giving voice to the female other that romantic artists merely controlled. He is generally correct in focusing not so much on Browning as a creator of independent female others as on his role as critic of romantic appropriation working broadly in their tradition. He provides an interesting reading of "Porphyria's Lover" both as a parody and critique of the Keatsian male Porphyro in "The Eve of St. Agnes." Browning reheats Keats's porridge to criticize his identification of sexual possession and permanence. "My Last Duchess" similarly parodies sexual and aesthetic possession. Knoepflmacher is most interesting in the roles he ascribes to the reader in making the woman speak (for instance, through the images that we make speak for the duchess). His study doesn't entirely answer Swinburne's critique of Browning cited in his conclusion: that Browning may be on the side of the female angels but still seems more often not to let them speak directly. Between the opposing views of the poet as Guidoian uxor-poet-icide and as the Victorian male who do the policewomen in different voices lies a complex truth of good intentions and a male ego working, as Knoepflmacher shows, in an essentially male tradition, no matter how subversively.

On the recurrent subject of Browning's relation to the Romantics we can set beside Knoepflmacher's observations on Keats and Shelley, Martin Bidney's rather similar, if less broadly aimed, study of the "Madhouse Cells" in relation to the Keatsian aesthetic (*SEL* 24:671–681). Bidney amplifies some of Knoepflmacher's observations about Browning as parodist and critic of Keats by a careful look at his earliest dramatic monologues. He finds these poems, read by the light of Keats's aestheticism, "defamiliarizing" Keatsian moments of identification of art and life by their grotesque parodies.

Discussion of Browning and the romantics has centered on the less well-traveled road between Browning and Keats; so in the matter of Browning's relation to his contemporaries it has been the commerce between Browning and Arnold, rather than Tennyson, that has provoked the most interesting discussion. In a fine article, "Two Versions of the Problem of the Modern Intellectual" (*MLR* 79:769–782), John Coates eloquently restates the traditional view of "Cleon" as an answer to Arnold's *Empedocles on Etna*. He is especially good at placing both poems back in the Greek context that both writers knew so well, in the process defending them somewhat against Frank Turner's vision of Victorians' misappropriation of Greek antiquity. Coates finds both Arnold and Browning using subtly appropriate examples from Greek history and culture to make contemporary cases of equally great subtlety. Cleon is read more interestingly as a late Greek of antiquity with a complex awareness—in that similar to Arnold and Arnold's character—of his own modernity. Browning's answer to Arnold is that we must accept the modern belatedness and move on from there—as Cleon himself finally refuses to do—not consume ourselves in lament over a lost past and its simplicity. In another good comparative study (*MLR* 79:783–796), Jane A. McCusker produces a different debate between Arnold and Browning, one she sees totally under Browning's control in the contrasting versions of Aristophanes (Arnold) and Euripides (Balaustion/Browning) in Browning's *Aristophanes' Apology*. McCusker makes a good case for the poem as a (rather harsh) personal evaluation of Arnold as well as his poetics. If there is no specific external evidence to back up the identification of Aristophanes with Arnold, there are unhistorical traits in Browning's characterization of Aristophanes that fit Arnold rather well, especially Browning's vision of the Greek poet moved by patriotism and cultural conservatism to let his genius work in "baser stuff" and let himself fall into a career of artistic deterioration. That's playing hard ball—but Browning, we know, made incisive judgments of his contemporaries and McCusker's view is far from improbable.

A final topic of interest this year, of perennial interest to Browning critics good, bad, and worse, is religion. Here Browning studies seem to be following the general current interest in Victorian religious thought in relation to modes of interpretation (e.g., typology) or general theories of religion and myth. Blair Ross, "Ripeness is All: Historical Perspective in Browning's 'Apollo and the Fates'" (*VP* 22:15–30), interprets this poem of old and new Greek religions according to a schema of progressive mythology that sees Christianity as a natural growth from paganism, that is, a higher mythic conception to answer to man's developing nature. Apollo is seen as both type of Christ and as learning in this scene the progressive nature of reality in which he, too, like the Fates he threatens, will be supplanted (by Christ). In an attractive interpretation of "Karshish," Michael J. Berens (*SBHC* 12:41–53) likewise sees Browning interested in the roots of religion in the human myth-making capacity. Berens demonstrates Karshish's inner conversion by the appropriate echoes of Christian language that appear spontaneously in his monologue: as if the working of faith within will reinvent the Christian vocabulary in anyone at anytime. Two articles on "Caliban upon Setebos" examine the weird theology of the speaker, neither entirely satisfactorily. Terrell L. Tebbetts ("The Question of Satire in 'Caliban upon Setebos,'" *VP* 22:365–381) has interesting observations on the contemporary use of Caliban as a term (including unsavory racist allusions that do not appear in Browning), on Browning's interest in the process of Caliban's thinking, and on Caliban's infantile psychology (à la Erickson); but his conclusion, that the real satire is on Benthamism, doesn't seem to me well proven. Another study, also interesting and also not entirely persuasive, is John Hunter Lammers' "'Caliban upon Setebos': Browning's Divine Comedy" (*SBHC* 12:94–119). Lammers offers useful Biblical and Miltonic echoes in Caliban but often seems to assert more than his evidence suggests about a conscious allusive web of intention in Browning. The idea that Caliban is a mini-epic of creation and redemption (rejected, of course, by Caliban as Cleon denies his insight) is interesting but Lammers' tiringly complex allegorical readings of Caliban's descriptions seem excessive. I note with pleasure plans by Linda Peterson and David Shaw for much needed broader studies in the area of Browning and hermeneutics and religious philosophy.

The past few years have seen truly splendid progress in basic scholarship on Browning. 1984's work gives this reviewer a relief from collating passages of text, checking lists of Browningiana, and scrutinizing lengthy footnotes with a microscope. Fine new editions, the Collins-Pettigrew Penguin/Yale of a few years ago, the Jack-Smith Oxford English Text Edition in progress, the much improved revived Ohio edition serve Browning well, though no additions have been made to the latter two in the past year. Philip Kelley and Betty Coley's masterful *The Browning Collections* of Browning books, manuscripts, and objects appeared in 1983 (dated 1984), finally giving us, along with the earlier checklist of letters, an authoritative source list of the so widely dispersed primary documents of the Brownings. In 1984 we had the beginning of a major new scholarly resource, Kelley and Ronald Hudson's long-awaited *The Brownings' Correspondence*, two volumes of which appeared during the year. The volumes bring the letters up only to 1831, before Robert's first extant one appears, so I will leave detailed review to my colleague and only notice here the sumptuous, traditional publication, with wide margins, generous spacing, and lovely plates, that Kelley and Hudson have managed to preserve by publishing with their own Wedgestone Press. Assuming the scholarship, especially the annotation, keeps up to the quality of the presentation, this may prove one of the great publishing achievements in nineteenth-century studies in our generation. The second volume does publish in an appendix the two, already published, letters of Robert Browning, Sr., enrolling and withdrawing his son at The London University. There is also an interesting publication of Sarah Flower's letter to W. J. Fox, now surfacing at Baylor, that included the only surviving copies of the two early poems, "The first born of Egypt" and "The Dance of Death," from which Kenyon established texts for these works.

The publication now becomes the authoritative text for these poems and is different in spelling, punctuation, and a few readings from all other editions based on Kenyon's transcription. It is also worth noting, though I do so against myself, that neither the traditional account of Browning's early verses nor my correction in *Browning's Youth* (1977) quite jibes with the end of Sarah's letter, omitted in Kenyon's edition. Sarah is clear that the author, "the boy" Browning, is already fourteen (which makes sense in terms of the date of her letter of May 31, 1827—Browning was born in 1812 and had already even turned fifteen by the time of writing). She says the poems were extracted from a "whole book full" and that he is "mad to publish them." The traditional story was that Browning wrote "Incondita" at twelve and showed them then to Fox. My version, trying to deal with Sarah's clear statement that these two poems were of his age fourteen, was that the two poems were later than "Incondita." We will now have to conclude that the date of age twelve given by Browning himself was incorrect (or even a deliberate attempt to make these early works seem mere boyhood scribblings, as he later referred to them with embarrassment) and that the "Incondita" were composed around 1826 and brought to Fox (who counseled delay in publication) sometime in 1827, perhaps as a result of this letter. Of course, the familiarity Sarah assumes in Fox with "the boy" Browning and the biographical accounts of a direct approach to Fox could suggest that there were two entire sets of manuscripts, one of age twelve and this later of age fourteen, or even that Fox was consulted earlier, knew of the poems, but never read them. The full publication of Sarah's comments leaves us more curious about Browning's earliest poems while even Kelley and Hudson's failure to find other documents from the period of Browning's youth that he took so much trouble to obfuscate suggests that our curiosity will find no gratification. Certainly it is interesting to find Browning as late as 1827, already turned fifteen, "mad" to publish poems he would later attribute to mere childhood.

Browning's current and future editors will want to note one other significant scholarly addition in 1984: Michael Mason's discovery of an uncollected fugitive, "Duty," that Browning published in Holyoake's *The Present Day* (*TLS*, April 27, 1984, p. 453). Mason supposes that the contribution grew out of an earlier association over the publication of the oddest of Browning's many odd editions, the Chicago and Alton Railroad *Poetical Works* by a friend of Holyoake's. It is a fine statement for Holyoake's ethical, secularist journal, but, alas, no important poem to add to Browning's canon. Finally, one additional contribution to the textual record, a long report on the manuscript of *Strafford* in the Lord Chamberlain's records of the British Library, deserves notice. I noted last year that the Oxford English Text editors were not aware that Kelley and Coley were reporting a manuscript in the form submitted for approval for stage production to the Lord Chamberlain and hence omitted this interesting variant from their text. Anneliese Meidl (*BIS* 12:163–188) discusses the numerous variants and omissions, primarily those introduced by Macready (with some help from John Forster), between this version and the first published edition. Meidl doesn't give a full list of variants but does indicate well the many important differences between this acting manuscript and the edition Browning brought out in part to establish his own competing version. The manuscript essentially confirms the biographical record of tension between playwright and director-actor—that Macready took major liberties with the young playwright's text in order to present it to the action-oriented, uncerebral theatrical audience of his time. The major variants in the manuscript give us a graphic record of the reasons for frustration on both sides.

Robert Browning: Year's Work, 1985

Browning scholarship this year has been enriched by the important publications, the third volume of *The Brownings' Correspondence,* the letters of Browning to Katharine de Kay Bronson, and the Ohio *The Ring and the Book*—which I haven't succeeded in seeing. The importance of Philip Kelley and Ronald Hudson's enormous project in *The Brownings' Correspondence* needs to be underlined now that the record has finally hit substantial Robert Browning material in the period that it covers, 1832–1837. Although Elizabeth's letters still predominate, there are twenty hitherto unpublished letters by Robert (Albeit three only snippets from bookseller's catalogues), making a relatively large percentage of the rather few letters available for this period. Given the incredible dispersion of Browning materials after the Sotheby sale there is no assurance that this collection is definitive. But the relative success of Hudson and Kelley's method is clear enough. They have been close to thirty years now at work cataloging Browning materials in a tremendously large number of public repositories or private collections. Their great catalog of the Browning letters and Betty Coley and Kelley's *The Browning Collections* gave us guides to the puzzle. They now are able to fit the pieces together and read the full record. That the record for Robert has been greatly slowed by the work on Elizabeth may bother scholars of the male poet. The mixture of Robert's early letters with the totally separate letters of Elizabeth in this early period may also seem a bother. Yet the value of this comprehensive method will come clear when the two streams merge and the intersecting puzzles are solved as one. In the meantime, the careful preliminary work pays off for Robert even in these early works by the wealth of supplemental material—gift copies, Browning circle letters, family materials, manuscripts, drawings—that Hudson and Kelley are able to lay out in solving issues of dating of context.

Browning notoriously destroyed most of the intimate evidence of his early life and the epistolary record, starting only at about age twenty-one, remains a scant one, even with these welcome additions. Most, while throwing some light into dark months or half years between 1833 and 1837, are relatively brief, showing the young Browning, like the far more well represented older one, a businesslike, unrevealing letter writer, whose flourishes mostly take the form of rather complicated and embarrassed compliments to his correspondents. Generally he wrote to his immediate audience, not for posterity. He reveals himself, therefore, only in letters to those close to him—Elizabeth especially. He did so earlier to a close friend, Euphrasia Haworth, in charming letters that one reads again here with pleasure. He also opened his mind, and to some degree his soul, as a poet, to his early friend from France, Count Amédée de Ripert-Monclar. The six letters published here, dating from December 1834 to August 1837, make a splendid addition to our knowledge of the precocious young poet of this time. They show a young worldly Browning commenting upon Monclar's favorite Bentham, post-Reform Act politics, and the development of railroads. Browning shares Monclar's family interest in history, edits an English review by Monclar of his historian uncle Fortia d'Urban, and, through Monclar and Fortia, joins the French L'Institut Historique. Most important, Browning shares with the friend who inspired *Paracelsus*, and to whom it is dedicated, the history of his inner development as a poet. A remarkable letter of August 1837 is really a brief *Prelude*, tracing the growth of his artistic sensibility, in early rhymes, music, art, wide reading—especially in the Greeks—and the composition of *Pauline*. It is the very rare self-explanatory voice that we always look for beside the lapidary achievement of Browning's art and generally find only in the Essay on Shelley and some of the letters to Elizabeth. Other letters also offer interesting critical observations on *Pauline*, that "pale face & slight shadowy figure," on the dramatic poetry of *Paracelsus*, and even on *Sordello*. Finally, these letters, filled with references to French literature from Rabelais to George Sand, and often in French, confirm our sense of Browning's wide reading in world classics and his interest in current Continental literature.

Philip Kelley's achievement as a collector, editor, and publisher has received, and deserves, high praise. This is a beautiful volume, sumptuously presented in the tradition of fine publishing, and carefully printed. We should also recognize the fine and careful work of co-editor Ronald Hudson, who shows himself almost always equal to the very difficult problems of annotating these letters. Except for a few cryptic personal references, indecipherable only because we know so little about Browning's life in this entire period, Hudson hardly ever needs to confess defeat. He has done a remarkable job on Browning's frequent, rather affected use of allusion. In the process he demonstrates again, as I have argued, that Browning had a very broad and central education in Greek, Latin, and European classics. Far from dwelling in the out-of-the-way crabbed learning of the autodidact, the poet most frequently alludes to Aeschylus, Horace, Virgil, Shakespeare, Pope, or Shelley and Byron, not to Sibrandus Schafnaburgensis. Hudson's excellence answers this reviewer's only remaining doubts about the quality of this monumental undertaking: clearly this is a truly major event of Browning scholarship. I can only add further thanks for all the other material these gentlemen give us: copious, choice illustrations—a few, like the sketches by Browning, Monclar, and Haworth, never before published; a list of supporting documents, together with publication of Monclar's commentary on *Paracelsus* with Browning's observations and explanations; seventy-five closely printed pages of contemporary reviews of Browning's work; full, well-informed biographical sketches of Browning's most important correspondents; a list of unrecovered letters and a few letters, published in the collection, by correspondents to Browning. We will stand as indebted to the editors' generosity in husbanding what fragments there are as we must be sorry for the poet's deliberate occlusions.

With the editorial assistance of Rita S. Humphrey, Michael Meredith has also produced a handsome, beautifully illustrated edition, in the Wedgestone format, of Browning's letters to a close friend at the other end of his life: *More Than Friend: The Letters of Robert Browning to Katharine de Kay Bronson* (1985). Meredith does an intelligent and scholarly job of editing Browning's (sometimes Browning and his sister's) fifty-eight letters to Bronson along with one of hers to him (Pen's Fannie evidently destroyed the rest) and nineteen others among Bronson, her daughter Edith, Sarianna, and Pen. Meredith also does us a generous service in reprinting Bronson's two fine articles (originally published in *The Century Magazine*) on Browning in Asolo and Venice, as well as a memoir by Daniel Sargent Curtis of Browning in Venice. If the material in the letters is generally familiar to us it is only because Bronson performed such a good service to Browning biographers in her charming and detailed articles. The letters themselves are what one expects in Browning's later correspondence, chatty, preoccupied with people and places, courtly (with still a trace of the prose Browning's tendency to embarrassment of style and manner). References to his work tend to the kind of merely external description that makes the stuff of Henry James's frustration with the social Browning: a new poem is simply "a more lengthy and elaborate affair than usual."

As important, perhaps more so, is Meredith's well researched and elegantly presented account of Bronson and of Browning's Indian summer relation with her. He gives a very useful history of Bronson herself, including her American background and her physical separation from her mentally ill husband, who died in any case in 1885. One of the great lion hunters of the Jamesian world of Venice where Browning spent many summers in the 1880s, she quickly became Browning's especial friend and most generous hostess, first at Venice then, finally, at Asolo where she made the poet comfortable in the little hill town of his youthful revelation. Meredith adds to his careful record of this friendship an interpretation of the emotional dynamics that will naturally interest romanticizers of Browning's love life but also will command respect as a very possible explanation of the background to some of Browning's more interesting last poems. In his reading, Browning fell in love with Bronson, eventually with a physical passion; by a somewhat Browningesque irony, she felt strong feelings too, but of idealizing reverence and protective affection for the considerably older lion she had in tow. This unequal romance, unconsummated and broken off by Browning's death after his idyllic visit at Asolo in Fall 1889, is hard to prove, just because its terms would be that Browning could not easily move to reveal his passion because he understood and appreciated the different quality of Bronson's feeling. Meredith is therefore forced to rely on evidence from the poems, including love lyrics in *Ferishtah's Fancies* and poems such as "Now" and "Inapprehensiveness" in *Asolando*. The process is thus inevitably a bit circular, the poem interpreted by the biography then establishing the biography. Yet the latter poems are striking enough and the biographical traces clear enough to be most plausible as comments on real feelings about Bronson. Nonetheless skepticism can create other stories, also plausible. Browning wrote these poems for publication: was he paying a compliment while reflecting, in his usual impersonal mode, on the experience of love? The problem is that we know Browning had certain motivations in his maturity that could also explain his close association with Bronson: his love of friendship, her hospitality and most useful connections, her help to Pen (one can hardly imagine that Browning was not aware of her well-provided daughter as a possible rich catch—to be more blunt than James usually is about the realities of this his world—before she married and Pen found another well-to-do American). Bronson herself recognized Pen as Browning's "vulnerable point, the heel of Achilles" and close association with the socially central Bronson would be a major asset to the painter son settled in at Venice himself. All this is only to say that we must be hesitant to see in this idyll a revival of deep feelings to be compared to those for Elizabeth. In the world of society in which the late Browning moved, it is not hard to believe that everyone, even a great poet, is, in James's phrase, working everyone else (even a rich, still somewhat innocent American) ever so delightfully and pleasantly. Certainly Meredith's scenario of a wild (but not wicked) old man's passion is more attractive and well argued. Meredith's exemplary scholarship allows us, in any case, to make the final call for ourselves.

The Ohio Browning, now under the capable leadership of Allan C. Dooley, has published its edition of *The Ring and the Book*. The poem was not included in the Collins-Pettigrew

Browning. This first modern edition with full apparatus should be of great interest. For future editors of Browning's work, Michael Meredith's well-informed study of Browning's revisions of the 1868 *Poetical Works* (*SBHC* 13:97–107) offers just the kind of close look at Browning's actual relations to his changing text that was not available when the original Ohio project began. Meredith shows that Browning took up opportunities in 1870 and 1875 to revise and correct the text substantially and suggests that the process shows the poet adapting and refining his use of punctuation. Meredith argues from the record that Browning was more attentive to those "mere stops" than he may have been given credit for; citing two volumes of the 1872 *Poetical Works* with Browning's corrections in them for 1875, Meredith shows how consciously Browning tried to weed out errors; yet the record also shows how easily printer's errors cropped up. Especially because we have no record of authorized changes for the 1870 edition, editors have good reason to continue to scrutinize changes in the final edition carefully against earlier versions. Finally, Mary Ellis Gibson (*SBHC* 13:11–19) offers some useful insights into ways in which the historical research of the poet's father fed his son with the facts, and an interpretative scheme by which to present them, in the Pope's chronicle of the dark ages in the Formosus passage.

There were four full-length critical studies of Browning, all of them worth attention yet also reflecting somewhat alarmingly—at least at first glance—the great diversity of our critical tongues at the present moment. William E. Buckler's *Poetry and Truth in Robert Browning's* The Ring and the Book (1985) is a strongly argued full reading of Browning's great single poem. It is long in close critical reading and moral reflection on character, broadly in a moral and New Critical tradition whose continuing strength is apparent in the exceptionally fine explications and useful corrections he offers in reading each of the books. Beginning with Browning's own self-reflexive statements in the poem, Buckler proposes a method of reading that takes seriously the poet's conclusion that "our human speech is naught." In his approach, we are tested as readers by realizing the limits as well as the strengths of each speaker's version of the truth, including the poet's own tentatives in the first book. Buckler is especially good in forcing admirers of Caponsacchi or the Pope to see the limits of even their privileged positions; similarly he forces us to acknowledge Guido's humanness (if not humanity) and his occasional just hits in his scatter shot of diverse articulations. Buckler shows no awareness of recent deconstructive approaches to character in Browning (Slinn, Hassett, or, more broadly, Tucker) yet his skeptical approach brings him, like his poet, naturally close to such criticism. Traditional critics may find his critique of the Pope as destructive as a formal deconstructive approach. A committed deconstructionist might be uneasy, as even this more pragmatic reviewer was, with the constructive idealization of Pompilia as innocent language nearest the truth. Her goodness does not necessarily privilege her articulation of the truth: one feels Buckler's own system often violated in favor of establishing in her some central truth. The biographical insight, that Browning wrote his poem in a complicated dialogue with the prophetic innocence of his dead wife, whom he found morally right, like Pompilia, but lacking in just the awareness of the intense wrongness of human speech, could have helped problematize this treatment of Pompilia. Buckler's feminist perspective, which sees the poem as especially about the failure of male human speech, leads him, perhaps like Browning, toward pedestal-placing of the good innocent woman, another form of male control, isn't it? These problems notwithstanding, this is a powerful interpretation that will take its place among the less than handful of major studies of Browning's poem.

Buckler begins his analysis with a discussion of Henry James's interesting tribute to *The Ring and the Book*. Ross Posnock, in *Henry James and the Problem of Robert Browning* (1985), makes the personal and literary relations between the master poet and master novelist the focus of a suggestive reading of the aesthetics of the two writers. Refusing to isolate literary from personal influence, Posnock tells a story of James's early infatuation with a forbidden book of his teen years, *Men and Women*, his social propinquity with the poet in society and artistic London culminating in their being close neighbors in

De Vere Gardens, and James's two stories *à clef* expressing both his acute awareness of Browning and the failure of their relation to attain any degree of intimacy. Following Bloom and René Girard, Posnock puts forward an interesting speculation about the influence of Browning on James. He finds Browning's personal influence a form of double bind, in which James is encouraged to imitate the dramatic poet but blocked by him from entering the poet's world of sexual maturity. In his exciting readings of "The Private Life" and "The Lesson of the Master" Posnock sees James dealing with Browning's threatening potency by creating a myth of the two Brownings, a myth that both explains and justifies James's own different vision of the artist as aesthetic monk sacrificing all (especially sexual) life to his art. For Browning scholars easily comfortable with the view that there were two Brownings, a private one and a public one, this much more complicated interpretation of James's message should be required reading. I found Posnock's readings of James's "appropriations" by rewriting of Browning's works, *In a Balcony* by *Wings of the Dove*, *Fifine at the Fair* by *The Golden Bowl*, *The Ring and the Book* of course by James's vision of the novel in that country, less persuasive as studies of influence, primarily because the evidence for rewriting is weak in the first two cases (Posnock is more persuasive where he shows James's mind concentrated on Browning, as in the argument for *The Inn Album*, which James reviewed, as prototype of "The Lesson of the Master"). His essays nonetheless stand as exciting comparative studies. They offer memorable critical discussions of the development of a theatrical self (as opposed to the sincere self of the Romantics or the solid, respectable selves of Victorian middle-class society) in Browning and James and the parallel development, in dramatic monologue and point of view narration, of an art of perspectivism. Posnock is a smart and agile critical presence who artfully blends interesting theoretical speculation and fine close readings (albeit with a motive) in the manner of the loosely identified new historicist school of critics. One can object that positions are interesting but tentative. For instance, one could read the Oedipal conflict that Posnock heavily outlines between James and Browning equally interestingly as an approach to a confession of homosexual attraction followed by rejection (Browning's private life being just that world of intimacy James was resolutely not invited in to share). My point is only that the new union of theory and history can create gorgeous but rather unstable theories. The book perhaps generally overstates Browning's importance to James by its special pleading; yet it is an exceptionally intelligent comparative critical approach to Browning and James's art.

Like Posnock, unlike Buckler, Loy D. Martin in his *Browning's Dramatic Monologues and the Post-Romantic Subject* (1985) engages strenuously with the explosion of theoretical work that has been challenging traditional modes of inquiry in literary study over the past twenty years. He is also an engaging writer who, indeed, dazzles at times with the interesting routines, from Jameson, to Darwin, to Marx, to the communication system of Alcoholics Anonymous, to the development of individualized languages for classes of people in the nineteenth century, to the Freudian revision of dreams in their transcript into language. More than prior writers on Browning who have created a dialogue between their readings of his work and contemporary theory—for instance Tucker, who consistently stressed deferral of closure in Browning, or Slinn, who read the poems rigorously from a deconstructive view of character—Martin allows his study to become something of a baggy monster. Unlike nineteenth-century novels in James's characterization, Martin's work is filled not with lots of life, but with lots of theory. It reads, and could profitably be read, as a kind of gallery of contemporary critical applications, Marxist, deconstructive, linguistic, Bakhtinian, Freudian, and, perhaps most self-consciously, literary historical. Martin is disarmingly open about the looseness of his overall approach. He offers himself as a bringer of new questions, even if the result of being so broadly inquisitive is not always to cast a strong light on the issues raised. Martin has the great virtue of being interesting wherever he works; if he sometimes churns heavy stuff dredged up from contemporary theoretical studies, he is genuinely interested in communication, not—as one suspects with some of our full-time theorists—mystification. We now have, as Arnold would wish, a very lively current of ideas, as contrasted to the not so distant days when Richards, Brooks, and Wimsatt seemed the only game in town. Martin is a bearer and sharer of his wide reading in theory; he displays the variety of tools available with only a touch too much enthusiasm and only a modest failure of skeptical discrimination. If he lacks the strength of decisiveness of one theoretical approach pushed to extremes he has the advantage of representing more fairly the excitement and confusion of our critical moment: where the elusive promise of bringing together so many independent strands of criticism after the New Criticism tempts us to brilliant but somewhat unstable syncretic creations.

Martin's ostensible aim is to provide an account of the production of the dramatic monologue, with Browning as major example but the broader issue as his ultimate focus. Such a question involves him in a broad discussion of the social conditions for kinds of literature and more broadly, as in his bright but difficult opening, in the theoretical premises to statements about literary production and society. At moments Martin seems embarrassed by the lack of specific social context he provides to uphold his neo-Marxist schema of a literary form responsive to a crisis in world view. Although his vision of Browning as a product of nineteenth-century capitalism nonetheless expressing his own dis-ease with Cartesian individualism through the creation of the dramatic monologue is suggestive, his work seems to me weakest in its attempts to relate literature and society. Similarly his interesting reading of "Childe Roland" as a version of Freudian writing of dreams doesn't disguise the weakness of this analysis as a representative description of the production of the dramatic monologue by the individual writer. Martin's smaller big question, which he avoids naming as how to describe the distinguishing qualities of the dramatic monologue (because he wished to define the genre not formally but in terms of its production), seems to me to find better answers. Rendering these answers also allows him to offer a number of fine readings of Browning's poems and constitutes the book—because of, as well as in spite of, the author's claims for his work as a broader inquiry into broader questions—as at least an interesting new critical (no caps.) study of Browning. Here he partly follows Tucker and

Slinn's work. One credits his statement that he completed the thinking before seeing their work; indeed the variety of critical methods at work in this book probably results in part from its long period of gestation in a mind that keeps up with contemporary theoretical trends and naturally resists closure. With Tucker, Martin sees Browning as rewriting his Romantic heritage into a language of processive experience that connects out into time and space and resists closure. With Slinn (or the less rigorous but oft more subtle work of Hassett), he sees Browning's work as deconstructing the stable idea of character (what he calls homogeneity of character). The current rage for Bakhtin and for the dialogical over the monological moves Browning's stock up, as Martin analyzes it, decisively, if ironically, by the dialogical nature of his monologues. Martin's interesting reading of the monologues by the light of Kristeva and Bakhtin as works emphatically turned to complex communication, combining voices of author and speaker, reaching out from the isolated individual to a community of language, mediating individual and social languages, even allowing dialogue between Robert Browning and Elizabeth Barrett Browning as well as between Browning and the British public that may yet come to like him, is one of the strong parts of this book; nor can a reviewer easily do justice to the subtlety of his arguments which stress not the ease of communication but the simultaneous presence of two poles in Browning's work—the self terrified in its isolation and the self full in its awareness of intimacy with others.

Martin calls himself, among other things, a semiotician, and his work also strikes out new ground in finding ways to describe, as opposed to interpret, Browning's language. Instead of (just) another reading of certain monologues we are given a description, generally from a linguistic perspective, of the peculiarities of Browning's language: for instance, the imperfected nature of the verbs, stressing action going forward and connecting metonymically to other times and places or the devices by which speech as conversational actions is indicated. Sometimes one feels, as often with structuralist or semiotic descriptions of literature, that this is a great effort to catalog and pronounce the obvious; yet in other places it gives us new knowledge of what makes Browning so very different a poet from the nineteenth-century romantic tradition. Martin is especially good where his habit of posing questions opens up whole new, seemingly obvious territories of inquiry: perhaps especially his fine observations on the ample baggage of conventional poetic devices (complex rhyme, meter, and stanza forms in Browning, highly artificial effects of sound in Tennyson) that go along with the new stress on poetry as seemingly real speech in the dramatic monologue. This is an imperfect book about the way in which the dramatic monologue was written but in some sense about the writing of a description of the dramatic monologue. As such, it leaves the reader with some of the reaction to the form itself: exhilaration at its immediacy and sense of ongoing experience and discourse, frustration at its relative incoherence, its frequent loose ends, its teasing, unresolved questions, above all its modern multiplicity of approaches and arguments.

The fourth in this year's impressive number of significant books on Browning takes us back from Martin's sometimes excessive theoretical eclecticism to fine traditional biographical and critical scholarship in Daniel Karlin's study of the love letters, *The Courtship of Robert Browning and Elizabeth Barrett* (1985). This is not to say that Karlin's monograph is a monolith or to fall into identifying innovation and creativity only with new theoretical schools of criticism. Karlin centers his work on a careful biographical history of Robert and Elizabeth's relation as created and revealed in their letters. But he moves easily and imaginatively across a variety of approaches to these exceptionally difficult examples of epistolary art. He is the first writer to attempt seriously to define the special nature and quality of these letters, at once very special biographical documents and exceptional works in the canons of both writers: for Elizabeth, exemplary products of a major nineteenth-century epistolary author; for Robert, as Karlin rightly emphasizes, the one exceptional attempt (along with the essay on Shelley) to write in a different form from his poems, to write "RB, a poem" rather than dramatic utterances. Karlin is astute in his analysis of the lovers' drama played out in the letters: the very different personal histories that flow side by side, each finding in the other a means to evolve and complete a personal myth long in the making. He carefully and lucidly plots the main events—Robert's first letter, Elizabeth's decision to let him visit, Robert's sudden and destabilizing declaration of love early in the correspondence (the one destroyed letter), Elizabeth's emotional distancing from her father, culminating in his forbidding her to go to Pisa for her health, the secret engagement and its tensions, and, of course, the decision to elope. Anyone who has seriously attempted the letters, which Chesterton famously stigmatized as letters from the Cherokee, will appreciate the order Karlin brings out of the poet's abundant chaos. He is especially good in assessing central issues behind the surface of the letters, such as their uneasiness over Robert's need to depend on Elizabeth's inheritance (threatening to mark him as a traditional fortune hunter) or Elizabeth's uneasiness at Robert's absolute insistence on her authority. His account essentially provides us with a piece, for these years, of the fully researched biography we are otherwise lacking.

He is as effective in analyzing the letters as special kinds of writing. He explicates and probes Robert's compulsion somehow to get beyond words to his real feelings in this one case and shows how this leads in practice to a dramatic monologue of RB that focuses on his own poetics: expressing his love effectively and dramatically, as Elizabeth shrewdly remarked, "with that pretension, too, to dumbness," by the rhetoric of insisting that language cannot embody the full conception. Karlin rightly stresses the importance of Robert's statements about the differences between himself and Elizabeth for his poetics as a whole and shows how Elizabeth is interpreted by him to take the place of the Shelleyan poet: one who *is* the poetry she speaks, who is the true poet yet also exists in violation, and indeed in a certain contempt, of all that Robert believes about the nature of language and artistic achievement. In this respect Karlin shows Robert's theories very much in accord with Martin's conception of his art as successive, open ended, extended in time and space. Karlin gives less space to Elizabeth (and perhaps somewhat underrates her work) but does show the different way in which Robert's influence only brings her to redirect her religious and apocalyptic poetics to glorify Robert and this world with the religious sanctification she had previously reserved to a better world far beyond Wimpole Street and its invalid's room.

The second half of Karlin's book presents chapters on salient topics in the letters. It suffers, as such structures are liable to, from repetitiveness with the history in the first part. Yet there are important new perspectives: for instance, on the way in which external realities such as London acquaintances become internalized in the private and highly symbolic language these poets so egregiously developed. I especially like the treatment of Mr. Barrett, whose patriarchal sins are made manifest but whose fictional place in the psychodrama of two lovers working to free a daughter from her dependence on dad is also emphasized. The comedy is how wonderfully he plays into the needs of the two lovers, doing just those things that will allow the daughter to re-create him from affectionate patriarch to mythical tyrant. One could even speculate (though Karlin does not) that he acted out unconsciously a repressed desire to rid himself of the superannuated child who had for so long, and so elegantly, staged her passive resistance to tyranny in the illness of her room. For better or worse she would now be Robert's problem, as he would be hers. I only wish Karlin had somewhat reflected back the realities of their complicated married lives on the splendid myths of married fulfillment Karlin so well shows the two master poets creating—each with rather portentous indifference to what the other is planning.

Karlin does a great service in forcing us finally to deal with the impressive anomaly of these letters, which have been neither the domain of the popular Robert-Elizabeth cults (this is very *un*-popular work) nor really a part of the canons of the poets. He has in this book drawn continuously on the excellent work of Elvan Kintner, who completed his exceptionally fine edition of the love letters just before his so unfortunate early death. He pays the tribute that Kintner would doubtless most wish—of showing how these difficult letters, now available to us because of his fine work, can take their proper place among the exceptional works of both poets.

With so many fine books on Browning this year, as well as excellent editions, I will have to be forgiven briefer mention of articles. Beside Martin's work can be placed the excellent article by Christine Froula, "Browning's *Sordello* and the Parables of Modernist Poetics" (*ELH* 52:965–992), whose generally persuasive reading of those very difficult self-reflexive passages in *Sordello* fill out Martin's description of Browning's poetics in the area in which he is probably weakest—the reader's part in the text. Froula also sees Browning turning from a Shelleyan poetics of inspiration to a world of change and uncertainty; she identifies the new poetic and political project of *Sordello* as one inviting the reader as brother and as made-to-see into the process of the poem, a stance that she identifies, perhaps too inclusively, with post-Romantic poetics generally. Her analysis, articulate where Browning seems only suggestive (or, as she notes, parabolic), in some sense completes the statement of *Sordello* where Browning sought a new role for the poet in history. She could well have observed that such an idea, once seized, would naturally redirect Browning's efforts from the reader-antagonistic, ironico-prophetic statement of poetics of *Sordello* to the reader involving and provoking art of the dramatic monologue, where our egregious critical history of varied readings testifies to the high degree of reader involvement Browning sought and obtained.

Warwick Slinn (*BSN* 15:1–9), in a critique of an earlier article by Ann Wordsworth, insists on maintaining the concept of the subject in a post-structuralist vision of the dramatic monologue. The subject, he argues, can only be thought of as something constituted by the text, but it continues to exist within the text and can't be merely washed out of our discourse on the dramatic monologue—an important point that could serve as a clarifying addendum to his own deconstruction of Browning's characters in his book. Two interesting general articles in which Browning figures deserve mention as well and touch on similar issues. Gerhard Joseph (*VP* 23:403–412) explores the premonitions of post-structuralist ideas of mirrored regression (the Quaker Oats box effect) in Victorian poets with ease and impressively broad learning. Herbert Tucker's fine essay, "Dramatic Monologue and the

Overhearing of Lyric" (in *Lyric Poetry: Beyond New Criticism*, edited by Chaviva Hošek and Parker: pp. 226–243), discusses elegantly the co-presence of romantic, lyric expressive and dramatic, historical and contextual qualities in the dramatic monologue. Beginning with a possible historical model in which Browning and Tennyson both react against J. S. Mill's idea of poetry as overheard feeling, or in any event react against the critical milieu in which Mill's opinions were set, he sees the dramatic lyric form as provoking, and re-enacting in the reader's experience, the conflict between rhetorical, dramatic communication and lyric utterance. Tucker offers the dramatic monologue as the test case for literary pedagogy and poetics in the twentieth century, with a brief turn-of-the-century rejection of dramatic for "pure" lyric leading to a re-assertion, in Modernism and New Criticism, of the speaker in poems. Finally, he finds deconstruction questioning the imaginative creation of character by its emphasis on the textual. His balanced judgment, that we should accept a new version of a reader's creative conflict between these two tendencies, without yielding one to the other—focus indeed on the emergence of character out of language—is commendably comprehensive yet, like the idea of lyric moments in the contextualized drama, productive as a practical approach to interpretation.

Pound's relation to Browning was a major critical interest, to set alongside Posnock's work on James and Browning. Most important is George Bornstein's fully researched and interestingly argued chapter "Pounds Parleyings with Robert Browning" (in his edition of a volume of essays, *Ezra Pound Among the Poets*, 1985, pp. 106–127). Drawing on manuscript material at the Beinecke he demonstrates a surprising specific influence of *Balaustion's Adventure* on the young Pound. There Pound learned to follow Browning in seeing his relation to an earlier poet not as a trial of competition and blocking anxiety but as an infusion of strength from craftsman to craftsman. At the same time, Browning's creative translation of Euripides can be seen to have encouraged Pound's other method for making past literature new. Bornstein locates this influence in the poem "To R.B.," which is more specifically related to Browning and Balaustion through manuscript sources: the poem is spoken by Pound's mask, one Cooper, who discussed *Balaustion* with R. B. Bornstein provides a full summary of Pound's long dialogue with Browning, in poems such as "Mesmerism," Pound's many Browningesque monologues, and the *Three Cantos* (1917) that closely followed Browning in *Sordello*. Although he identifies a period when Pound did feel the need to criticize and throw off some of Browning's influence, he sees him ultimately as an example of a kind of poet, with his stress on craft and on the atemporal co-presence of all great works of art, who is less susceptible to Bloomian anxieties of influence. Jonathan Ward ("Pound's Browning and the Issue of Historical Sense," *BSN* 15:10-28) also provides much detail on Pound's long and developing relation to Browning. He essentially embroiders on Jacob Korg's article *(ELH* 39:420-440) in which he saw Pound moving from an earlier romantic sense of history, which he identifies with Browning and Carlyle, to a more objective division between history and myth in the final revisions of the early *Cantos*. There is, I believe, an overstatement of Browning's disregard for historical accuracy in contextual poetry (as also in Bornstein's comments on this issue: Browning's errors follow his limited scholarship not a romantic disregard for accuracy) and also an overstatement of the "objectivity" in Pound's accurate but rather notorious substitution of massive quotation for historical judgment and political acumen.

Of studies of individual poems, two notes on "My Last Duchess" by L. M. Miller—on the context in Renaissance connoisseurship—and George Monteiro—on Frà Pandolf—(*VP* 23:188-195) are of interest, especially the implication from Monteiro's source that the original of the friar had gotten into amorous difficulties. Russell Goldfarb (*SBHC* 13:59-69) continues a current process of revaluation of Fra Lippo Lippi in a careful article that raises questions—obvious enough when one looks at the friar aslant his beguiling rhetoric of naughtiness—about his moral justification. As with a number of famous monologues that attract revisionary readings, there is need for some way of putting the problem of the many possible stances of the reader at the center of the interpretative act. Is there any way in which we can determine that one or another reader's position is implied or demanded by the act of the poem itself? Jeff Karr suggests some interesting parallels between Paley's *Evidences* and "Caliban upon Setebos," though the attempt to read the poem precisely as a version of natural theology in a Darwinian world leads to more qualifications and complications than his scheme wishes. Certainly this is a key, if not the key, to the poem. William Butts (*SBHC* 13:24–36) takes as a premise the multiplicity of satiric reference in the poem. He focuses instead on the Menippean satire on Caliban's mental processes, a model for the poem that has the advantage of explaining the general reader's pleasure while allowing for the variety of interpretations of satirical reference that have appeared and doubtless will keep on appearing.

Following the work of George Landau and the dissertation of Linda Peterson, Glenn Everett ("Typological Structures in Browning's 'Saul'," *VP* 23:267–279) makes a convincing demonstration of Browning's conscious use of typology as a structuring device in "Saul." The interpretation is doubtless now in a general way familiar for this monologue of a Biblical character but Everett works out the details persuasively, especially the conversion of images from natural to typical in the development of the poem. He raises interesting questions about what use such an interpretative method was to a Victorian aware of alternative skeptical structures of experience (heaven does not generally open up for Browning's characters). One could even ask to what extent Browning is using the tradition self-consciously, portraying a religious mythological nature rather than making his own testimony through a sacred monologue. Anne Hiemstra (*SBHC* 13:47–58) also suggests some interesting archetypes in *The Ring and the Book*. Finally, Ann P. Brady's study of Guido's sexual treatment of Pompilia (*BIS* 13:137–164), placed in a broad condemnatory survey of his and Arezzo's churchmen's patriarchal predecessors in the Church—Paul, Augustine, Aquinas, et al.—complements Buckler's stress on Browning's attack on misogynist traditions. Browning's position could probably be stated more specifically as a condemnation of the social system of arranged marriages (soon to be replaced in the time of the poem by what Stone has called affective individualism) that placed an unwilling bride such as Pompilia essentially in the position, as Brady points out, of a prostitute. Her collation of passages shows that Browning deals rather forthrightly with the problem of her sexual relation to Guido.

Having slogged through reviews of so many critical books and articles this year, perhaps I may be permitted a broader concluding note. This is only to observe what may seem an alarming schizophrenia in the critical world, if the output in this special field is typical, as I believe it is. We have totally different critical discourses in the work of Martin or Posnock, highly influenced by recent theoretical work, and that of Buckler and Karlin, who innovate within the now traditional Anglo-American modes of moral observation and close analysis or biographical and psychological contextualization and critical commentary. I believe that the point to make from this year's work on Browning as an example is not that we aren't two critical nations at the moment—rather obviously we are; nor is it that some are hopelessly outdated and some are with it; nor is it, I think, that we await some synthesizer who can make all these discourses one by a brilliant work of translation (which is not to say it isn't worth the effort: Posnock's work talks to Karlin's about the myth of a private sexual life, first created by Robert and Elizabeth long before James; Karlin uncovers the explicit poetics that translates into Martin's description of Browning's linguistic world; Buckler, like Karlin and Martin, shows Browning's preoccupation with the limits of words and his skeptical analyses of characters in *The Ring and the Book* are, in effect, deconstructions of monological interpretations of any speaker—unless Pompilia miraculously speaks out the white light which, Karlin tells us, Browning believed Elizabeth did). Rather, we should say that there is critical vitality on a number of fronts, some more established, others following out new conceptions. The good work that has appeared this year in both older and newer criticism hardly suggests that more traditional modes of discourse have played out their usefulness; indeed, Karlin's book, of the four, will probably have the greatest overall impact on our larger vision of Browning because it opens up not just an approach but an entire part of his canon; nor does it indicate that new theoretical conceptions of literature and of the relation of literature to experience can be dismissed as ways of approaching an individual writer. There is room for good work from a variety of approaches; the need is always for the exceptional work that makes us see a writer/his work, no matter how familiar they have become, with new eyes.

Robert Browning: Year's Work, 1986

As in so many years recently, 1986 saw steady and impressive work in developing the basic scholarly knowledge of Browning's texts and context that has been for so long badly required. To begin with texts: with the attention given to the new Penguin/Yale and Oxford editions of Browning there has been a tendency to count out the once famous—or infamous—Ohio edition. It has its very serious problems; it stopped publishing for many years; but it is not dead. A decent fifth volume appeared in 1981 covering the last of the *Bells and Pomegranates* through the first half of *Men and Women*. It is finding capable direction and bibliographical competence in managing editor Allan Dooley. The old problems with the copy text and with inadequate knowledge of manuscript materials have been essentially licked (I won't rehearse my evaluation of these technical issues in the Ohio text which I presented in *VP*, 1982; the procedure and most of the Introduction remain the same). We now have from Ohio (1985) a rather exciting event: the publication of *The Ring and the Book*, books one through four, edited by Roma A. King, Jr. Collins-Pettigrew did not include *The Ring and the Book*, which had been previously issued in the same series in a text edited by Richard Altick of the 1868–1869 first edition. Oxford has a very long distance indeed to go before it arrives at the great epic of Browning's late middle age.

Altick's edition quietly asked the dangerous question that everyone now seems to dare ask about texts: why prefer an author's last intention to his earlier one? The Ohio edition, which suffered badly in the reviews for its difficulties in identifying Browning's last intentions, oddly now does well when we begin to accept the idea that there are many legitimate texts, from different points in the author's life, that different readers, for varying reasons, will wish to consult. The old Ohio's notorious idea of the author as a continuously innovating medium seems where many of us have come to, after all the controversy over Wordsworth and Shakespeare. In its almost as notorious recording of all variants leading up to the copytext, Ohio gives each reader a kind of kit to create his or her preferred text. The Ohio edition offers a virtual rare bookroom full of texts for any Browning poem where the determined critic can trace the author's changing intentions and craft for any particular line—as well as the occasional interference of the printer. Unlike Altick, King offers us the text from Browning's old age, the 1889 second impression of the 1888–1889 text. For this text, unlike many of the earlier poems, there are, in fact, few changes from the first edition to the copytext. Because Ohio is now careful not to authorize and endorse changes made by printers' errors, one could argue that this is a very reasonable choice for a reader's text. Browning touched up word choice or phrasing here and there rather than rewrite the text, as he did some others, especially *Pauline*, by favoring his mature judgment over that of his earlier self. (Like Morse Peckham, who did a separate edition of *Sordello* to show how often one could argue changes in successive texts were the printers' rather than Browning's, I incline to suspect that there could have been more justified editorial emendations than the two and a quarter pages chosen here.) What is interesting is the text of the manuscript of *The Ring and the Book* that can be reconstructed from the variants. We can see quickly how Browning's conception developed into the classic phrasing of the text we know. Without a trip to the British Library and days of hard labor we may easily appreciate the pains Browning took, as he put his text in shape through manuscript, galleys (apparently not extant for books one through four), and revisions (in Beinecke: Ohio provides readings of page proofs and corrections on the proofs, as well). The poem that proclaims our human speech naught was created with great care; having the full record of this care in the text offers some great advantages to compensate for the cumbersomeness of the Ohio presentation.

A spot check of some four hundred lines (no errors at all) shows that the editors are transcribing the text carefully, as they did in the fifth Ohio volume, though not always in the earlier volumes. King offers a useful and concise chronology of events in the story (oddly a chronology of history and fiction, *The Ring and the Book* and *Old Yellow Book* at once), a description and account of the sources, and a history of the composition of the work. The latter seem even too brief, omitting a great deal of Browning's comments on the work in progress, its relation to Elizabeth, and his odd offers to other writers of his quarry. The notes themselves are an important update and addition to detailed scholarship on the poem. Any annotator of *The Ring and the Book* has the advantage of standing on the shoulders of giant (if sometimes nodding giant) antiquarians, Treves and Cook. King was also fortunate in being able to draw upon the good work of Altick's edition of the poem. King is now the last word: his annotation is generally as full as Cook's and as authoritative as Altick's. He gives essay-like commentary on perennial thorny subjects—Molinism, St. George, the ring and the ring metaphor, Pompilia's literacy. He wins kudos for identifying the philosophic sin and has other small but important triumphs such as the meaning of "Quiet as Carmel" as reference to the nunnery. More generally valuable is the wealth of Biblical reference he rightly concentrates on identifying. Years ago Minnie Machen's little book on *The Bible in Browning* pointed out how rich the verbal echoes are. King adds tens of such identifications. He explicated the many literary allusions consciously used by Browning's speakers. We have only to remark how free Browning is of verbal echoes (as opposed to direct allusions) to any text except the Bible, in tremendous contrast, say, to Tennyson: not a proof of Browning's limited education only in the Bible—the poem is packed with a very wide literary culture in its direct allusions—but indication of Browning's refusal to work in other poets' syntax and lexicon. A special problem in *The Ring and the Book* is the "real" history: should the annotator, as Cook often does, make it his business to write a running history of the historical events as he, as opposed to Browning, now sees them based on presumed superior powers as a scholar and the fuller historical record we now possess? The temptation is irresistible; the rewards, satisfying the reader's curiosity naturally roused by the historico-epical poem, making one's own Bloomian strong reading of the poet's text, are considerable. I like Altick's quick treatment of such issues. I have, grudgingly, to admit that King's added commentary on the history is hard to resist: one has a curiosity about the texts beyond the text. Too often the spirit, as with Cook, is simplistic: the real truth versus the poet's lies. Historians now tell us history is itself a matter of fictions and fictions. One fears for the beginning student who is led down the path that proclaims the poet's truth naught and every scholar's words the simple facts.

Annotation in this volume continues, in one respect, the Ohio tradition: they do not curb their eloquence. Notes begin well with much new research; they end in pedantry. Like Pettigrew in the same series, Altick has the virtue of pithiness: a great virtue for an annotator. Compare his on *alembic*, "distilling apparatus" to King's "A simple apparatus for making distillations" or on *Domus pro carcere*, "house arrest" to King's "Literally, a house for a prison: a condition corresponding to our 'house arrest.'" If there are no longer notes on Venice as a major Northern Italian city there is still the old (and so natural to teachers of the poem) Ohio desire to tell all, with excessive notes on subjects such as the geography of the sea of Galilee, the Pope's Jubilee, Cicero as a Roman statesman and orator, and comfits. A general editor, insisting on condensation in each note, would have done wonders and kept the reader's attention on the poem itself.

With these weaknesses, this is nonetheless a major piece of work, excellent in its sensitivity to literary effects in the poem and unflinching from hard points. Combining such an excellent text and useful apparatus with such a high level of annotation, the Ohio *The Ring and the Book* promises to be perhaps the most valuable contribution the edition has made so far: an acceptable scholarly text of Browning's great single poem.

That other seemingly endless publishing project, *The Brownings' Correspondence*, came out with the fourth of the forty or so projected volumes. The size of the venture will show its worth when it comes to the years in which Robert and Elizabeth's lives ran together: the synoptic letters will give us a great deal of day to day detail on both poets, with the special illumination that comes from so many crosslights. In the meantime, the plan rather swamps poor Robert in the *far* more abundant letters of his talented future correspondent and spouse. In the earlier volumes this effect was perhaps easier to overlook. Robert's rare early letters also began later than Elizabeth's so one was content to murmur: his time will come. But here we are up to the quite public Robert of 1838–1840, the time of Macready and *Sordello*, the young man making his way as an established force in the new Victorian generation. And still we wade through pages of entirely unconnected material to find the few Robert letters (or if we are reading Elizabeth's far more vivid chronicle of this traumatic period in her life we are rather rudely interrupted by somewhat too formal and artful letters by an unknown man accepting or regretting invitations to dine). Perhaps it would have been better to throw consistency somewhat to the winds for the period before the convergence of the twain and give us one slim volume of all Robert's early letters. Certainly both the scholar and the general reader would prefer it so.

Of the 181 letters in this volume, 28 are by Robert, and they are an even smaller proportion by bulk. Another five are to Robert. Except in the love letters, whose importance as a kind of high poetics as well as high drama Daniel Karlin's book recently and rightly emphasized, Robert was generally neither a revealing nor an artistic letter writer (whereas throughout her life Elizabeth is one of the more interesting correspondents of the century). The letters in this volume are not an exception. Only three, to Fanny Haworth, have some of the personal projection and literary flamboyance of the love letters, muted in proportion as this seems to have been a controlled flirtation in comparison to that full-hearted love affair. A few other letters, notably one to Domett and one to Macready, are also full and interesting reading. The majority are simply brief notes of two or three sentences, aimed as the great majority of Browning's letters are at accomplishing a piece of business cordially and efficiently.

This is not to say that the Robert Browning letters here are unimportant. We have so little in the way of primary evidence of his early years that even brief notes are of special value, often throwing the only light we have on months of his life. Of the twenty-eight letters by Robert, sixteen are here newly published (three of those to Browning are also additions to the record). This considerable supplement to prior volumes of Robert's letters certainly continues to show the fruits of Philip Kelley's years of preliminary research. He has found good letters in such less-than-well-known literary collections as the Dunedin Public Library, Dunedin, New Zealand or the Southwark Central Reference Library in the poet's old stomping grounds. Among the new letters is quite an important one in the series to Haworth, which includes interesting references to Procter and to L. E. L. as well as the curious information that a horse named Paracelsus was running at St. Leger. There is also a brief but warm letter, in French, to the French friend Ripert-Monclar—from the series of interesting letters that had long been known by, but were not available to, Browning scholars. Other, less intrinsically interesting letters provide a good deal of useful information about Browning's serious efforts to advance his career during this transitional period. A number show him nervously sending copies of *Sordello* or receiving the warm but not generally positive responses of literary friends—Landor (Browning values his critical judgment very highly; he returns that he looks forward to reading the poem but that Browning overrates his acumen), Procter (he is about to read it), Milnes (Browning hopes the poem pleases), Ripert-Monclar (Browning recalls how they used to talk about Sordello), Harriet Martineau (she hopes the poem will prove a crown to him). Of course it was to prove more a crown of thorns than of laurel, at least in the short run, and other letters show us the young poet moving quickly to cover for his tactical error by pushing plays on Macready and offering more popular works and plans for popular publication to publishers such as William Smith. Other brief letters show us Browning writing to the scholar John Payne Collier for information about the ballad *The Atheist's Tragedy* or planning to take Landor and Tennyson (the books) with him to Italy. Apropos of that 1838 (*Sordello*) trip to Italy, the editors generously include a full transcription of Browning's brief diary entries on the voyage, from the Toronto MS. Here we can pinpoint the very day Browning was off St. Vincent, how he came into Venice to his appointment with roughhewn humanity, and exactly the days and places of his almost pilgrimlike experiences in the heights of Asolo.

The volume is as handsome and generously executed as the preceding three: beautiful print, paper, and cover, lovely frontispiece and illustrations, full supplementary materials, including a record of other documents relevant to this period: a fine product made in America by Philip Kelley's intelligent, lean, and efficient Wedgestone Press with proper support from NEH. Annotation, by Ronald Hudson, is generally up to the high standards established in earlier volumes. DeVane and Knickerbocker's *New Letters* are corrected for dating of one important letter (that to Macready, now of August 9, 1840) and Hudson often gets hard references others missed (e.g., young Edward Denison, Bishop of Salisbury at age 36). Here and there one looks for a bit more: for instance, what was that *Atheist's Revenge* ballad? Could a clearer discussion be offered of the Shelley volumes (as indeed it is in *New Letters*) that Browning sent to Moxon? In reading the accessory materials one is oppressed by thirty-seven pages of Barrett materials, much about issues that Jeannette Marks already has explored in more detail than most anyone could wish, and only four entries for Robert. Surely there is more, including those in Macready's diaries, cited even in the notes themselves—or do I misunderstand the system in this appendix? Many of the annotations, including identification of that horse named Paracelsus from the *Times*, are exceptional bits of scholarship; the full printings of published reviews for the period is a great service in itself, often the result of more than ordinary searching and scholarship. Despite reservations about the premature marrying of Barrett and Browning in the endpapers and motto on the cover I continue to believe this is an extraordinarily important and generally excellent edition, a major addition to our knowledge of both poets.

Some interesting specialized studies also valuably illuminated special corners of Browning's life and associations. Patrick Waddington's interesting little book, *Browning and Russia* (Baylor Browning Interests) bears a date of late 1985 but didn't appear on my desk until later. It deserves its modest place on the full Browning shelf next to Korg's study of

Browning and Italy or Gridley's *The Brownings and France*. Browning had only two important connections with Russia, in contrast to the immersion in Italian and French literature and life: the interesting trip at the beginning of his career in 1834 and the fine late poem "Ivàn Ivànovitch" on a Russian subject. Waddington has made no newsworthy discoveries about either of these connections but, with his excellent knowledge of Russian literature, language, and history he has provided a remarkably detailed record of what can be known. Through the accumulated detail of his researches into Browning's early visit and his careful review of the possible sources for the poem (none of them in fact directly Russian) he leaves us far better able to form a critical assessment of Browning's interest in this, then, rather marginal and ill understood culture. Research into state papers has, alas, not revealed specific references to the young English poet traveling with the Russian diplomat Benkhausen (Waddington prefers the Slavic Benkgauzen), but it does clarify the origins of the trip in a crisis over Rothschild refinancing of the Russian national debt and the duration of Browning's stay in St. Petersburg (one month). Better, he gives us a realistic circumstantial picture of the world of Russia and St. Petersburg that Browning would have experienced, including the carnival fair on the Neva that he considered using as a setting for a drama. The wealth of details about various Western versions of the sleigh and wolves story of Browning's poem makes an interesting history in itself, especially because the origin of the tale remains unclear. Waddington also offers a comparative account of Robert and Elizabeth's political attitudes toward Russia (not much in Elizabeth's favor) and a summary of Browning's relations to Turgenev (neither very cordial nor admiring).

In another fine piece of scholarship, really of modern antiquarianism, John Coulter (*BSN* 15:2–19) presents new evidence about the Browning residence at New Cross based on an entire archive of the Haberdashers Company, which owned the land on which the Browning family residence after 1841 stood (and who finally succeeded in pulling it down and erecting row housing in 1890, thus obliterating all memorial of the residence). Coulter's new evidence and excellent careful work allows him to establish the exact site of the Browning house, telegraph cottage, somewhat to the west of my own speculation, and also to obliterate the one possible visual impression that has survived. Coulter's prints of the nearby area do confirm the impression we have from the letters that the Browning family lived at New Cross in a very comfortable area of country homes, still outside of London's encroaching and enormous development. The two servants in the Browning household indicated by Coulter's new records, while fewer than the three or five servants of some of their grander neighbors, certainly confirm the sense of substantial comfort we have of the family. This is an excellent work in those incredibly dusty local records, where a good deal more research could be done on the social context of Victorian literature.

A final, very competent, and useful work of biographical scholarship is Meredith B. Raymond's substantial article on John Kenyon (*SBHC* 14:32–62). Raymond offers a full account of the Brownings' friend and generous patron, based on careful work in a great variety of published sources as well as some unpublished work (some presented at the end of the article). There may be minor additions and adjustments when the full record comes out of the Browning correspondence but this will stand as a very thorough, well-balanced, and thoughtful summary of the life and work of this interesting person. Kenyon, as Elizabeth wrote Robert, was something of a "Sybarite of letters" rather than a full man of letters. He avoided mental labor and strife of heart and lacked the "faculty of worship" (which she believed Robert had in good measure). If he indeed was no Robert (or Elizabeth) he was a man of importance in his day whose philanthropy is especially memorable. He gave the Brownings substantial support during his life and a fortune at his death, settling once and for all the question of what porridge Robert Browning would have. One of the effects of that fortune was to allow Robert to move into his patron's shoes, as a prominent participant in literary society as well as literary production. Kenyon's poems, on toleration, on the limits of his own abilities, and on many an occasional subject, were no wise up to Robert's, as Kenyon knew. As a literary man of the world Robert never could come near

Kenyon's high and genial style. "Kenyon the Magnificent," as Robert called him, seemed to know every writer of importance in the two generations of English literature up to his death in 1856. His magnificence in generous support for literature and charity (he left money to ninety persons at his death) and in the famous hospitality of his literary breakfasts (where the fare was far above porridge) was accompanied by less of the older Robert's boisterousness and self-proclaimings, less of Elizabeth's posing and moral domination. He was a Pickwick or Jarndyce, but also something of a Skimpole, who preserved a childlike love of life's joys. If Dickens couldn't imagine the combination, real life could, and also gave him a sense of refinement in appreciation of the arts and delicacy about others' needs. Biography delights in such unbelievable and attractive hybrids, where no novelist could dare offer such a patent fiction. Raymond tells a pleasant and interesting tale comprehensively and very well.

In contrast to these important advances in editions and scholarship there was considerably less important critical work, a good deal less than the prior year. Perhaps energies went into the unusual Browning conference at Southwestern College, close by Philip Kelley's trim and attractive world headquarters for the Browning correspondence at Winfield, Kansas: an interesting gathering of scholars and a fine exhibition of Browning manuscripts; or perhaps critical studies are being delayed in publication for the centennial year in 1989. Mary Ellis Gibson's *History and the Prism of Art: Browning's Poetic Experiments*, announced for 1986, in fact appeared too late in 1987 for review here. How much there is still to explore on the subject of Browning and history is clear from Lee C. R. Baker's "The Diamond Necklace and the Golden Ring: Historical Imagination in Carlyle and Browning" (VP 24:31–46). Using Hayden White's theoretical approach to all history as necessarily involved in fiction-making, Baker distinguishes between Carlyle as historian as romantic ironist and Browning as historian as unself-conscious mythmaker. The final turn of the essay, in which Baker evaluates Browning's insistence on myth-making as his particular strength, doesn't seem persuasively argued. Yet Baker's critique of Peckham's position that Browning can be seen as an historical relativist aware of the limits of all positions including his own is a useful one, well presented.

George Myerson has a cogent and well presented essay on *Paracelsus* in *Browning Society Notes* (15:120–147), a journal that deserves better circulation in the United States (it is *not* like the original Browning Society publications: indeed it is rather intelligent and even intellectually bold, as is that other misnamed, or too modestly named journal, *Browning Institute Studies*). Myerson explores Browning's sources for the poem in Crollius and Paracelsus' *Philosophy Reformed and Improved* (1657, in English) and Agrippa's *Of the Vanity . . . of Artes and Sciences*. He uses this source work to establish a newer and more interesting point: that Browning has a thesis about Paracelsus as a scientist, as well as a romantic quester. Using Kuhn's paradigm for the emergence of modern science in the breakdown of the closed Neoplatonic or Hermetic system of magus and magic and its replacement by an infinite and objective system of scientific exploration, he shows Browning criticizing Paracelsus' initial role as subjective possessor of truth (Book I) but explaining his final vision as the successful discovery of the universe as open, objective, and infinite (Book V). Finally, he defines Browning's view of science as exploring God's infinite universe in opposition to totally secular paradigms for the universe. This is an important interpretation that raises our judgment of Browning's historical ability in the areas of intellectual history and history of science.

Samuel L. Chell's *The Dynamic Self: Browning's Poetry of Duration* (1984) shares Myerson's view that Browning discovers in Paracelsus contrasting ideas of time that are essential to his work. Unlike Myerson, he is not interested in the scientific implications of the new time of infinite extension but in time itself as at once subject and structure of all Browning's poems. Chell adapts Bergson's concept of time as duration within experience rather than, on the one hand, eternity removed from life or, on the other, mere material motion in a straight line (as in clock time). Chell then essentially makes a reading of Browning's poem from *Pauline* to *The Ring and the Book* with the theme of time as his central truth. We read Browning's message about time as ultimately a psychological and spiritual one: the dynamic self, to remain dynamic, must remain in time. Time as change may be creator or unmaker, but it will prove a truly destructive element only to the character (or reader) who attempts to evade the process. Dynamic selves accept experience by intuitively building on past and present in inner consciousness. If Sordello generally refuses process and tries to thrust in time the concerns of eternity, the lovers of "By the Fireside" richly mature, not by freezing the good moment as an epiphany out of time but by building their self-consciousness on a sense of past and present. The Browning philosophy of time, which is surely convenable to many concerns in Browning's poems, ends even with the old central truth—incarnation as the symbol of the reconciliation of eternal and ordinary time.

There is something too static in this approach, which too often accepts the model of old time in which a philosophy of life (even an attractive, pulsating one) is read into and out of Browning's works. And Chell indeed can see his activity not only in relation to Tucker's work on Browning's evasions of closure or Hassett and Slinn's concerns with definition of character in Browning, but also in harmony with the traditional cause of answering Jones and Santayana's claims of barbarism in Browning. A more complex system for talking about time would have helped (Bergson is no longer the only starting place: I do count one mention of Poulet, although there may be others I couldn't find in this indexless book). A structure that explored Browning's varieties of views of time rather than began, dissertation-wise, with a formula—even the elegant and brief formulation of Bergson that Chell provides—would have thrust the criticism more into the moment and away from the general exposition of a position. The point is not that Browning had a good or bad theory of time (isn't even Santayana's poise and civilized permanence attractive to all readers of Browning sometimes?). The point is that Browning is much preoccupied with time in his work. Indeed strong readings could see individual poems—"Pictor Ignotus," "Abt Vogler," "Andrea del Sarto," or "Cleon"—revealing a deeper drive toward release from the wheel of time or the Heraclitean/Browningesque flux in which they are found.

Chell's own reading, of *Pauline, Paracelsus*, and *Sordello*, of monologues on love, art, and religion, of *The Ring and the Book*, are generally not as challenging on the subject of process as Tucker's or no probing about the substantiality of character as Slinn's. They are nonetheless well worth consideration. At their best they stress not only the thematics of time but also time as structural element in the poems. He makes many interesting points about the time tenses of poems as modes of presenting issues of time (to be compared with Loy D. Martin's more technical observations on "The Being Written" in his *Browning's Dramatic Monologues and the Post-Romantic Subject*, 1985). Chell also makes interesting speculations on time in the consciousness of the reader, especially in *The Ring and the Book*—though these are not fully worked out into a system of reader response (or reader manipulation). Chell is certainly correct in calling our attention to the centrality of time in Browning's poems: his implicit definition of a Browning monologue as a compression into a few lines of the consciousness in time of a lifetime is an excellent starting point for his explorations of the tremendously different time systems of different poems.

Another work, also actually published in the fat year before this lean one, Harold Bloom's *Robert Browning* (Modern Critical Views) is a collection of articles and selections from earlier years. It does feature as Introduction an interesting article in which Bloom revisits his own career-long preoccupation with Browning's revisionary company, especially Childe Roland. Bloom is among the extremely few major, general critics who have insisted upon wrestling with Browning's obviously central, exceptionally eccentric, place within the canon of English poetry. No critic is more exciting to read on Browning: without a major work on Browning himself (as, say Shaw, Tucker, Ryals, or even Miller—a long section in *The Disappearance of God*) he has, by his controversial strong readings of Browning as antithetical quester, probably come closer to dominating critical discussion on Browning than anyone else since Langbaum. His revisiting here addresses metacritically his own obsession with the antithetical quester in "Childe Roland" and, as with most obsessions, succeeds especially in repeating the obsession: how can we relate Browning's quest (to put it briefly and badly) to that of Shelley? Moving through a dazzling group of interpretations of Browning's poems on music, of "Andrea del Sarto," of "Childe Roland" (once more briefly but impressively) and of the stunning lyrics of *Asolando*, all of which he reads by the light of both Nietzsche's deconstructive formulas and Freud's familial interactions, he arrives finally and unexpectedly at the neglected poem "Thamuris Marching." Here is the quester once again, doomed to defeat but happy in the sublime moments of earthly joy, a fellow traveler as poet of earth to Shelley as poet of divination. Perhaps the problem of reconciling Browning to the Shelleyan model of the poet is there laid to rest. But evidently such good readings, which keep insisting on "strong" readings of poems against their apparent grain, also read Browning generally against the grain. Bloom focuses obsessively on the few poems in which he can read the character as a version of Browning himself, as one reads poems of most of the Romantics. Even Andrea del Sarto, whom he grants is not like Browning, is still presented as a projection of the poet's situation. To find him citing Betty Miller repeatedly, without much criticism of her simplistic equations between Browning as man and Browning's characters is not surprising. More essentially, the poems are read *as* Romantic poems, as quests for the self-definition inhabiting poems. That an objective poetry of earth might demand an entirely different poetics, closer to systems of irony and rhetorical structures more amenable even to Both, Iser, or Riffaterre than to Bloom, doesn't seem to occur to him—or when it does such canonical approaches to "poetry always dramatic in principle, and so many utterances of so many imaginary persons, not mine" are swept away with majestic contempt. We are fortunate to have in Bloom such an inspired misreader of Browning, whose strong cuts *à rebours* force us to set aside our whittling commentaries on individual monologues and face the major issues in defining a poetics for Browning.

The collection is an interesting addition to Bloom and Munich's useful earlier compilation of critical essays. It somewhat oddly mixes classic statements in the relatively recent history of Browning criticism (since Langbaum, say, and beginning with him, in fact) with less well-known but attractive essays, not necessarily in the mainstream of critical concerns, such as John Hollander's lovely "Browning: the Music of Music." Tucker's central work appears briefly near the end of the collection. In between is a long reprint of Bloom's own familiar reading of "Childe Roland" from *A Map of Misreading*. That Bloom leaves out entirely major modern criticism of Browning (Hillis Miller, Shaw, Ryals, even Slinn's provocative work) while publishing so many essays essentially sympathetic to his approach is bothersome; Armstrong sees "Mr. Sludge, 'The Medium'," in her intricate interpretation, as a kind of failed quester; Tucker is the most Bloomian of the new theoretical critics; Ann Wordsworth's fine Lacan-inspired essay on the gaze in Browning is also Bloom-inspired and is in fact reprinted from Bloom and Munich's earlier collection; Steven Shaviro's reading of "Caliban" is another Freudian study of a quester. Bloom has a right to choose criticism he finds convenable and offer a very personal recent critical history. The rest of us would be better served by either another broad collection of the major approaches to Browning from Langbaum to the present, or, what is probably of more use now, a collection of the newer theoretical approaches (Shaviro, Tucker, and Wordsworth stand for them here) that have been revising our way of looking at Browning in the 1980s as much as Bloom himself did in the 1970s.

Vincent P. Anderson's *Robert Browning as a Religious Poet: An Annotated Bibliography of Criticism* (1983) is a useful work of critical bibliography, also really a contribution to the history of Browning criticism. Many readers may not find the subject promising since it must surely take us back not so much to Browning's exciting poems on religious subjects but to those studies of Browning as a religious leader, as an answer to the problems of faith for our time, as a poet of the incarnation, and all the rest, that began with the original Browning Society and continued with Berdoe, Charlton, and their successors —and seems to go on and on, if one looks at Books in Print, as the reprint houses keep churning out these antiques of Browning scholarship to their helpless customers, the unsuspecting or very thorough university librarians. I should say immediately that Anderson lacks the ironic perspective and close wit that made William Peterson's study of the Browning Society such fun to read. (Anderson does call Hickey's "Glorious Robert Browning" an "unfortunate title.") But his thorough and modest commentary provides a very useful anatomy of these and the many other kinds of attitudinizing on Browning and religion that have characterized the unfolding reception of this controversial part of his canon. We have had heretical Brownings, skeptical Brownings, Brownings very sure of God and pessimist Brownings, existential Brownings, Brownings preoccupied with a central truth and Brownings swimming in phenomena, Brownings for whom God is love and Brownings for whom He refuses to come. I suggest that anyone interested in adding to this (on the whole) not too impressive literature first study Anderson's general summaries and useful annotations. Excerpts from some contemporary reviews at one end and summaries of dissertations at the other, both not definitive, are also useful; and Anderson helpfully notes the relevance of general critical and biographical works to his central issue.

Ashby Bland Crowder, in a long article, "Browning and Women" (*SBHC* 14:91–134), enters a passionate area in a quiet and orderly way. After a review of Browning's relations with women, he summarizes Browning's attitudes toward various topics relating to women. He leaves the poems to the side and treats the letters as so much expository material. This approach raises some questions: letters are not essays but reactions to dynamic and changing real situations. Still Crowder is aware of this problem and does tease out of this somewhat alien material a fairly coherent profile of Browning's warm, generally positive, sometimes confused attitudes to women. He liked women physically, liked to touch and hold them—the collected evidence seems to raise that old question of whether Browning had some kind of secret life before Elizabeth or after her death—but he also could criticize women for showing physical affection in public, and then again get rather too physical himself for some of his dinner companions' tastes. He believed generally in women's ability to achieve aims as high as men's but pooh poohed their being allowed in to the hurly-burly of Parliament. He believed strongly in rescuing poor women bullied by patriarchal dragons—so they could begin a new life as strong mentors and leaders of their rescuers, who would sit at their feet. What does man want? Crowder's odd methodology, leaving out all those poems on these subjects, at least allows a dispassionate comparison of what we think we see in the splendid poems to what we are sometimes only amused (or sorry) to find in the prosaic letters. George Ridenour also treads on ground that feminist critics dispute when he attempts to show the parallels to *Aurora Leigh* in *The Ring and the Book*. Robert creates Pompilia in the image of Marian Erle, herself indebted to the real Elizabeth, despite the difference in class. Verbal echoes, even the phrase "the central truth," point back to Elizabeth. Robert's epic follows his wife's in its realistic material and melodramatic treatment. Yet, here's the rub: Robert's melodrama is better, "more consequentially melodramatic," than his predecessor's (predeceasor's). Shouldn't the next point be a version of Nina Auerbach or Adrienne Munich's views of the two poets' relations: Robert misprisions Elizabeth with his distorting and defeating work; his ring, as Munich has said, surrounds and cancels hers: poetic posy proves stronger poetry. At least such a point of view would strengthen Ridenour's significant comparison.

Finally, two articles tried out new approaches to Browning's work that should prove productive for other critical efforts. In his "The Arrangement of Browning's *Dramatic Lyrics* (1842)" (in *Poems in Their Place: The Intertextuality and Order of Poetic Collections*, ed. Neil Fraistat), George Bornstein reminds us how carefully Browning paired dramatic lyrics in the original volume and shows the important lights attention to the poet's ordering can throw on the themes and art of the poems. Like Yeats, Browning crafted his individual volume to create a larger poetic design that gave special kinds of significance to individual works. Bornstein's interesting summaries of themes in these generally matched and interlocking poems shows how productive this approach can be. Because Browning later reorganized these poems in collected editions—a fact that Ohio and Penguin/Yale have preferred to ignore in their orderings—

his original orderings take us back to some troubling questions about choice of text. We have some argument for reprintings of the original edition as well as the artificial text we have—later texts in original publication order—in the standard editions.

Sarah Gilead's "'Read the text right': Textual Strategies in Bishop Blougram's Apology" (*VP* 24:47–67) takes us, once more, into the breaches (or gaps) of this labored, and frequently labored over, monologue to try out some new critical models. Drawing on Huizinga and Caillois' ideas of play, and on Herbert Tucker's concept of the ducal reader who attempts closure, she sees the three personas, Blougram, Gigadibs, and the narrator as all playing a game of trying to frame and bring to closure the others: a lively critically current article that is also somewhat too rushed, unfocused, and tends finally to create its own distorting frame of triple game for what is mostly the verbal pyrotechnics of only one player.

Good as some of these studies are, important as the Browning texts being published are, the year's work leaves me forced to conclude that this was not a boom one for Browning—a dip in the overall index after last year's high volume of activity. It has given me a chance to do belated justice here to some works from that year. I won't believe, after such very lively debates between the older New Criticism and the newer theoretical work in the early 1980s, that we are moving into a critical age of tired or sullen silence.

Robert Browning: Year's Work, 1987

In 1987 another installment appeared in the excellent progress this decade has made in editions of Browning's texts with even more promised or out in 1988. If this work was stricken through with doubt and eventually stopped for a long period in the seventies by the controversy over proper copytext and other editorial procedures, it has now been resumed with assurance in a textual age built on acceptance of reasoned disagreement and variety. Collins and Pettigrew gave us a competent working text of Browning's poems, and Collins and Richard J. Shroyer now (1988) have out with Garland a complementary edition of the plays, newly edited with full textual apparatus. Ian Jack's Oxford edition moves slowly but magisterially ahead. In 1988 appeared the third volume of the Oxford edition and also the second volume of the Ohio *The Ring and the Book*, the only fully edited modern version of Browning's epic.

The monumental edition of the Brownings' letters also continued at its impressive pace. Editors Kelley and Hudson issued volume five in 1987 and have six out for 1988. The fifth volume, the one to be reviewed here, takes the correspondence from January 1841 to May 1842. It is de facto a feminist volume with Robert out-epistled by his future, still stranger, wife, by a huge margin. I have noted the difficulty that the editorial convergence of the twain before their time makes for the scholar of either one, though there is the advantage of seeing synoptic accounts of similar London literary events. There is so little Robert here that this theoretically useful effect is in fact pretty much absent. Obviously, when their lives begin to come together, the joint printing will be extremely useful. In the meantime we can search through for the occasional terse, often slightly embarrassed note by Robert among his isolated wife's flowing correspondence. One is, as always, impressed by the editors' thoroughness and system in finding such scattered letters, but also by Robert's own thoroughness in covering over his early tracks. For the period of volume five there are only twenty-one letters by Robert, of which only six were previously unpublished; in addition, one is fully published that was partially printed before; parts of another, from an obscure Sotheby catalog years before the famous sale, rank as a discovery. There are six letters to Robert, all previously published. In such a faint record the recovery of each scrap or brief note is an achievement. The new letters are brief; they show Robert citing Apuleius to Mrs. Jameson, and, in another, professing his passion for Correggio, sending a copy of *Pippa Passes* to Ripert-Monclar in good formal French, asking Macready if he has yet read the manuscript of *A Blot in the 'Scutcheon* and, in another, thanking him for a season's pass to Drury Lane. Alfred Domett's previously unpublished letter to Robert just as he left England is a warm one; he tells Robert to write for the world and for him in New Zealand. Nothing especially revealing here, but as in prior volumes, carefully edited and well annotated. Having tried myself, I was not surprised but sorry Hudson could not nail down John Poole's six lines quoted in the long letter to Fanny Haworth of 1841. In the same letter Browning's interest in Polidoro da Caravaggio through his famous Andromeda print might have been noted. The additional apparatus in the appendices, a bonus in beautiful volumes produced at commendably low prices, includes sketches of Carlyle and others, usefully focused on relations to the Brownings, related correspondence (almost all, here, on Elizabeth), and the especially helpful reprints of contemporary reviews (here of *Pippa Passes* and *King Victor and King Charles*). As Ian Jack has noted (see below) to read these original responses is to see a work like *Pippa* with eyes stripped of the conditioning created by years of reception: it is, as indeed it still is in many ways, another difficult work by the author of *Sordello* and rather shocking in its materials, tales of passion and "common courtezans of the poorest class" (*The Spectator*, April 17, 1841).

Richard L. Purdy possessed a private collection of letters, journals, and other papers relating to Browning's youthful friend Amédée de Ripert-Monclar. This collection has now gone to the Beinecke where it is open to all and has been extensively drawn upon by Kelley and Hudson. I can record here my gratitude to Professor Purdy for a delightful day's quick look at these materials while still rejoicing that they are finally in the public domain. We have a special treat now in being introduced to these materials most graciously by Professor Purdy himself—through belated publication of an article he wrote in 1945 (*YULG* 61:143–154). Although the information it cites is generally available in the published letters, the article is a clearly written, beautifully balanced summary that reminds us of the unpolemical, untheoretical, and humane scholarly values of a very different age of literary study. It is good to have the collector's introduction finally before us.

While textual work on Browning has continued to provoke and extend fundamental issues that make his editions major cases in point in current debates on editing practice, critical discussion of Browning has at least reflected well the promise and confusions of our conflicted, and now rather prolonged, moment of fundamental reexamination of theoretical principles. At times the year's work has even suggested a division moving almost to schizophrenia, both between traditional close textual analyses and theoretically inspired new critical enterprises and among those multiplying and spawning approaches themselves.

A substantial critical study, Mary Ellis Gibson's *History and the Prism of Art*, has its own problems with diffusiveness. But it has the singular virtue of critical comprehensiveness and coherence. It has not forgotten the historical enterprise that survived wave after wave of onslaught from the New Criticism but has recently seemed abandoned in our theoretical ferment—or driven into the strange byways of the so-called new historicism. We were trying to understand the Victorian period in all its exceptionally complicated relation to the emergence of the modern mind and world when we were interrupted by the literary philosophers with their hard questions. Gibson gives us a very useful, well-researched, and well-presented context for Browning's interests in history. She rightly avoids those old narrowly focused quarrels over the accuracy of Browning's historical assertions—the interpretation of *The Old Yellow Book*, Hulking Tom's relation to Lippi, and the rest.

Instead she shows us how to understand the historiographical complexities of Browning's context, the ways, for instance, in which the new demand for a history based on accurate evidence of Ranke and his school is not inconsistent with a focus on point of view and cultural context. She intelligently places Browning among emergent concerns with context, spirit of the age, cultural history, and the relativism of perspectivism in historical thinking by drawing on both works and biography, for instance the important personal influence of both Browning's historically preoccupied father and his friend/mentor Carlyle.

Gibson brings her definition of Browning's historiographical outlook to bear on interesting interpretations of *Sordello, The Ring and the Book,* and a number of the central historical dramatic monologues. If these do not have the excitement of, say, Herbert Tucker's readings, they are nonetheless contributions to reading Browning from a particularly well-informed and well-considered point of view. She frequently returns to central problems of how to read a Browning monologue that she rightly takes up from Langbaum, and she is right in effect to insist that new critical perspectives cannot eliminate those troubling though now aging questions—questions well raised by Langbaum but never well answered by the New Criticism, which indeed found Browning a major stumbling block to its usual preoccupation with aesthetic wholes and metaphor. Better than many of the more recent critics of Browning who have reached out more and more eclectically to a potpourri of critical approaches, Gibson moves reading of Browning along a path that is central to American critical discourse while she also adds something new. This somewhat bold approach may please no parties in our world divided between old Turks and young smarts. It at least pleased me. I felt I saw some new approaches I should have worked out, but had not, and I saw some new problems that might take me further. Her interest in a rhetoric of the monologue, with a reader driven to seek out a context and apparatus by which to find an author's point of view to put against the character's reminds us of the kind of dynamic of reading Browning we have too much overlooked since Langbaum's groundbreaking work. At the same time, I was often as uncomfortable with her implicit movement toward a notion of an authorial intention (the poet's point of view) as both New and newer critics will be. Yet substitute reader for author, as she often does, and we are very close to a reader-response approach to Browning. Her use of Wayne Booth, especially his later, less well-known *A Rhetoric of Irony*, offered a clear and rather precise way to speak of the historical ironies generated in Browning's work and also to suggest their frequent indeterminacy within such a rhetorical and normative way of reading (Iser's affinities with Booth, critical and historical, are well known; their unwillingness to release the reader from seeking a correct, normative reading is also a major similarity). With such familiar American tools, Gibson finds her way to a vision of Browning's ironies not unlike Clyde Ryals' (to whom she perhaps owes more than she acknowledges) as well as to notions of disclosure and historical openness or finality not so different from Tucker's. Her insistent interest in the veer Browning takes from romantic historical ideas of coherence and prophecy is quite productive in demonstrating Browning's strong rereading of a major romantic issue.

Having said so much positive, I must register a number of dissatisfactions. The intellectual historian and historiographer would rightly look for an even broader picture of historical movements in the nineteenth century and find the linking of Carlyle, Ranke, and Burckhardt, even with her excellent special pleading for their similarities, somewhat misleading. The theorist will find discussions of spatiality very one-sided, and apparently unaware how important the attack on spatiality has been in post-structuralist thinking, rather in contrast to Loy D. Martin's confusing eclectic but theoretically very sophisticated study of 1985. Readings of poems are often less illuminating than the general context she brings to reading history in Browning. The argument for Browning's relation to twentieth-century poets on history is both too long and too short: too long merely to serve as a reminder of the general value of his work, too short to deal with this large subject in itself in any meaningful way. Finally, while there are good general observations about Browning's relation to the difficulties of language in his insistent confrontation with history, the final chapters seem to go off on a tangent on Browning's diction. This is a large critical book that perhaps tries too much. The ideas and scholarship are always interesting; a good deal of cutting and editing would have created a better, and probably more influential, book. It is an impressive work of synthesis and consolidation of scholarship and critical thinking and certainly deserves to be read, studied, argued with.

The same should be said of David Latané's Jr.'s *Browning's Sordello and the Aesthetics of Difficulty* (University of Victoria English Literary Studies, 1987), a work far less likely to obtain the reading it deserves. It appears in a good monograph series rather than an excellent university press, perhaps because of editors' prejudice these days against studies of individual authors or, worse, specific subjects. We have all had to read many a vacant survey that skims across our desks from fine presses and skims across a number of writers to present at too great length its article-length central idea. By contrast, this little book (a merciful 132 pages) actually leaves one with the sense of knowledge advanced in that central gaping darkness in Browning studies, *Sordello*. Latané's, like Gibson's, is an example of a criticism that successfully unites analysis, historical scholarship, and theoretical sophistication. He builds on the fine work of both Tucker and Ryals on the early Browning, offering a sophisticated restatement of the first's view of *Sordello* as a work of Romantic Irony and working comfortably in the second's vision of the poem as a workshop of dis-closure and rebeginnings. His own contribution is especially to rethink the art of *Sordello* in terms of recent interpretive theories of reader response. I have in past reviews noted the good prognosis for such an approach to Browning and even did something about it in a study of rhetorical similarities between Donne and Browning (*John Donne Journal* 4:253–257) and a separate article on the subject (see below). Latané's book-length beginning of this subject has the great virtue of grounding a model for critical activity (look at the work as something that calls for certain kinds of activities or responses in the reader) in an historical survey of the way in which Browning, and the late romantic generation in which he began, conceived of the reader's role. This bright, skillful, and original approach to Browning thus brings the double cannon of thoughtful Constance, Iser, and Jauss, response and its historical horizon, to bear on the young Browning's most ambitious engagement with his reader.

The lore of *Sordello*, which we all know, tells us that few readers were up to Browning's onslaught. But Latané shows us that Browning very much followed the model for serious works of his day (his examples include *Sartor Resartus*) of appealing to a fit audience of the few who could provide an active response, hard thinking, and imaginative work. The work, as Browning's Preface to *Paracelsus* proclaimed, is so many stars, with so many gaps and rifts in its narrative texture, that the reader must himself make into a constellation.

Latané's own relation with his reader is skillfully managed: he uses Iser as a standard model of a conservative reader-response approach (the work has a rhetoric which controls the kind of response the reader makes) while also siding with us (and Fish) on its limits. He persuades us of the use of such an approach by a great deal of evidence of Browning and his age's awareness of reader response by many a similar name. He then explicates *Sordello* in language we can follow far more easily than that of the poem while showing us how much Browning built his poem on thematics of reader issues and by very heavy demands on his readers. Thus shown the hard work we should have done, who would complain, especially as we are given the option of making our own reading, when Latané hits the most complex passages of the poem. I liked especially his careful unwinding of the levels of reader in the work—the friends Browning addresses, the great poets the narrator summons to hear or snooze over his tale, the real audiences, including Salinguerra himself, to whom Sordello sings, the People as an historical figure for the ultimate audience poetry aims to help, and all of us readers. We last were given by the poet the large task of being brother poets and makers-see ourselves. Some of Latané's observations on historical interpretation come close to Gibson's own and would have benefited from her fuller historical context (his allusions to Romantic history are too broad and vague). At moments when even Latané falters among the many voices, elliptical allusions, riddling parables and manifold aporias and hiatuses of the work, one is tempted to see this reader-response approach as merely a way of justifying a poem in which the poet left all the work of making any sense out of his story and its self-reflexive themes to his poor reader. Indeed, Latané's excellent collection of different comments on *Sordello* by Browning's contemporaries includes just that astute complaint. But whether you smell the civet they make perfume out of in your brotherly cooperation with the author or mere skunk, you, dear perplexed reader of *Sordello*, will find this one of the few works that actually helps explicate and describe the poem. Latané rightly sees it moving always in at least three dimensions, the text reaching out to us with questions, demands, and especially blanks to fill. This is a very well-written book, filled with excellent new historical digging (for instance on the familiarity of Browning's material in his day or on the theme of Rome in contemporary literature), sophisticated in its theoretical references and argument, coherently fashioned into a fine book on *Sordello* that also allows us far better to see the poem's relation to the usual Browning canon—beginning with its own Epilogue on the connections of *Pippa Passes* to *Sordello*.

Latané's mediating work between theory and history acknowledges his debt to Ryals's fine book on the early Browning. Ryals adds an interesting footnote, but I hope also work toward a new book about middle Browning, on *Christmas-Eve* (*FNT* 17:39–44). Using his central critical trope of Browning as ironist, he warns against the temptation of reading this work as a statement of the biographical Browning's position. The speaker combines seriousness and levity and reveals himself as ironic author of a fiction at the end.

A fourth study, a longer article, also begins to build toward a less polarized criticism this year. E. Warwick Slinn, "Consciousness as Writing: Deconstruction and Reading Victorian Poetry" (*VP* 25:67–81) is an exceptionally lucid and well-argued approach to Browning's own exceptional "Two in the Campagna." The refinement over his more broadly argued deconstructionist book on *Browning and the Fictions of Identity* is impressive, especially in moving toward a less radical stand on identity as mere fiction. His explanation of Derrida on Freud on writing is the kind of "theory" of deconstruction that will hardly persuade those not enthralled by the deconstructionist master's enticing games. Consciousness is not to be precisely defined by Freud's model of the child's mystic writing pad (plastic over a wax base) but it helps Slinn moderate excessive deconstructionist claims of the end of consciousness. The model is now of a subject that writes and is written simultaneously, aware of itself but thus aware of consciousness as being controlled by language as it controls it. Such a model yields a splendid interpretation of Browning's poem—which is among his very finest just because it is a monologue whose speaker is so aware of the shaping forces of its language. Here, Slinn persuasively shows us, the Browning speaker is most free and yet most aware of how little control he can have of his consciousness as it exists in his language. Slinn then is able to explain the way in which the poem grows to an awareness of the desire of consciousness to reach stability by its own obliteration—as here, in love, or, in Slinn's interesting parallel in Arnold's *Empedocles,* in death. A fine article that is good to see in *Victorian Poetry,* where it may help bring a better dialogue between our critical schools.

Two articles on *The Ring and the Book* also show critics working more familiarly with current critical theory while making contact with central traditional critical issues. Kris Davis (*VP* 25:57–66) counters simpler views of an heroic Caponsacchi with a penetrating look at the priest's passivity and his sense of being pushed by his experience of Pompilia into a kind of crack, between church and sexuality, comfort in this life and security in a larger moral order. Davis' article usefully insists on the complexity of the character as his words create him set against the heroic images others create for him. Ever since *Hamlet*, such perplexity is of course the mark of the authentic hero in the modern world and need not conflict, as Davis seems to imply, with the heroic image others have of him. Adam Potkay (*VP* 25:143–157) is more wide reaching but also more insistent, in a way that verges on dogma rather than theory, on his poststructuralist schema. He easily shows that Guido was of the deconstructionist's party all along. In this he does rightly emphasize the character's interesting stress on antihumanistic dark truths: the instability of character and the multiplicity of interpretations and perceptions. The trouble is this view is too easily given the day: Guido is neither defined nor saved at the end, Robert is just another character, ditto the Pope and Pompilia, relativism is all, sometimes a ring is only a ring. The tension between skepticism and Browning's roundabout and comprehensive way of shaping an experience of seeking truth is lost in mere theory. The characterization of the opposite position, as leaping to sudden closure, is really a caricature. Potkay comes very close to inventing Gibson's argument about historical point of view; his argument could be strengthened by following hers on the kind of truth that can yet emerge from a history built on skepticism and many perspectives.

If I do say so myself (for I am guest editor with editor Adrienne Munich), volume fifteen of *Browning Institute Studies* (1987) is sometimes more polished but on the whole less effective as an updating of traditional close criticism of Browning and a dialogue between theory and practice. The editors say as much in their perhaps too arch (but interesting) introduction. The volume is a special edition, based on papers submitted to a well-attended international Browning conference at the rather improbable location of Southwestern College, Kansas (in the home town of the Browning letters enterprise). Articles, on Lippi, on Galuppi, and on "Pan and Luna" continue prior debates, Joseph Dupras perhaps most strikingly by giving us the other view of Lippi seen under the sign of reader's judgment rather than sympathy: this, he cleverly argues, is not Browning's ideal figure for the artist but—well— a very fast-talking libertine brother both in his life and works. Where Gibson would say we give Lippi understanding through historical placing and context, Dupras argues, perhaps too much from Browning quotations from outside the poem, that there are serious moral and aesthetic questions being begged, where we should beg to disagree. There are two good articles on *The Ring and the Book* with a broader scope: Allan Dooley interestingly explores epic and anti-epic tendencies, rightly stresses the transformation of traditional epic (as in

Wordsworth or Pound the poet emerges the hero) and also the Bloomian process of the strong poet submerging and altering his predecessors. Munich's own contribution holds up the ring metaphor to scrutiny one more time, now to analyze its Etruscan origins and to examine brightly its implications as a transformation and strong overcoming of a female symbol, itself a symbol of the work of the dead beloved herself: a continuation of the discussion of psychic and poetic conflict between the two very different heirs of romanticism yoked together by Victorian marital love. Ian Jack's article on *Dramatic Lyrics* is a rich first fruit of scholarship from his work on the Oxford edition. He points out how little we have looked steadily at the oddity of this classic volume as it was first published, how many fundamental questions, such as dating of many of the poems, we have left unexamined, how easily we have let conjecture and error slip into the record. My own contribution to the volume, which I leave the reader to judge, is another approach, in the same large critical areas as Latané's work, to the reader in Browning, here defined as an overhearer to the dramatic monologue.

Two substantial articles, both interesting but of uneven overall quality, deserve final mention. Kenneth Maclean's "Wild Man and Savage Believer: Caliban in Shakespeare and Browning" (*VP* 25:1–16) adds little to the extensive literature on the monologue as it gracefully places both Shakespeare and Browning in the thematic tradition of the wild man. His stress on the unchanging quality of Browning's Caliban in contrast to Shakespeare's leads him not to tease out much vitality from the monologue itself, which he sees primarily as reducing all liveliness of perception to materiality and death. The combination of great energy with a limiting intellectual system is more dialectic or dynamic opposition than reducing system. Laura Haigwood's "Gender to Gender Anxiety and Influence in Robert Browning's *Men and Women*" (*BIS* 14:97–118) attempts an intertextual reading of Robert and Elizabeth with some success in showing us a dialogue of themes and images, especially Robert's comments in his poetry on *Sonnets from the Portuguese*. The article suffers from indecisiveness over whether Robert was a boasty male who encompassed and silenced his wife (the theme well presented by Nina Auerbach a few years ago and by Munich in the article mentioned above) or a sympathetic husband who left Elizabeth the room of her own poetics. Haigwood starts tough but lets Robert off rather easily by the end.

    I think I see my way to ending with at least a more positive ring than in past years on evidence that the critical ferment of our time may be producing a new brew, more generally palatable to all students of Browning; that we may even be approaching a time when theory and analysis will work together to extend the understanding of Browning as remarkably as the debate in editing has extended our knowledge of his texts.

The Decade's Work in Browning Studies

When I was volunteered to write a summary of the decade's work in Browning criticism and scholarship for *Victorian Poetry*, this did not seem a too much larger task than the year's evaluations I have been turning out for most of this decade—only one-thousand percent. It was, in any event, not the entirely appropriate, but far too ambitious, task of a summary and evaluation of the century's work. The common wisdom is that criticism, and even editing practices, have (as you like it) finally come of age/gone entirely crazy or to the dogs of late so that recent critical history should, in any event, stand alone, case unparalleled.

In fact, I find now that I am not so sure that the subject easily stands alone. The more I think about what we have said and learned about Browning recently, the more I am seeing patterns that go right back to the century of criticism—so much of it seemingly outdated and overworn—since Browning's death. I should not be so surprised: one of the many things we have been learning by relearning is the dependence of all cultural products, including our own genteel work of criticism, on the work that preceded it and on which it necessarily feeds—feeds much more than we like to admit, with our Romantic and overreaching faith in the originality of critical genius. As modern theoretical criticism has tended to diminish belief in the absolute originality of creative genius, it has seemed only to leave critical originality, by vanity or courtesy, still standing as a hopeful exception. All the recent work in criticism, so new and original, looked at again, seems at least firmly rooted in the past. By the same token our residual Romantic faith in a few Promethean and determining new critical approaches and individual critical movers and shakers bumps up against a growing sense that an invisible hand of critical history has moved us all along a few heavily channeled critical canals. Doubtless certain critical barges catch our attention far more than others, blazoned with sharp thinking, festooned with wit and excellent writing. But the more I assemble the pieces of the picture, the more I begin to see the preoccupations that create our critical culture, that indeed give us as firm critical horizons as those of any other age and make true originality, except as small moments of innovation on the current drift, unimaginable. What will criticism of Browning look like at the bicentenary? We can't know or we would be there already. All we can know is that the scene then will have great historical sap roots in our own—though what now seem the major elements to my eye in 1989 may look like so many irrelevant miscellanea put in one of those time capsules to the desperate reviewer of 2089 who—God love you—should take an interest in what we thought of our contribution at the time.

Perhaps I dare say that the future historian of the reception of Browning in the 1980s will be likely to say very much what we all always say of Victorian culture: it was a time of change and a time of continuity, a time that thought it was undergoing major changes and achieving major conservations. (And of course it thought it was the best of critical times and the worst of critical times.) The sense of great change, great conservation, momentous consequences hanging on the resolution, was nowhere more evident, or strident, than in the set of critical issues turning on the current debates variously labeled deconstruction, post-structuralism, or more broadly, post-modernism. And here the historian, like ourselves, may see the intense disagreements of the time as often more apparent than real, concealing by their shrill opposition the tacit agreement about what issues are central and worth discussing.

Certainly this is the area of Browning studies, as of literary study in general, where there has been the most action—and most lively discussion. I hope I will be forgiven if I begin, like the author of *Sordello,* by summoning up a worthy from the past to focus this discussion and suggest how deeply seated it is in perennial preoccupations of Browning criticism: I call as undeconstructive a figure as G. K. Chesterton himself—a pre-postmodern, pre-modern, indeed by preference medieval man. Yet his mature fictions, no less than his early tortured drawings, were haunted by a vision of a world in which nothing exists beneath appearance, all things fall apart, noses, as in *The Man Who Was Thursday*, keep deconstructing. In fear of such a postmodern world he of course called up a ruddy solid man, a kind of Yeatsian fisherman of poetry, the good Robert, English as old ale, creating a super-solid neo-Chaucerian world of fictional people. Never mind that many are villains, fast-talkers, or self-deceivers: they are at least real fictions, with no complexities of difference between art and life, from an age when writers' hearts beat hard and their brains ticked high-blooded. If Chesterton could shore up a vision of Browning's unified sensibility against the ruin promised by the coming century, Santayana, of course, saw him not as the solution but the problem, a force of barbarous emotional chaos threatening to overwhelm organization and order. Browning's position as a contested case—a figure of either reassuring solidity or disturbing disintegration—has persisted through the rage of modernism for order and into the rage of post-modernism at order. The issue could of course be traced back to Browning's own confused vacillations between an objective and subjective role for the poet and these conceptions have also persisted in the debate. Those seeing Browning as a creator of objective and hence "real" characters have focused on explaining their genesis or on the moral issues that naturally come to the fore when we imagine fictional characters as people much like those who live in real Valladolid. Jacob Korg's *Browning and Italy* (1983) continued this tradition in focusing on the relation between Browning's life (in Italy) and his works (Italian scenes—though mostly from literature not life) and in arguing for the influence of Italy in leading Browning to an objective poetry based on a substantial world of real men and women. Or William Buckler, working in a close analytical and in itself somewhat skeptical tradition associated with the New Criticism in his *Poetry and Truth in Robert Browning's* The Ring and the Book (1985), nonetheless emphasized moral issues in evaluating Browning's characters, on the presumption that an essentially mimetic art demands an evaluative and moral criticism: how lifelike and convincing are they? what does one say about their values and actions? Or, in an apparently different mode of criticism, Samuel L. Chell in *The Dynamic Self: Browning's Poetry of Duration* (1984) used Bergson (and not Poulet) to stress the coherence of internal experience and internal time in Browning's rendition of the consciousness of time of a lifetime compressed into a dramatic monologue (and we remember that stream of consciousness itself could function either as an extreme of realism or as its subversion). The combination in Chell of a substantial and referential view of the nature of Browning's art (creating coherent consciousnesses) with an argument stressing Browning's belief in immersion in the destructive element of time and defending Browning against Santayana only suggests on how many different levels of criticism these issues played out their oppositions.

On the level of character, the most obvious and most recurrent arena for debate in Browning criticism, the case for insubstantiality and deconstruction was made most emphatically by E. Warwick Slinn in his *Browning and the Fictions of Identity* (1982). Here again, far from creating a totally new approach to Browning, Slinn had distinguished predecessors, for instance in J. Hillis Miller's early phenomenological criticism, *The Disappearance of God,* which stressed a common experience in Browning characters rather than their solid individuality, or in W. David Shaw's focus on argumentation, which created not so much a vision of substantial identity as Kierkegaardian levels of being in character (*The Dialectical Temper*). Drawing on the full-blown poststructuralist dogmas of the necessary fictive non-referentiality of language, Slinn subjected Browning to a rigorous reading on a "dramatically based model of man as artifice." As in Leo Bersani's seminal study of character in fiction, *A Future for Astyanax,* substantial characters, all those men and women, are dissolved not merely into dramatis personae but a "shifting series of dramatic hypotheses, unified only by a self-perpetuating consciousness." Each monologue deconstructs its own appearance of creating coherent identity. Slinn has somewhat moderated his views in later, interesting articles (e.g., *BSN* 15:1–9: *VP* 25:67–81) but his position, in its extreme deconstructionist first form, found echoes in later criticism, for instance Adam Potkay's somewhat reductive reading of *The Ring and the Book* (*VP* 25:143–157). A less influential work, in some respects less challenging in its approaches to individual poems, Constance Hassett's *The Elusive Self in the Poetry of Robert Browning* (1982) is also a more useful approach to the broad issue of substantiality of character. Hassett in effect argued for discriminating between constructivist sheep, known by the experience of conversion that creates a coherent personality within, and incoherent goats, who, like Guido, are mere artifices of their own will to persuade or perform. She allowed us to see Browning's presentations of character historically, set in a moment (though perhaps it is one of those historical moments that keeps recurring) when the notion of character is in crisis between creation and decreation and thus problematic.

Two finer works of criticism, by Herbert F. Tucker, Jr., and Clyde de L. Ryals, and a suggestive one by Loy D. Martin, with many parallels, took these issues to a different level of critical discourse. Tucker's justly celebrated *Browning's Beginnings: The Art of Disclosure* (1980) looked less at the idea of character than at the way in which Browning's language and poetry works. As such his explicitly Derridean investigation of difference in Browning as a process of avoiding closure picked up much of the strength of the New Critical focus on careful analysis of verbal structures. (Tucker's model explication of Cleon's too well-wrought urn perhaps exemplified the liaisons as well as contrasts between Yale past and more recent.) Starting with an elegant restatement of Browning's convoluted relation to Shelley—differing from whom, he learned to always be differing even from himself—continuing with a thorough rereading of that gateway to Browning monologues, *Sordello,* Tucker elegantly unrolled the process of Browning's poetry in which renewal and new beginnings displace each movement toward artistic finish or completion, thus both enacting and creating modern poetry.

Some of the excitement of Tucker's work—in which we felt a new critical mode really offering a new experience of the work—was repeated in Martin's eclectic, fitfully brilliant and opaque work, *Browning's Dramatic Monologues and the Post-Romantic Subject* (1985). His notion of processive experience paralleled and drew strength from Slinn and Hassett on

Browning's characters, from Tucker on the structure of the poems. To this he added the conceptual schemes of Bakhtin and Kristeva (also suggested by Susan Blalock, BIS 11:39–50) as a way of recognizing the openness and freedom of Browning's poetic world: rather than direct and control his characters he enables them to create a complex system of communication, combining voices of author and speaker, reaching out from the isolated individual to a community of language, everywhere allowing in the monologue a dialogue of social values and of ways of representing reality.

Ryals' work, *Becoming Browning: The Poems and Plays of Robert Browning, 1833–1846* (1983), comes closest to Tucker's in giving us an entire way to reread Browning. Apparently something of a glutton for punishment, Ryals moved from his earlier studies of difficult late Browning to the early difficult (or sometimes tedious) work. What he found there is a different, though often compatible model to Tucker's, more rhetorical than deconstructive, for Browning's ceaseless rewritings of himself. If in Tucker's view Browning is always beginning over again, in Ryals' he is always becoming, moving to position himself at a higher level of being or consciousness. Ryals labeled the process Romantic Irony and stressed the way in which greater breadth of consciousness is always paid for by ironic self-awareness, often both of the limitedness of everyday life and matters and also of the insufficiency of any mythic fabrication of one's becomings into higher intellectual and spiritual states. Such an approach, here focused on the overall strategy of Browning's art, whether in his early long poems, his attempts at drama, or his first monologues, parallels Hassett's to character in that it leaves room for deconstruction and construction, working simultaneously to offer, take back, offer again. The pattern is a familiar one in *Paracelsus* with its ironies of aspiration, attainment, failure, aspiration in failure, and of course in the essential mode of narrative creation/destruction in *Sordello*. Like Tucker, Ryals was especially good in opening up Browning's long deplored early masterwork as the critical entrée to his poetics that it is. Also like Tucker, he was somewhat less impressive when he turned to the fruit of that poetics, the early success of the *Bells and Pomegranates* monologues—though both are excellent on *Pippa*.

If the postmodern, poststructuralist controversy enacted itself in Browning criticism as a restatement in new terms of issues central to Browning since his own distinction between objective and subjective poetry, the equally current and vivid feminist movement in criticism found voice through new articulations of equally old issues: namely the issue, beginning in the 1840s, between Robert and Elizabeth. Who dares judge between a wife and her husband? the traditional wisdom asks. "I," said Victorian critics, who of course regularly preferred Elizabeth and, later, saw Robert as an obstacle to their curiosity about her. "I," said Besier, DeVane, and also so many male and female sentimentalists in and out of Browning societies who fixated their gaze on the rescue of poor Andromeda Elizabeth from dragon Edward Barrett by Perseus Robert—a Caponsacchi determined on rescuing his Pompilia and having her too. And "I," have of course said feminist critics of all persuasions who regularly begin with a view of the marriage of the poets and, from that, fabricate their reading of the works. Here, while there has been important work on the long neglected Elizabeth herself, one must begin by saying that there has been far less important work on Robert than that promoted by deconstruction. Feminist approaches to male writers are a relatively late phase in the rapid evolution of feminist criticism since the mid seventies; the first explicitly feminist book-length study of Robert appeared only this year. The most seminal work, also perhaps the most extreme, was an article by Nina Auerbach, "Robert Browning's Last Word" (*VP* 22:161–173), whose general approach has been followed, with equal wit and panache, by Adrienne Munich (*BIS* 15:69–78). Beginning by deconstructing the idyll of rescue and happy Victorian marriage, they saw the conflict between two types of poets, two sexes, worked out in the poems, especially *The Ring and the Book*, where Browning's final one word more, after his spouse's death, serves to appropriate (or, in Munich's adaption of the ring metaphor, encircle and enclose) Elizabeth. If Auerbach's argument led her to understate the strength of Browning's treatment of women, especially the relatively great truth spoken by Pompilia, other approaches to Browning's treatment of women, focusing on the same issues, somewhat overstated both Browning's "feminism" and the place of

Pompilia in the poem. Buckler's study of *The Ring and the Book* virtually excepted Pompilia from the careful scrutiny of the limits of human truth in words that he brought to bear on the other speakers. Ann P. Brady's recent *Pompilia* (1988) followed U. C. Knoepflmacher's argument for Browning's anti-patriarchal feminism (*VP* 22:139–159) with some illuminating detail on Guido's very specifically sexual tyranny. The work romanticizes both Pompilia and Caponsacchi as saintly discoverers of pure love. The tendency to turn Robert into either a husband devil or a writer of feminist saints' lives was usefully corrected by Ashby Crowder's summary of Browning's perplexed and perplexing attitudes to women (*SBHC* 14:91–134) and William Walker's look at Pompilia's rhetorical strategies (*VP* 22:47–63).

Perhaps the most significant work on Browning and women has been free of direct feminist intent but also centrally focused on the Brownings' relation. Lee Erickson's *Robert Browning: His Poetry and His Audiences* (1984) traced Robert's movement toward writing for an audience of one, his spouse, though this study of a very special reception situation was weakened by his failure to acknowledge the differences and conflicts Auerbach stressed. Daniel Karlin's *The Courtship of Robert Browning and Elizabeth Barrett* (1985), one of the more original works on both poets of the past decade, drew on Elvan Kintner's splendid edition of the love letters to provide a striking analysis of both the psychodynamics and mythopoesis involved in this marriage of true, and very complicated, minds. His analysis of the necessary mythmaking in the damnation of Edward Barrett and the inevitable mutual misprision of poet and lover by poet and lover gives a firmer base on which to develop future stories, whether biographical or critical, of the two poets.

Another major field of critical activity of the past decade, what the New Criticism called the affective fallacy and we have come to call reader-response criticism, has also been a steady area of activity in Browning studies. And like feminism and deconstruction, it has very substantial roots in Browning criticism, along with the coordinate reception studies that also emanate from Germany's critical school of Constance. Study of Browning's reception, before we knew it by that name, featured serious evaluation of the aims and limitations of Browning's age in William Peterson's book on the Browning Society, *Interrogating the Oracle* (1968). Robert Langbaum's classic study of the dramatic monologue in many ways derived its importance from the recasting of traditional genre studies into what we would now call a reader-response mold. Experience in *The Poetry of Experience* is not only the subject of the poem but an action in the reader, who evaluates the poem on the somewhat restricted response coordinates of sympathy and judgment. Langbaum's relative success in speaking excitingly about Browning at a time when the New Criticism signally failed with him, might have suggested the productivity of this approach, under its new name and theoretical formulations, in the eighties.

Erickson's book, mentioned above, was the closest thing to recent full study of Browning's reception. His approach, with its interesting summaries of information concerning Browning's critical fortunes among his contemporaries, opened up a number of subjects but was also marred by its diffuseness and lack of critical self-definition. His shift to an author-centered criticism to propose the rather strained thesis that Browning moved from writing to people generally to an ever narrower target, first Elizabeth and God, then finally God alone, drew his attention away from the full and rigorous study of the context in which Browning's works were received that we need. John Woolford's recent *Browning the Revisionary* (1988) also contained useful information on Browning's critical reception, especially the shocking failure of *Men and Women*. But his main focus in a critically syncretic study was also reader-centered, on Browning's reactions to his contemporary readers' responses—in his next work, where he revised his prior work in a careful response. The dialectic of author and contemporary readers was productive of new approaches to Browning—for instance Woolford's focus on the "structured collections" of monologues in the 1863 reordering of poems, in *Dramatis Personae,* and in *The Ring and the Book*. Woolford's definition of a Browning sequence of poems as a strategy to bring the reader into active work of interpretation often left me in doubt whether he was uncovering Browning's structure or merely providing his own response to (that is, his interpretation of) the themes he found in the group of poems. But as an approach that tried to define Browning's relation to his Victorian audience from his point of view—the critical terms here are strategy or response—it was more convincing than Erickson's. Finally, David DeLaura, in a subtle study of interrelations and to some extent intertextuality between Browning and Ruskin (in *Victorian Perspectives,* ed. John Clubbe and Jerome Meckier, 1989), used Browning's famous comments to Ruskin describing reading as a form of skipping over glaciers as a starting point for fine observations on Browning's demanding, sometimes teasing relation to his reader. He saw Browning positioning himself between the removed classicism of Arnold and the blunt moralism demanded by many Victorian readers—indeed, where Ruskin would have the artist, though he failed sadly to appreciate it in Browning.

Woolford's study, especially the good sections on the political attitudes implicit in Browning's strategy to involve the reader in the poems of the 1830s, can profitably be set beside the more specifically reader-oriented work of David E. Latané, Jr., *Browning's* Sordello *and the Aesthetics of Difficulty* (1987). Latané usefully located Browning's strategy toward the reader in contemporary attitudes, stemming from the Romantics, about the necessary challenge to the reader made by serious works of literature and he provided a just summary of basic theoretical issues in reader-response criticism. His work was especially helpful in unwinding the mummy's sheet of *Sordello* by showing us both the thematics of reader issues in the poem (the many readers it conjures up, including ourselves) and in offering a model reading by the active reader. Christine Froula, "Browning's *Sordello* and the Parables of Modernist Poetics" (*ELH* 52:965–992) also intelligently discussed readers in *Sordello.* The dramatic monologues, where reader-text interrelations are most productively at play in Browning, have received less attention. Dorothy Mermin's *The Audience in the Poem: Five Victorian Poets* (1984) looked specifically at the varieties of listeners in the poems and their relations to the speakers. Herbert F. Tucker, Jr. (in a contribution to *Lyric Poetry: Be-*

yond New Criticism, ed. Chaviva Hošek and Parker, 1985, pp. 226–243), drew upon Ralph Rader's concise generic taxonomy of 1976 (*CI* 3:131–151) to tease out the conflict in the reader's experience of a dramatic monologue between rhetorical, dramatic communication, and lyric utterance. My own article (*BIS* 15:105–112) attempted to configure and calculate the dynamics among speaker, listener, and the reader conceived as an overhearer. Perhaps it is worth stressing the reader-oriented approach implicit in so much traditional Browning criticism. Those "new views" of familiar speakers of major monologues that were so common a product of the New Critical emphasis on interpretation of individual poems paradoxically forced us to transcend all single perspectives by displaying the variety of plausible interpretations available to successive readers. If clever special pleaders and devil's advocates, those attractive/despicable wits of the Browning critical world, have been less prominent recently it is perhaps because a more theoretical decade asks for broader views rather than interpretive tours de force alone. Still I enjoyed many briefer articles that forced us to see another side of a monologue we knew thoroughly and had settled in one pattern or a few: for instance, Joseph A. Dupras' (*BIS* 15:113–122) and Russell M. Goldfarb's (*SBHC* 13:59–65) reversal of our usual sympathetic response to that genial and worldly imprecision and genius Fra Lippo Lippi. Andrea as a Rabelaisian carnival figure anyone? She or he who should be tired of critical one word mores (as I confess I sometimes am) would be tired of criticism itself.

Studies of influences and sources, a preoccupation in Browning criticism since the days of the first Browning Society, have been themselves heavily influenced by the large critical shadow of Harold Bloom who has, of course, generally been at the center of thinking about tradition and intertextuality. Although Bloom himself has never written extensively on Browning, he has given him a central place as a major poet in the tradition and the first strong successor who had to grapple with Shelley's influence. Indeed this central agon of the imagination was already very present at Yale, through the work of Pottle and DeVane, as a model case for Bloom's rethinking of influence in psychoanalytic terms. Bloom's reading of Childe

Roland as antithetical quester, a Romantic reading of a Victorian poet with which we have, most of us, been uncomfortable, has been among the most influential, and provocative, rereadings of Browning since the New Criticism. In his introductory essay for his Chelsea *Robert Browning* (1985), otherwise not a particularly representative or useful selection of contemporary essays on Browning, Bloom eloquently revisited this central critical preoccupation. His importance has been felt more emphatically in the work of his students, especially Tucker's elegant restatement of the Shelley-Browning relation, not to mention productive parleyings with his view in Erickson's, Martin's, and my own study of the early Browning. Important as Shelley's influence obviously was, I argued that we must also see Browning in a broader relation to central English and continental traditions. Two articles on Browning and Keats, U. C. Knoepflmacher on Keats and Browning's feminism mentioned above, and Martin Bidney on "Madhouse Cells" (*SEL* 24:671–681) have at least begun to fill in the picture of Browning's broader romantic heritage. John Coates reached back to Cervantes to interpret "How It Strikes a Contemporary" (*SBHC* 11:41–46) and I argued for Donne's formative influence on Browning's development of the dramatic monologue (*John Donne Journal* 4:253–257). Two full books and one booklet filled in Browning's relations with Italian, French, and Russian literature. Korg's book, mentioned above, was a compendium of source work on the poems with an Italian setting, especially those on art, though less helpful on Browning's relations to serious Italian writers, classical or contemporary. Other complementary studies of Italian sources were made by Mary Louise Albrecht (*SBHC* 11:47–60) and Allan Dooley (*MP* 81:38–46). Roy Gridley, *The Brownings and France* (1982) was exceptionally useful in detailing Browning's reading in and enthusiasm for French writers, especially contemporaries such as Balzac (his favorite), Stendhal, and Flaubert. Mark Siegchrist's *Rough in Brutal Print* (1981) thoroughly presented the lurid French legal sources for *Red Cotton Night-Cap Country*, showing Browning's distortions and changes without denying him his creative rights, as so many commentators on *The Ring and the Book* have, to lie in the service of imaginative truth. Finally, Patrick Waddington's little book, *Browning and Russia* (1985) provided a detailed account of what little Browning did know of Russian writers (on a personal level, mainly a not very cordial relation with Turgenev) and examined sources of "Ivàn Ivànovitch." Browning's problematic relation with Arnold was reexamined in two good articles, John Coates's "Two Versions of the Problem of the Modern Intellectual" (*MLR* 79:769-788) and Jane A. McCusker's study of Arnold and *Aristophanes' Apology* (*MLR* 79:783-796). DeLaura, in the study mentioned above, drew upon both articles to position Browning in opposition to Arnold but in fundamental agreement with Ruskin. The article, using the letters DeLaura previously published, was important for its fuller view of Browning's debt to Ruskin in his poetics—a big improvement over the endless retelling of Ruskin's gracious recognition of "The Bishop Orders His Tomb." It also offered an interesting appendix on Browning's distrusting use of Arnold's key term, "culture."

The investigation of Browning's own influence on contemporaries and successors, also a topic with a long pedigree in Browning studies, found fertile, largely untilled soil, in a non-poet modern, Henry James. Ross Posnock's *Henry James and the Problem of Robert Browning* (1985) again showed the influence on influence studies of Bloom: his elegant argument from both biography and textual comparison suggested that Browning was a central and troubling figure of potency to James. (*Men and Women* was a forbidden and therefore dangerously attractive book to the young James.) In Posnock's original formulation James created a myth of Browning to overcome his influence, much as Browning did of Shelley and, again like Browning with Shelley, he proceeded to encompass and to rewrite Browning's work in his own fiction. The study was a good critical approach to both writers, with interesting ideas about the development of the theatrical self, as opposed to the sincere self of the Romantics, and the use of perspectivism. I was less persuaded by the comparative readings and somewhat unsure of the cross discussions from biography and society to the works: like New Historicist studies that it resembles, there was both originality and a certain degree of idiosyncrasy.

The relation to Pound continued a valued old chestnut in discussion of Browning and modernism. George Bornstein (in his edition of *Ezra Pound Among the Poets,* 1985), offered a full review of Pound's Browning, emphasizing the way in which Pound's renovative relation to past writers allowed him to learn from Browning and build on him without the distortions and displacements of Bloomian anxiety. Jonathan Ward (*BSN* 15:10–27) focused more narrowly on Pound's recasting of historical poetry as he worked through and then away from Browning and, in his penultimate chapter, Loy Martin interestingly underlined the difference in sensibility and relation to the past that led Pound, and even Eliot, to transform totally, and finally abandon, the dramatic monologue. Finally, Bornstein also looked at Browning's relation to Yeats (*Yeats Annual* 1:114–132) and here we end back in Bloom's main-traveled road with Yeats reacting to, and attempting to swerve away from merely following, Browning and Tennyson's first generation reaction to and swerve from Romanticism.

Many major topics in Browning studies over the years have found contemporary critical restatement, though often less satisfactorily and thoroughly than one would wish. There is the old one of Browning and religion, the issue that moved the Browning Society—those pale, unsatisfied ones in their quest for another answer to the crisis of faith of their time—they being unsatisfied by the Tennysonian turbulence that had contented an earlier generation. Vincent P. Anderson's serviceable *Robert Browning as a Religious Poet: An Annotated Bibliography of Criticism* (1984), with excerpts and summaries, served to remind us how regularly Browning has been reread to fit each generation's religious preoccupations. We have had heretical Brownings, skeptical Brownings, Brownings very sure of God and pessimist Brownings, existential Brownings, Brownings preoccupied with a central Truth of Incarnation, and Brownings swimming in phenomena, Brownings for whom God is love, and Brownings for whom he refuses to come. Woolford's book restated Whitla's emphasis on the Truth of Incarnation. Hassett's study of how Browning adapted ideas of conversion and apocalypse in his presentation of character offered a more original study of Browning's particular moment—putting to secular use major aspects of religious tradition. The same was true of Glenn Everett's "Typological Structures in Browning's 'Saul'" (*VP* 23:267–279), which followed generally the work of George Landow and also Linda Peterson's excellent summary, "Biblical Typology and the Self-Portrait of the Poet in Robert Browning" (in *Approaches to Victorian Autobiography*, ed. Landow, 1979). Everett rightly raised questions about the implications of such a traditional mode of interpretation, here again consciously and perhaps also historically used, in an essentially secular literary form. Peterson's more recent article, "Rereading *Christmas-Eve*, Rereading Browning" (*VP* 26:363–380), provided an important reflection on Browning's awareness of hermeneutic problems arising in religious issues and spilling over to all forms of interpretation. Her elegant interpretation of *Christmas-Eve* saw it as an enactment and demonstration of the problems of religious interpretation, whether typological, based on historical tradition, or rational and mythological. In her persuasive view, we are driven to accept the impossibility of privileging any one interpretive stance; hence Browning's poems employing typology necessarily question and historicize the biblical interpretive structures they offer. I was less persuaded by her special pleading for the poem as a turning point in unleashing Browning's reader to multiple interpretations of monologues (the history of criticism of "My Last Duchess" alone says the moment was far earlier).

Other good interpretive articles have focused on religious issues: Blair Ross on progressive mythology in "Apollo and the Fates," a typological poem outside the Christian system (*VP* 22:15–30); Michael Berens, on "Karshish" (*SBHC* 12:41–53), also concerned with religion as universal myth-making; and John Lammers and Jeff Karr (*SBHC* 12:94–119; 13:37–46) on "Caliban Upon Setebos." Lammers read the poem as a mini-divine comedy ready for his allegorical interpretation; Karr noted parallels to Paley in order to read the poem as a version of natural theology in a Darwinian world; both were helpful, neither fully persuasive.

This relatively weak addition to thinking and knowledge on the topic of religion found a parallel in the even weaker record of studies on two other great issues, politics and science. Here the earlier critical history itself is less rich, except in regular complaints (such as this one) over the failure to explore such obvious subjects. Yet on first sight the failure seems to have been also Browning's, especially in science. His apparent interest in evolution in *Paracelsus* yielded to uninformed positions later in his career. Only George Myerson, in an article on the science of Browning's *Paracelsus* (*BSN* 15:20–47), returned to this apparently barren field. Drawing on Kuhn's paradigm for the emergence of modern science, he interestingly plotted Paracelsus' growth as one toward scientific as well as moral awareness. Browning endorses the modern scientific view of the world as open, objective, and infinite, though he draws back from a totally secular vision of the universe. We need other studies that similarly examine the implied, if often confused, attitudes of Browning toward the emerging scientific disciplines, hard and soft, of his century.

Politics was a more conscious and habitual theme of Browning's, though we look in vain, as we do in so much nineteenth-century British literature, for the central work overtly about politics. Here three studies have at least raised the discussion to interesting levels of discourse. John Woolford, in an article (*BSN* 14:1–20) substantially repeated in his recent book, offered a thoughtful analysis of Browning's early liberalism as an author's position. Browning's ideal of power, stemming from what Woolford called Puritan anarchism, made him reject the author's authority over the reader, an elegant way of explaining the embarrassed attempts at sharing authorship in *Sordello*. In somewhat parallel terms to the early study by Lawrence Poston (*PMLA* 88:260–270) of Browning's political skepticism as an ironic view of the relation between nobility and power, Woolford interestingly reviewed the themes of renunciation and abdication of power so clear in some of the plays. Robert Viscusi (*BIS* 12:1–28) found a different, also intriguing, way of unmasking the political positions of the apparently apolitical professed liberal. His study of imperialism in Browning's celebration of Italy avoided the simplicities of classic Marxist imperialist theory by its sensitivity to the positive side of Browning's liberal culture, his ability to balance and hold in suspension various views of a subject, here both the Italy of classical Rome and that of Dante. In this decade of renewed and highly abstract Marxist cultural/literary theory Loy Martin's formulations of a social drive for an event in literary history—the production of the dramatic monologue—were predictably abstract and unfortunately lacking in specific social context. His thesis of a crisis in bourgeois Cartesian individualism leading to a work (of art) alienated from its producer (the author, who cedes authority, here not in the first instance to the reader but to the indeterminable dialogic subjects of the dramatic monologue), leans heavily, almost certainly too heavily, on a single long interpretation of "Pictor Ignotus." It is a way of thinking about the relation between a literary form and a cultural-economic context (superstructure and infrastructure) useful enough in itself but much too speculative in form. Obviously we badly need more comprehensive and fully worked out approaches to both Browning's own discourse on politics and society and his larger place in a rapidly changing Victorian world.

The coordinate subject of history was of course much more directly a concern of the poet and has elicited regular critical comment since, from the only somewhat useful research into the real history behind Browning's poems, undertaken with the rather naive aim of seeing how true Browning's poetry was to history, to the sophisticated historiographical comments of Morse Peckham. There have not been many persons writing about Browning and history in the last decade, but fortunately there was one good article and a substantial, well-developed book. Lee Baker (*VP* 24:31–46) drew on Hayden White's rhetorical approach to history writing as necessarily a form of fiction making to contrast Browning and Carlyle. He found Carlyle a romantic ironist (as Ryals has found Browning) but Browning an unselfconscious mythmaker. From this analysis he criticized Peckham's view of Browning as an historical relativist, aware of the limits of all positions, including his own. Mary Ellis Gibson's *History and the Prism of Art* (1987) was a much larger and more impressive approach to the complexities of this major subject in Browning. She cast a wider net, avoiding reductive descriptions of Browning's involvement with history. Her overall position on Browning's historiography was closer to that of Peckham than Baker. She emphasized Browning's affinities to Carlyle as relativist and ironist: she rightly stressed the concern with history Browning learned in his family, from father and half-brothers. She accepted the influence of Ranke and his school in Browning's concern with sources and accurate evidence but saw this as compatible with a perspective on history that stressed context, cultural history, and the relativism of perspectivism. Clearly there is still an issue that will not go away, as Baker rightly insisted, in Browning's countervailing push—let us call it a force of desire against its own skepticism—to have the record mean something and mean for good. Yet it is Browning's persisting relativism and even skepticism, as Gibson competently showed in her good discussions of the rhetoric of the poems on historical issues, that creates the objective plenitude of his art against the reductive mythmaking of his heart. Better, perhaps, to see the tension between the two historicisms, romantic/prophetic and relativist/skeptical as the determining site of the poems. Gibson makes a case for affinities between Browning's historicism and that of twentieth-century writers; but again, this should be balanced against other points of view, especially Ward's article and the section in Martin's book, both mentioned above, on the differences between Browning and Pound's historicism, which take better account of the radically antihistorical vision of much high modernist art.

A complementary, interesting, and relatively unexplored topic, Browning's relation to the heart of darkness in man's prehistory and in his psyche at least found one able analysis in Dorothy Mermin's "Browning and the Primitive" (*VP* 20:211–237). Here again Browning is surprisingly in touch with the newer historical—here anthropological—work of students such as Edward Tyler, who saw primitive cultures as the origins, not degradations, of civilized societies. And here again, as Mermin ably showed, Browning counters his own expanding, implicitly relativist vision with his heart's need to impose a Christian mythological pattern—albeit a very sophisticated progressive one—on the span of human history. As interesting was Mermin's sense of Browning's preoccupation in his later works especially, with primitive urges, sexuality, violence, religious ritual, often revealed through dreams and other unconscious phenomena. In this she followed Samuel B. Southwell's *Quest for Eros: Browning and "Fifine"* (1980). Southwell explored a similar terrain of intellectual history, relating Browning's use of the term "soul" to the emerging concept of the unconscious as outlined by Lancelot Whyte's *The Unconscious Before Freud*. Like Mermin, he generally saw Browning involved in the fertile discussion of myth, anthropology, primitivism, and sexuality that led both to modern anthropology and Freud. His provocative analysis of *Fifine at the Fair* seemed more problematic, just because his argument wanted to show what Browning wished to say but dared not. Such an author-, or biography-, centered reading was naturally more effective in suggesting external influences on the poem—the presence of Browning's complicated feelings for the dead Elizabeth, for example—than in fully proving his thesis, that Browning's hidden meaning, the meaning whose name he dared not speak, was a vision of cultural unity built on acceptance of the sexual drive as a central life force. Yet his approach rightly reminded us how very much this poem, which we have tended to treat as a casuistic or metaphysical sport, was involved in the new ideas of woman, sexuality, and primitivism. This area of Browning should not be romanticized into a confrontation between Mr. Browning and the dark gods. Mermin especially sets us on the right track by seeing the emergence of these modern myths of myth, sexuality, and primitivism in Browning as a part of a general intellectual movement in his culture to which, unlike developments in the natural sciences, Browning was rather precisely attuned.

I might end this summary of criticism by daring ourselves to look directly sometimes at the white light that Browning himself mostly avoided: the poetics stated or implicit in his work. What theoretical statement can we find in Browning or create from our reading of his works that might seem somewhat to suffice as an explanation of his unique imagination? Of course answers exist everywhere in all these special studies of aspects of Browning's work. We have been less ready, despite the heady theoretical dialogue of our day, and despite some heavy theoretical statements about Browning, to try a direct art of Browning's poesy. Despite his reticence as a self-explainer, Browning's own statements are not irrelevant. "The Essay on Shelley," as Thomas J. Collins well showed some years ago, offers an elliptic but often stunningly useful system of criticism for speaking of his work. "The Essay on Chatterton," too, as Donald Smalley and I have emphasized, provides ways of talking about Browning's poetic argumentation and his sense of his own development. We have recently had added to this Browning's rather wonderful letter of August 1837 to his French friend, Count Amédée de Ripert-Monclar, in which he sketches his history of his own growth as a poet. In the study of Browning and Ruskin mentioned above, DeLaura, who gave us the unusually self-reflexive Ruskin letters, well used them to define precisely the similarities between Browning and Ruskin's poetics. Christine Froula's article, also mentioned above, has called our attention to the poetics that are somewhat more than half stated in *Sordello*. Her useful discussion in effect completed the statements of *Sordello* as a poem about the nature of poetry, seeing Browning advocating a turn from a Shelleyan poetics of inspiration to an exploratory and open-ended engagement with experience, in which the reader is involved in the process of making the poem. Her more direct attempt to formulate a poetics from Browning's agonizing self-inquiry into his art in *Sordello* built upon, or had clear parallels to, the excellent reading of the project of the early Browning that we have had especially in the books by Tucker, Ryals, and Latané.

Perhaps most important, Daniel Karlin's study of the letters of Robert and Elizabeth has amply shown what a helpful ring of keys they are to unlock both poets' poetics as well as their hearts. The problem was of course following their private, allusive, and especially elliptic (indeed filled with actual ellipses) way of discussing their ideas and aspirations for their poetry. Karlin saw Robert creating Elizabeth to take the place of the Shelleyan poet and then using this formulation to reestablish his own view of himself as different from this romantic idea of a poet who is the poetry he speaks.

By contrast, Browning is almost morbidly aware that he speaks not as the linnets sing but through the forms of poetry and the cultural artifice of words. Since Rader's 1976 article, mentioned above, there has been little work directly on issues of genre in Browning, nothing to compare with the earlier work of Donald S. Hair in *Browning's Experiments with Genre* (1972). Exceptions might be Martin's book, which as I noted brought various theoretical perspectives to bear in explaining the production and nature of the dramatic monologue, or the genre discussions implicit in reader-response approaches to the dramatic monologue. There have been few works—William Butts on Menippean satire in Caliban (*SBHC* 13:24–36) and Allan Dooley on *The Ring and the Book* as epic and anti-epic (*BIS* 15: 137–150) are two exceptions—that look directly at Browning's parodic genius in recasting and replaying traditional genres with seemingly effortless dexterity and unlimited resourcefulness. John Woolford's recent book called attention to a special kind of genre in Browning, which he called the structured collection of groups of dramatic monologues.

There has also been nothing on the varieties of resources in language in Browning to compare with Park Honan's 1961 *Browning's Characters*. With some success, both Martin and Gibson risked making their already somewhat prolix books too diffuse in order to include chapters linking their general topics to analysis of style and diction. Gibson saw Browning's commitment to the objective detail of recorded history and to accepting life lived through history finding its parallel in a language filled with colloquial speech, hard, knotty, and difficult style, and the resistant "clayey soil" of specific words for real things, people, places. She then suggested a system of variation from this standard diction by which characters are satirized through grandiloquent speech or elevated by sincere lyric. This was useful for certain poems but, unlike Honan's study, it tended to reduce Browning's infinite variety too much to one plain song—that indeed of an essentially prose Browning. In a chapter on "The Being Written" Martin used a linguistic analysis, primarily of progressive verb forms, to show on a local level how Browning finds a way of communicating open-ended process rather than closed and complete being.

As he acknowledged, this was a systematically formulated parallel to the similar analyses of processive effect in Tucker's readings of Browning's poems. Oddly, the analysis of individual poems is more persuasive, because it seems clearly to hold true for the poem in question. Martin's broader description of "typical" Browning linguistic effects left me uneasily aware of its unscientific form and uneasy about the intimidating computer studies, comparing Browning's usages to norms in other poets (or average great poets!) that could back a proper linguistic study.

Objective scholarship will always be with us—and indeed we have great reason to be thankful for the painstaking and careful labors in the vineyards of a number of biographical scholars and editors. The emphasis for the eighties should be on the fine work of editors. In biography there have been no full-length studies to succeed Irving and Honan's 1974 *The Book, the Ring and the Poet* or, if I do say so myself, my own 1977 study of the formative period and culture, *Browning's Youth*. Donald Thomas' survey biography, *Robert Browning: A Life Within a Life* (1982), merely retold others' tales, often without even using the latest scholarship. Gridley's study of the Brownings in France provided important new information and a gracious account of the Brownings' infatuation with France, Paris, and all things French. Korg's study of Browning and Italy, with less new information and a far less surprising story to tell, did recount gracefully Browning's once lyric, later somewhat tired love affair with Italy. The much briefer fling with Russia was carefully reported, with some important new detail, in Waddington's study. Perhaps most important, Daniel Karlin's reading of those perplexing and voluminous love letters from the Cherokee, also noted above, provided the best plotting and psychological analysis of the real courtship years that we have. We should be grateful for a number of other special studies in biography, John Coulter's (*BSN* 15, nos. 2–3:3–19) identification of the Brownings' residence at New Cross from work in local records; Richard Purdy's (*YULG* 61:143–153) gracious summary of the relation with Ripert-Monclar, now available in the record of the letters as well; and Meredith's Raymond (*SBHC* 14:32–62) well-researched and well-presented account of the Brownings' magnificent Maecenas, John Kenyon. These most illuminating stabs into the relative dark of Browning's biography suggest how much more could be accomplished through determined biographical research. Honan's treatment of the late Browning, my own of the early life and culture, and many of these specialized studies rightly begin with the assumption that the biography of Browning is not complete in detail, is filled with traditional myths and pieties that need critical examination, and is, like criticism, and despite its dependence on the good gold of fact, finally a matter of individual fabrication and interpretation—and thus always beginning over again with each new student of the poet and his life.

This survey of the decade's work in Browning studies, which seems to me to be reporting in fact some substantial new strengths, if also some relative weaknesses, in our contemporary current of ideas about Browning, is structured to end in any case on an upbeat. I have been suggesting how much more than we may like to think our critical approaches to Browning have grown out of and built on the tradition of discourse about him and his work. In the record of editing this is more obvious. The work of generations in assembling and editing the full record of Browning works and letters has been coming to remarkable fruition. The achievement of the last decade was striking. From its position as one of the weakest (and indeed even rather ridiculed) areas of basic scholarship in Victorian literature, Browning studies now stand fair to be one of the best and most sophisticated. And, as often, sophistication here has come in the maturing theoretical study of editing to mean both great knowledge and also a willingness to live in awareness of diversity and differences of opinion. Oddly, it was more lack of knowledge than of sophistication that brought Browning editing efforts in the 1970s into disrepute. The now notorious first four volumes of the Ohio Browning foundered especially over the ignorance of the entire Browning world about Browning's own writing, editing, and publishing practices and the location and even existence of certain manuscripts and revises. That lack has been and is still being rather massively corrected. Part of the problem was the incredible dispersion of Browning family letters, manuscripts, and books at the great Sotheby sale in 1913, at which the entire remains of the poet's literary life were sold off in large lots, often to other booksellers who kept breaking them down and dispersing them to buyers throughout the world.

Philip Kelley and Ronald Hudson, lately assisted in part of their work by Betty Coley, have done us all a truly major benefit in tracking down as many of these materials as they could and cataloging them carefully in two essential works of reference: *The Brownings' Correspondence: A Checklist*, published by Kelley and Hudson in 1978, and *The Browning Collections: A Reconstruction* (1984), compiled by Kelley and Coley. The latter completed this great task of reassembling the collection in catalog form in a magnificent way. It gave Browning students—both those of Robert and Elizabeth—a single invaluable source for locating manuscripts, proofs, revises, corrected copies, notebooks, diaries, address books, memoranda, and even all the known copies of *Pauline*. 2519 books of Browning or his family were identified—albeit some, here, as in other parts of the *Reconstruction*, only by booksellers' references—as well as presentation copies, association copies and manuscripts, and even lists of likenesses and photos, works of art, and household and personal effects, including 37 known locks of hair of the Brownings! We are now far more in control of the primary information available on Browning than on most other Victorian writers: a major, foundational achievement.

Kelley and Hudson, whose grasp seems surprisingly well suited to their bold reach, have added to this great work with the very solid beginnings of another—publication of *The Brownings' Correspondence*. There have now appeared seven volumes. All, certainly including the most recent (1989), maintained impressively high standards not only of comprehension and editorial accuracy—which we expected—but also of scholarship and annotation, where Hudson's work splendidly complemented Kelley's assembling and editing. The publication, a cost-efficient operation through Kelley's Wedgestone Press, has also been splendid: handsome, spacious, beautifully illustrated volumes that recall fine academic editions of an earlier decade. The generous inclusion of reprints of all contemporary reviews of the time period at the end of each volume has been a bonus that has already proven of great value in critical and reception studies, where we can all substitute our own appraisal of what the critics of the age said for the inherited, usually reductive and anecdotal, wisdom about Robert's reception.

With all this, the student of Robert may be nonetheless not a little disappointed to find how little of him has appeared in the seven volumes so far, where he is outwritten by his spouse-to-be far more than seven to one (volumes 6 and 7, June 1842 to October 1843 have, respectively, 19 and 7 letters to and from Robert and 147 and 225 to and from Elizabeth). Doubtless the Robert Browning scholar would have been better served for the early period, before the convergence of the twain, by one separate (and rather slim) volume, though already in volumes 6 and 7 some references to each other and different perspectives on contemporary events—for instance, Elizabeth's interesting comments on Macready's damning Robert's new play *A Blot*—show the eventual advantage of full combined publication when they do couple. On the face of it, there were also few major additions to Browning's record for this period, perhaps mainly the letters to Ripert-Monclar that had been in Professor Purdy's private collection. Browning has been on the whole very successful in covering his early tracks. Yet just because of the scarcity of information on his early life, we should be doubly appreciative of the comprehensive method that has presumably brought virtually every scrap there is to proper publication. To take the most recent volumes again as examples, 9 of the 16 by Robert in volume 6, and 3 of the 6 in volume 7 were previously unpublished. If most of the new letters are, as typically with Robert, brief, unrevealing, embarrassed, or all three, they also often provide important new details for what are otherwise entirely blank months in the record or, sometimes, offer new perspectives—as the letter in volume 6 showing Robert asking Macready to help him divide *A Blot* into three acts from five and planning to revise the play "while the printers have it in hand"! The editors' inclusion of a further section of supporting documents is also helpful, but here probably they will find their record less definitive; I also thought the biographical sketches, often of well-known folk, usually unnecessary, though they might interest the casual reader, if there are any, of these volumes.

Complementary to this excellent, ongoing work have been Ian Jack's collection of letters to James T. Fields, Browning's American publisher (*HLQ* 45:185–199), and Michael Meredith's handsome book, *More Than Friend* (1985), publishing the letters to his affluent American Friend in his autumn years, Katharine de Kay Bronson. Meredith annotated these interesting letters carefully and also provided a graceful and informative introduction; I must say I was skeptical of his attractive thesis, that an autumn friendship was also more: an Indian Summer passion. The mystery of Browning's late romantic life would seem to be other than we naturally think: not who was he with after Elizabeth but why was he generally still with her (love, guilt, convenience, habit?). Daniel Karlin's edition of Robert and Elizabeth's *Courtship Correspondence* (1989) is an attractive selection, about one half of the letters in the full, monumental Elvan Kintner edition and a good deal less than that in bulk. It is a reader's edition, focusing on the love tale to the exclusion of much of the literary and other gossip. I am not sure why the text had to be re-edited: annotation is itself useful, giving the common reader much of the helpful perspective and analysis provided in Karlin's earlier fine book on the letters. Finally, Mark Samuels Lasner (*BIS* 15:79–88) ably provided the context for his discovery of Browning's interesting first letter to Rossetti in William Allingham's commonplace book.

As for manuscripts other than letters, Craig Turner well edited the odd journal of Browning's envious and rather untrustworthy cousin in *The Poet Robert Browning and his Kinsfolk by his Cousin Cyrus Mason* (1983). Turner impressively eschewed overplaying his material, giving us an objective and critical view of this document which, brought out otherwise, could have generated any number of new Browning myths, those hydra things. Another odd but interesting set of documents, the acting versions of *Strafford, A Blot in the 'Scutcheon,* and *Colombe's Birthday,* published in facsimile, without apparatus, and too quietly in a Salzburg series by James Hogg (from the Lord Chamberlain's collection in the British Library), is now available from Longwood (U.S.A.) along with Hogg's companion volume summarizing criticism of Browning's plays. The edition complements Anneliese Meidl's (*BIS* 12:163–188) report of the *Strafford* text.

So much new information, very much including investigation in the 1970s of two separate records of Browning's revisions of the first ten volumes of his 1888–1889 *The Poetical Works* (the Dykes Campbell copies in the British Library and a list for volumes 4–10 at Brown) and useful commentary on Browning's publishing practices by Ian Jack (*BIS* 15:161–175) and Michael Meredith (*SBHC* 13:97–107), have improved, or are still improving, all three new editions of Browning's work. After the fiasco of the first four volumes of the Ohio Browning we have had a rare corroboration of Milton's faith that truth would not be put to the worse in a fair grapple with falsehood. We now have three acceptable versions of truth about texts of Browning's works and a fourth announced as on its way. The only completed text was that in the Penguin/Yale series of *The Poems* (1981) begun by John Pettigrew and finished by Thomas J. Collins. The two-volume text, which has already become accepted as the current usable scholarly edition for classes and most students, accepted Browning's last wishes as known by the volumes of *The Poetical Works* emended by his authoritative corrections for the second impression of the first ten volumes. The editors have implicitly followed Morse Peckham's persuasive argument, made by his edition of *Sordello* (1977), that editors must scrutinize the final text for printers' errors introduced in successive editions or even the poet's own repeated mistakes. There are corrections indicated, though perhaps fewer than one would suspect to be there. Annotation was a particular strength, with Pettigrew's pithy and often witty definitions throwing added salt in the wounds the original Ohio volumes received in reviews of their long, pedantic notes or identifications of Venice. The weakness of this edition was mainly outside the editors' control: Penguin/Yale had already issued Richard Altick's *The Ring and the Book* in the series; Altick's interesting reprint of the first edition is not compatible with the editorial principles of the Collins-

Pettigrew edition nor does it pretend to full annotation. Penguin/Yale also did not find room for the plays; as part of plans to base a concordance on the edition, the plays now have appeared in a separate volume published by Garland (1988) and edited by Collins and Richard J. Shroyer. This is a compatible scholarly text, though again one suspects more errors than are found (Oxford found eleven needing emendation to Collins and Shroyer's six). They have not used some manuscript variants for *A Blot* and *Colombe's Birthday* on the view that these are not in direct descent; but Oxford does use them profitably. The annotation was competent, though neither as full or incisive as Penguin/Yale. The brief history of criticism of the plays is a helpful summary essay. The edition will serve its immediate purpose but is not likely to have the practical use of the Penguin/Yale text, which rightly has been having its day while the two editions in progress are slowly appearing.

Ohio has in fact got its act together and come out with a competent volume 5 (1981) of its *Complete Works* as well as two very useful volumes, 7 (1985) and 8 (1988) of three planned on *The Ring and the Book,* which has no other full modern edition. (Volume 6, despite some notices to the contrary, has not yet appeared.) Ohio now incorporates manuscript variants and has a good argument for its only slightly different choice of copy-text. (They use the second, 1889, impression of *The Poetical Works* for volumes 1–10 rather than 1888 as Penguin/Yale and Oxford, with the updated rationale that Browning's actual changes may amount to more than the two records of changes Penguin/Yale and Oxford use and that the later text is reliable because the plates were changed only where Browning called for changes.) They are now especially suspicious of the copy-text as one that may carry forward or create error. Volume 8 emends the text in twenty-two places and restores lost line breaks accurately. The texts in my examinations were very accurate, unlike the earlier volumes, and annotation was far better focused than before and yet often generous and well researched.

The special value of the Ohio text was in fact one of its features that first provoked most vehement criticism. By providing a record of all the variants, now from manuscript through earlier collected editions to final copy-text, Ohio gave each reader a way of establishing Browning's text at any point in its, and his, career. The implicit challenge to notions of an author as a solid thing existing at only one point in time, when his definitive text was created by his fiat for all time, so troubling in the early 1970s, now seems reasonable enough (*pace*, Professor Crowder). For different critical purposes we require or prefer different texts. Browning did not generally rewrite his texts as remarkably as a Wordsworth or a Yeats; but he did continuously innovate (as the original Ohio editors rightly noted). For our practical purposes we may have good reason to prefer the earlier *Pauline* or the manuscript of *Paracelsus*, the first edition of *Dramatic Lyrics* (as George Bornstein has argued in an essay in *Poems in Their Place: The Intertextuality and Order of Poetic Collections*, ed. Neil Fraistat, 1986), or, as John Woolford's recent book interestingly suggests, even to go back to the reordering Browning himself imposed on his dramatic monologues when he collected his works in the 1860s. Ohio gives us the kit to build the text we need: guarantee not valid if not used cautiously and wisely.

The Ohio editors plan—someday—to return to those early volumes and correct. Meanwhile Ian Jack and his associates have published three of the excellent volumes in his projected *The Poetical Works*. The copy-text was the same as that chosen by Penguin/Yale and it has been especially carefully scrutinized for errors by comparison to manuscripts and revises, wherever available, as well as earlier editions. Jack did not give full variants but he usefully indicated those that seem most important and clearly marked his own emendations. In the case of *Pauline* and *Paracelsus*, he published the earlier versions (*Pauline*, 1833, and the manuscript of *Paracelsus*). We were not given everything we might want or need; rather, and this is true throughout Jack's edition, we were given the editor's personal but well-seasoned and judicious choices of what seems especially important. (I might say I would have welcomed more parallel texts, say of the first *Dramatic Lyrics* or *Pippa Passes*, in volume 3.) Oxford's glory has been its scholarly introductions and annotations. Here Jack has made especially good use of the full biographical record available in the letters, published and unpublished. The introductions really update and replace DeVane on most issues relating to the works published. The notes are especially strong in providing a literary context for Browning, a particularly difficult task for a poet so concerned not to sound like his predecessors. And Jack has not been afraid to befriend the reader and help him through cruxes in meaning, especially in his fine notes on *Sordello*. Each of the three editions of Browning has notes with different emphases worth consulting. Jack's are, however, generally fuller than Penguin/Yale and better focused than Ohio.

In sum, I think we have great reason to be pleased with the development of all three editions. Penguin/Yale is already available as a very respectable text for the serious student, a great improvement over what we had in general use before, with sharp and lively notes. Ohio, back on its feet, offers an acceptable scholarly text, full annotation, and a unique library-in-one of Browning's different texts. Its *The Ring and the Book* is immediately useful as the only scholarly text. Oxford is on its way to being the most authoritative and reliable single text, the choice for critical work and the most helpful compilation of information on a poem. If this were not plenty already, we have plans announced by Woolford and Karlin for another text, in the Longman's Annotated English Poets series, that will feature publication of poems in their first printed form, a rival text, in effect, to that of all three other editions.

On this note, with such plenty of good editions on or in hand and promise of a rejuvenated, younger Browning to come, I will end this review. With all the controversy in our current critical, and even editing, worlds Browning has not been neglected. Our criticism has shown him as an especially interesting test case for many of the current critical approaches, or for their opponents. The good of this is of course that we are taking the problem of reading and understanding Browning seriously; we are challenging former readings and approaches, which go dead in any case with mere repetition; or we are being challenged to defend our positions, exhibiting the rationale behind our customary procedures. Major work in editing Browning has both made important new information and texts available and helped us to rethink more carefully our relation to those texts. Put all this in the time capsule and see what it will look like—important or minor—another centenary from now. The level of activity, even the amount of disagreement and excitement over it, assures me that Browning at least will survive for another hundred years.

Robert Browning: Year's Work, 1989

The centenary of Browning's death produced scholarly gatherings in various places—Venice, the Armstrong Browning Library, CUNY, the MLA—and centennial essays, promised or, as in the case of an Australasian collection, actually published during 1989—*Browning Centenary Essays,* a special issue of *AUMLA* (71:1–181), edited by Simon Petch and Warwick Slinn. The volume deserves to be ordered for your libraries for the generally high level of discourse throughout the volume and in particular for the contributions of Petch ("Browning's Roman Lawyers," pp. 109–138) and Slinn's own summary contribution ("From Textual Reference to Textual Strategy: Critical Responses to Browning's Poetry," pp. 161–181).

Victorian Poetry had its centennial issue on Browning. The strength of the volume, for I do believe it is worthy of the occasion if not a major event in the 100 year critical history, is rather in the area where I have been finding Browning studies strong over the past decade: as in the *AUMLA* volume there is a persistent and highly intelligent attempt to relate traditional views of Browning to the broadest theoretical issues that have been rousing our profession. Nor is there a lack of established critics. I note especially the two central essays by two of our finest Victorian philosophical critics, David Shaw and Warwick Slinn, who in a sense only happen also to be among the usual suspects by their continuous interest in relating Browning to currents in Victorian and contemporary philosophy. Their essays, both grouped under works on *The Ring and the Book,* might better have been featured first, as establishing broad theoretical concerns for the more specialized but equally probing essays by other contributors. For both critics, among the very few who persistently attack the hardest questions between philosophy and practical criticism in the Victorian period, Browning is clearly still very much alive, a writer one comes back to again and again to test out historical or theoretical issues in philosophy and literature. Browning is also alive for them, I have to say from these essays, for very much the same reason he was important to philosophical and religious critics at the end of his physical lifetime, because his notoriously difficult work especially allows the critic a great deal of room to find his own interest in him. Of the two, Shaw, who has been exploring so well the long undervalued Victorian discussions on philosophy and literary theory, is stronger in relating Browning's theoretical statements to Browning's contemporary scene; and I found his placing of Browning's work in relation to nineteenth-century hermeneutics generally or to Jowett's particular theory of Biblical interpretation extremely suggestive. But the subtitle of his article is "*The Ring and the Book* and Modern Theory" (pp. 79–98) and his direct aim is to show that Browning foresuffered and prejudged our current critical debates. I found this provoking: in the good sense because Shaw does effectively show what diverse attitudes to interpretation are encoded into Browning's text; in the bad sense, because Shaw's excessively rhetorical approach allows him at times to start reading a sermon on Browning's answer to the problems of (critical) faith of our time. (Indeed, the text moves from a modest Browning is "prophetic of" to "Browning shows" toward the end.) Shaw is weakest in the vagueness of his references to contemporary criticism, which sometimes have the vacancy of straw men. We can understand Guido and Tertium Quid as deconstructionists. But references to structuralists, finally settling on the lawyers, are too vague and sweeping to be recognizable. Petch's view that they are in fact closest to deconstructionists seems a better move in this game. Caponsacchi and Pompilia are myth critics, but this seems only to amount to their well-known myth-like mutual rescue. Shaw's (not Browning's, who will be read again by current lights in his bicentenary) lesson from Browning is a sensible one, that "dreams of transparent meaning are at best consoling fictions" though we rightly seek the ever elusive truth by "entertaining such fictions."

He may yet grow a deconstructionist (clearly the generally distrusted, generally attractive Molinists of our time). His point against deconstruction, that those who know our human speech is naught are presuming to know with certainty that others can't know with certainty, is the central paradox of the Cretan liar used by Slinn in his article (pp. 115–133) and Slinn's study begins with a broad argument against reading *The Ring and the Book* for more than consoling fictions, against looking for a romantic position of transcendent truth based on a privileged status for aesthetic discourse. There are only various fictions, no moment that escapes discourse. Slinn's essay is most interesting where he goes beyond the (dare I say party line) assertions about the arbitrary relation between referent and sign, the impossibility of a transcendental signified, the post-Cartesian consciousness, and looks at the way in which monologues speak of their own production, so that each part of the epic calls attention to the shaping force of discourse that both gives it its claim to truth and tells us it is only one of many possible such discourses and thus can make only a limited claim. I liked also his rereading of the ring metaphor, both subtle and original, as also a master display (sign) of the prevalent concept of production in the work as a whole. Slinn tantalizingly reads Browning here and there as an Hegelian; this, too, has the danger of finding in Browning only what happens to interest us at the current moment; at this point the references to Hegel are as brief as Shaw's to current positions in theory, and that is, once again, a problem.

Browning knew that the Americans and Italians appreciated him and that he had friends, too, in the antipodes; and that still has to console him for certain slights at home: alas, a conference planned at Oxford, in these days of renewed hard-times, tub-on-bottom, thinking was killed, evidently because there was no profit in it. The original Society did come through with a handsome centenary volume of *Browning Society Notes,* actually in the year, featuring a small book-length essay by Mairi Calcraft on Browning's London (19:3–134). It is generally an accurate summary of what we know of Browning's London, from his childhood to old age, and rightly reminds us that this Waring of poets was nonetheless very firmly rooted in the great metropolis. Maps and photos of scenes associated with Browning make it an ideal guide to Browning's London; and it provides proper warning, suitable for moral reflection on the comparative endurance of bricks and books, on the massive obliteration of so much of Browning's physical world.

With so much interesting activity in his honor, and more still on the way, Browning should have every reason to be gratified at his longevity; his pleasure at hearing of positive notices of *Asolando* even on his deathbed in Venice suggests that wherever he is in the wind-grieved Apennine or further south by cicala, cypress, and sea, he is indeed pleased. And he can be pretty sure that he will live on to ask his mortal question a hundred years from now. So much centenary publication forces me to be briefer in noticing other significant articles. Blair Ross's study of the magus tradition in *Paracelsus* and "Fust and His Friends" (*SBHC* 16:86–104) usefully placed Browning's presentation of these characters in relation to recent scholarship in the Renaissance, especially the emergence of science in a cult of the ideal immersed in the material—which is not to say (though Ross is unclear on this point) that Browning fully shared this ideology, only that he knew it well. A philosophical reading, rather than another reading of magus-philosopher Browning, was the aim of M. W. Rowe's study of "Two in the Campagna" (*BSN* 18:36–47). I found the clarity of thinking in this attempt to apply philosophical discussion of consciousness (Sartre, Nagel, Cavell) helpful in understanding Browning's dramatic meditations on the interpersonal. "The Pied Piper" manuscript, in Browning's copy of Wanley, was reported as now at Baylor (*SBHC* 15:55, 69; 16:30–41) and the subversive figure of the piper explored at length in a study by David Goslee (*SBHC* 16:42–51). At two ends of the spectrum of influences on Browning, William Brewer convincingly and interestingly related Browning's portrayal of Caponsacchi and Pompilia to Dante and Beatrice (*SBHC* 16:7–17) and James Loucks (*SBHC* 16:35–40) offered Trimalchio's Feast in the *Satyricon* as a plausible source/analogue for "The Bishop Orders His Tomb."

The Centenary year provided a good opportunity to take stock of what we have made of Browning in the hundred years since his death. I took the occasion to turn the year's work report into a "Decade's Work" review as part of the special edition of *Victorian Poetry*. My review, which focused on the play of modern critical approaches to Browning in the 1980s and on the substantial achievements in editing that have begun to let us see Browning plain after 100 years, happens to have been nicely complemented by a much larger work in review of criticism covering the entire century and some of the reviews during Browning's lifetime. We will all be much indebted to the labor of love, of Browning if not always of what we have done to him, that Philip Drew has put into *An Annotated Critical Bibliography of Robert Browning* (1990) for the Harvester Wheatsheaf series, though I regret that its date, and the full table of works for 1989 that I face, oblige me to put off a full review of its strengths and omissions until next year.

Drew observes that Irvine and Honan's still standard biography of Browning has the weakness of enjoying "the opportunity to display an impudent disrespect for Browning and to present him in an unfavourable light whenever possible" (p. 22). This is rather strong and might better fit Betty Miller's deliberately debunking life. But Browning has certainly suffered in our esteem from post-Stracheyan biography's quest for the unpleasant facts hidden beneath Victorian reticence and reverence as much as many less eminent Victorians. Despite rumors of love for a half-aunt and Miller's better proven claims that the boy Browning actually loved his mother, the great scandal uncovered in the life of this Victorian has of course been his relation to Louisa Lady Ashburton, the rich and well-connected widow, friend of his in the 1860s and enemy from about 1873 until his death. She was mentioned only once in the authorized account of Browning by his enduring friend, Mrs. Orr, and only once by Griffin and Minchin in their first edition. But the letters published by Hood and those to Blagden (edited first by Armstrong and then re-edited by McAleer), and subsequently those to the Storys edited by Hudson, uncovered a much richer tale, which has become the central scandal in recent biographies, beginning with a supplementary chapter added to his and Griffin's work by Minchin in 1938.

It was a classic Victorian cover-up, as can be seen from the discreet discussion of the entire issue, without naming it at all, by Mrs. Orr (pp. 284–286). She speaks of "some leaven of bitterness" behind *Fifine* and explains that it had to do with difficulty in leaving behind the past, his "spiritual allegiance" to Elizabeth and his consequent difficulty in accepting the present when it came to him "with friendly greeting." He was "injust" to what it brought and this in turn reacted upon himself and, eventually, his work. Both William Raymond and DeVane filled in the lacuna in Orr's biographical explanation of *Fifine,* as did Minchin, by the information that Browning had been going through the major dark mood of his life after betraying Elizabeth in an awkward proposal to "Loo" Ashburton, a proposal that brought the additional chagrin of failure: his uncouth and direct references to his own motives, which should have been understandable enough to the woman who had inherited a great fortune from her brief marriage to the much older Ashburton, brought on a rage and led ultimately to permanent estrangement.

The dark mood has of course become a central concept in Browning criticism, explaining the recommitment to Elizabeth in *Balaustion's Adventure* and very likely the unpopular harshness of *Red Cotton Night-Cap Country* as well as the sexual contortions of *Fifine.* In modern biographies the story itself has accorded well with the wish to see Browning not as Victorian St. George but as representative human being, complete with confused motives and sexual disturbances. Both standard works, by Miller and by Irvine and Honan, give the episode a major place in the narrative, though in fairness one should say that both accounts are rather sympathetic to a difficult business, as if they are more comfortable with Browning when he is indeed caught with his trousers down than when he appears the perfect Perseus. Only William Whitla offered another reading of the complicated record of letters alluding most elusively to the facts of the matter; he suggested that the proposal came rather from Loo and that the poet was then caught up in the wake of a woman scorned, and nearly drowned (*BSN* 2:12–41). His argument was more effective in suggesting possible weaknesses in the predominant, reverse, view than in proving his case, which generally depended on the same material and a faith that Browning consistently avoided considering marriage.

Clyde Ryals kindly called to my attention a recent life of Loo, *The Ludovisi Goddess: The Life of Louisa Lady Ashburton,* by

Virginia Surtees (1984). Despite the date, it has received almost no attention and missed the standard lists of works relevant to Browning; yet it deserves careful scrutiny because it presents some new evidence and makes a full case that the proposal was the Lady's; most important, the argument opens a way to eliminating Browning's dark period as a biographical event, or relegating it merely to the troubles over son Pen at Oxford; and it implies a renewed view of Browning as simple and unchanging in his spiritual fidelity to Elizabeth. If true, this would indeed chasten not just recent biographers' but our collective impudence for having cast Browning unjustly in an inglorious light.

The new evidence in this murky business is important: two new letters from Browning to Loo, evidently in her family Northampton Papers, dating from December–January, 1870/71. The first merely arranges to send Pen to visit over the holidays. But the second contains some characteristically awkward language in which Browning fends off her invitation to him to join them (as Browning quotes her back, that she "wished for me much"). He declines: "If I secure no good to you, and therefore to myself, by a great exercise of self-denial, there has been one more great mistake made by me who have made many—but few that, by reason of this difficulty, looked so like the right course—never very attractive you know! If it is clear to me, at any time, that I can give you a moment's pleasure with no pain . . . [no distance] shall separate us. Perhaps some instinct will tell me when I am really wanted" (p. 143). Surtees reads these excuses for not visiting in 1871 (the proposal, whoever made it, seems to have been in 1869 and not, as Minchin supposed, in October 1871, when Browning did pay another visit to Loo) as also comments back to the proposal: he has chosen the "right" but (politely) "never very attractive" course of "self-denial" and now does not wish to give the (disappointed) friend unnecessary pain, though he would like to be friends. This is plausible, but it is not quite the sure evidence we need in this quandary; Browning could merely be exercising his usual rotund awkwardness in refusing invitations, making the first section equivalent to "it would be a pleasure, but"; the pain to her, which lies behind the reason why it is a pleasure best not now indulged, could refer to the distress generally attributed to her distaste for a proposal based on too much honesty, or even overmuch protesting, about a heart buried in Florence and marriage sought for the good of his son. Interpretation could even run the opposite direction and find in the "this difficulty" an impasse over a too honest (or emotionally and sexually dishonest) proposal and in the "when I am really wanted" an invitation for her to come back to the original offer, still hanging between them.

The only other new evidence is a later letter that follows the final break of October 1871, that second visit to Loo's vastness in Scotland when she "wanted to have the air of shutting the door in my face with a final bang,—fancying that she could coax me round the back-way the very next day" (and note here too the tantalizing ambiguity of all these documents: was she finally refusing him and then finding that he would be darned if she could keep him as a friend—in at least the English, if not French sense of the word—and literary lion? Or was she enticing him to visit so she could save face by appearing as if she were refusing him when he had in fact refused her, naturally provoking his resentment?) Browning writes in July 1872 a kind letter of sympathy when Loo's house partly burns.

Surtees's account leaves me more open to the possibility that the Lady pursued the gent, but in no way sure. There is clearly room for a fuller try at a narrative that pulls together all the evidence into a persuasive whole (and Surtees doesn't mention Lord Acton's confused but confident report that he had inquired about the matter and found Browning *had* proposed). And this will need to include, as Honan rightly argued, awareness of what we find as a mood behind the works of the time. I think it would be a mistake to rush to a new position of imprudent respect for Browning that saw him as the faithful householder easily resistant to wealth and power in the form of even a Ludovisi goddess, faithful for ever in some easy way to his now long-dead saint. I would begin with Mrs. Orr's certainty that some bitterness was working in Browning at this time, quite visible in his works; and I would add a pretty good assurance that the always courtly though sometimes awkward Browning would have done all he could to placate a disappointed admirer, if there had been no emotional involvement on his part. I might even consider going back to the generous stance Minchin took, seeing this as really a clash of emotions and personalities between "two high-spirited, impulsive" people, another case of modern love gone sour, rather than a simple matter of who refused whom. We can be pretty sure there was some kind of parleying between them and certain that it led ultimately to a very serious bitterness and estrangement on both sides that left its mark as late as the satirical portrait of her in the *Parleyings* themselves.

Michael Meredith and The Browning Institute appropriately commemorated the Browning year with an attractive reader's edition of Browning, *A Centenary Selection from Robert Browning's Poetry* (1989), with a general Introduction and useful notes by Meredith. Otherwise there was less to mark the year in the generally active world of Browning's texts than in criticism, though another volume in the fine Kelley and Hudson *The Brownings' Correspondence,* where Elizabeth is still writing the lioness' share, did appear (noticed last year). The fourth volume of the Oxford Browning is announced for later this year. The major event would certainly have gratified the poet: the completion with the third volume of the first full modern edition of his epic poem, edited by Roma A. King (volume 7) and King and Susan Crowl (volumes 8–9), in the Ohio *Complete Works*. I already reviewed volume 7 here favorably in the review of works in 1986 and, more briefly, volume 8 last year. I'll have to leave review (also largely favorable) of the final volume for next year, as the special centenary publications have already overfilled my space.

While I am on the subject of Browning's moods, I'll end this centenary review with some reflections on Browning's temper, and ours. Two articles, by Mairi Calcraft (*BSN* 18:3–13) and Ashby Crowder (*BIS* 17:93–113), have reexamined the issue of Browning's disposition when he wrote about that minor painter in distemper, Pacchiarotto. Crowder's study of Browning's revisions, mainly in the reworkings he deduces between the manuscript and printed version (Browning usually did his rewriting on proofs and revises), gives a good account of the poet's manner of working on that poem. The principle, even in attacking that awful Austin, seems to have been, write in anger; revise at leisure, which Crowder calls working in good temper, though Browning was not above adding another cudgel-swipe at the critic: "my Hop-o'-my-thumb there" became "Quilp-Hop-o'-my-thumb there": good tempered like the hit-man smiling at you as his truck comes on fast! Calcraft defines Browning's temper more precisely in seeing this as a poem about controlling distemper, with unruly feelings beneath the somewhat forced good humor of the surface. The issue of proper copytext for Browning's poems has been, and probably will continue to be a source of some distemper among Browning's well-meaning critics. At an MLA conference two years ago I summarized papers on editing Victorian texts by pointing out that the big disputes of the nineteenth century were those over textual issues—the Higher Controversies, so to speak—not those over mere hermeneutics. And I suggested that this might yet be true in our age, where the disputes over theory have so far been the most visible ones, now that the idea of author's final intentions is being questioned. We actually received some hate mail after the session—though not, I hasten to add, from any Browning scholars. Now Crowder answers (*BSN* 18:47–54) in the studied good temper he has been studying and asserts that, in Browning's case, final revisions "nearly always represent an improvement in his poems: and that different arrangement of poems that Browning made, and most modern texts avoid, are unimportant." I do agree that in most cases Browning did not rewrite his texts thoroughly, so that we do not generally have totally diverse early and late versions, and his changes are most often judicious. But the Oxford edition has already thought it worth offering companion texts of *Pauline,* Woolford's *Browning the Revisionary* has made important claims about the order of Browning's dramatic monologues as he regrouped them, and he and Karlin have announced a text based on Browning's first published versions of poems. Obviously there is room for further discussion and even for possibilities of distemper. But in this pleasing year for the poet we can imagine he would also be pleased to know that we are taking him and his works, text of his youth or text of his Indian summer, text understood in the light of one theoretical horizon or in that of another, so seriously.

Robert Browning: Year's Work, 1990

The centennial (or centenary, if you prefer) of Browning's death, in 1989, brought us back to existential questions about Browning's longevity as a poet. Browning might well mutter from the Abbey, like his own Bishop, "Do I live, am I dead?" What he heard from his readers should generally have pleased him. The Browning Societies, whose activities brought him the recognition for which he was starved and a certain kind of enthusiasm that embarrassed his reputation as it created it, still live—objective correlatives of the general reader's abiding interest in this poet. The poet might truly be gratified to find himself a school classic, one of the few Victorians (along with Dickens, George Eliot, the Brontës, and maybe Trollope) still read everywhere by growing minds—well, at least a few familiar poems, which at least give his central artistic invention a place in the educated consciousness. That worldly, unflappable poet might be astounded by the activities of the large English studies profession: an institution still forming in his day, whose present size and pompous extension might be beyond even his imagination. On the whole he would also feel vindicated and pleased, if now and then a little puzzled as well. For there has been a great deal of writing—still appearing in 1991 and too much, in any case, to be fully reviewed last year or this—by this new kind of critic whose business includes appropriate centenary markings and remarks, valuations and evaluations.

They (we) are certainly an international organization: as English spreads as the world language, getting to be a great worldwide group acting in consort by some mysterious precept of unison—like the early Christian Church . . . or the Mafia. The toniest observation was in Venice itself, in late November (not quite on the sad 12th of December), where the Giorgio Cini Foundation, in the Palladian Isola di San Giorgio Maggiore restored and owned by the Foundation, hosted in doganal splendor an international assembly of critics, scholars, and writers for three days of papers and discussion of Browning. Since this is not *Vanity Fair* (and I do mean the magazine) this reporter will not try to describe this Veronesesque gala or attempt to note the personages who floated by. Suffice it to say that the gondolas cost too much that year too and in new Europe's new Italy there were no poor peasant girls to be seen. Two significant publications that ensued command mention, especially as they could easily be lost to readers here or in England, which would be unfortunate. The first, a catalogue of a splendid exhibition, *Robert Browning A Venezia* (1989), mounted by Professor Rosella Mamoli Zorzi to accompany the complementary theme of the conference, Browning E Venezia, is a handsome record of an important exhibit (unfortunately only in Italian). Even with the selected pictures it is able to print, it is perhaps the most evocative of the many accounts, fictional and more non-fictional, of Browning's golden years and death in Venice. The many sketches (including some attractive privately held Sargent drawings of some of Browning's set of friends and a sketch of the poet's confectionery funeral barge by Ralph Curtis), photos (can that be Browning struggling up the enormous stairs of that cold folly of son Pen, Ca' Rezzonico? probably not), fine paintings (a picture of Mrs. Bronson from a private collection showing her handsome but extremely cool in temperament), and memorabilia, all set our imaginations free to reenter that glamorous Anglo and American-Venetian world that we identify with Henry James and Sargent himself as well as with Browning. The inclusion of sketches, diary entries, and letters from private collections and Italian museums and libraries makes this not just a pretty memento but an important record of materials for Browning's many visits to Venice.

The proceedings of the conference itself have been published as *Browning E Venezia* (1991) under the editorship of Sergio Perosa.[1] Browning would certainly have been gratified at the high level of interest in his work by Italian English scholars

---

[1] The following review of this collection, omitted from this essay originally, appears here for the first time—1997 note.

who are re-engraving Browning into modern Italy's ancient heart. But I should start by stressing that this is an international work of criticism, with about two thirds of the text, *in English*, by American and English scholars. It is a work that shouldn't be ignored by that majority of us Anglophone critics who don't read beyond French and German criticism. We all await the Silicone Valley notebook translator that will bring the world's critics truly into one discourse, and those of us at the conference were fortunate enough to have simultaneous translations. It is a shame that some of the fine essays by Italian contributors will be mainly inaccessible. I note especially the extremely lively interweaving of *Beppo, Pippa*, and a decoding of "De Gustibus" by the fine critic Giorgio Melchiori (pp. 95–108). I also need to stress the value of many of the essays in this collection because it appears not only under foreign title but also in such apparently amateur form. The printing in the volume is execrable (it makes those old early Ohio volumes of Browning look very good by comparison!) and is thoroughly unworthy of its distinguished sponsors. Translating machines are hard but we do have (and so does Olivetti) spell-checkers readily at hand.

The essays' central subject, Browning in Venice, elicited two excellent studies in biography that should not be lost to the text's mean appearance. Michael Meredith (pp. 85–94) offers a gracious account of Browning as reader of his own poetry. In his last years in Venice the poet would read to a rather public audience, in effect anticipating our contemporary poets' primary mode of seeking audience and publicity for their work. Here, as usual, Browning not only leads the way for the poets but does so by borrowing from the novelists: as with Dickens, one can even speak of Browning—as Meredith shows in his account of strenuous readings of two or three hours right up to that of November 19, 1889 when he recited proofs from *Asolando*—reading himself to death. Most important is the impression of Browning's own reading of his work that these performances suggest: strongly dramatized with quite varying tone and manner for different speakers, from a very solemn Saul to a "*buffo* imitation of the querulous Italian—very humorous" of "Up at a Villa—Down in the City." Zorzi's study (pp. 117–124), a condensation from her catalogue, brings a uniquely Venetian shading to an account of Browning's associations among people and palazzi in Venice in the 1880s—a most useful study that should be made available in English.

A number of the other essays focus on works with Venetian settings, including a study of the carnival in *Fifine* by Barbara Melchiori (pp. 109–116). Venice and Asolo in the Veneto, with their early and late associations for Browning, are inevitable sites for sightings of Browning's relation to the romantics (Shelley and Byron doubtless drew the young man there as much as Sordello's story) over a lifetime. Superficially Browning would seem to repudiate his earlier romanticism in the attack on Byron in *Fifine* (another visit to Venice inspired by the philandering Byron) or in the explicitly anti-Wordsworthian revisiting of Asolo in the "Prologue" to *Asolando*. But John Woolford's study of the former poem as a rewriting of *Sordello* (pp. 233–251) usefully sees Browning revising his own revision of romanticism in his youth. In the earlier poem, a realistic humanism opposed romantic aspirations for human perfection; in *Fifine*, Browning can accept the place of the visionary (Juan's dream over Venice) in the poet's understanding of man. This is a fine essay stalking major game in Browning; it is easy to see the other side in these two most "metaphysical" of Browning's works: the seer still present in the poet's stance and self-preoccupation in *Sordello*, the beneficent confrontation with the real (as Barbara Melchiori's essay points out) in the carnival of *Fifine*. Woolford also handles the sexual real of *Fifine* so delicately that it hardly exists as phallic fact in his essay, though it is certainly there in this provocative poem as the archetypal stone on which the pinnacled stones of Venice are modeled. Similarly, Giorgio Melchiori's fine essay suggests that beneath the attack on Byron's grammar and morals was a central reusing of the style—"*leggero e divagatorio*"—of *Beppo*: which Melchiori interestingly defines as the introduction into poetry of Sterne's digressive, consciousness-centered way of writing. In one of a number of essays on *Asolando* in the volume, Angelo Righetti (in Italian, pp. 273–283) also points out (as Harold Bloom has) that the apparently anti-romantic theme of the "Prologue" is of course a revisiting of the central romantic theme of dejection and failed imagination.

On the broader subject of Browning and Italy, J. B. Bullen (pp. 71–83) expertly defines Browning's historical myth of the Renaissance (a word he finds Browning nowhere using in his poetry) as it developed in reaction to the Catholic vision of earlier Christian art promoted by Alexandre Rio. He sees Browning, like Jameson and Ruskin, refocusing on earlier works of the Italian artists, with relative downgrading of the late Renaissance figures such as Guido Reni who originally interested him. At the same time, Browning reacts to Rio (whom he read by 1846; or does he react more to Ruskin himself?) by reasserting the values of "Renaissance," as they would later be formulated in Burckhardt or Symonds, including Lippo's realism and Giotto seen as involved in a civic and political ideal: a useful essay to set beside David DeLaura's study of the painter poems (*PMLA* 95). Daniel Karlin (pp. 325–337) reminds us how interesting Browning's last study of Italian painters still is: "Beatrice Signorini" reconfigures the issues of male-female relations and artistic genius of "Andrea del Sarto" into a very different tale in which patriarchal marriage is both life's ideal (life's infinite moment for the mediocre baroque painter Francesco Romanelli) and exposed as a refuge for the male who recognizes his inferiority to the woman of genius—here Artemesia Gentileschi. In Browning's fable the narrator speaks of his central character rather than giving him Andrea's tragic dignity of self-definition and throws the problem directly to us: love is best—for the second rate?

Philip Drew (pp. 179–191) contributed a pleasantly polemical essay (a by-product of the book on Browning criticism reviewed below) challenging the Browning critics to take on the task of criticizing rather than dismissing Browning's late poetry. His point, which chimes with Giorgio Melchiori's sense of Browning's position between Sterne and Joyce, is a good one. We must not dismiss out of hand—as in some sense both James's comments about a poet on the novelist's side of the street and Wilde's famous quip have encouraged us to do—as not good because not conventionally poetic the later works in which Browning experiments with a poetry closer to prose. On the other hand, I have to report that most of the rather many essays in both English and Italian in this volume looking at the late Browning do not face squarely the problem of poetic valuation that Drew poses; he may not (and probably should not) be particularly pleased despite the attention given later Browning by this centenary volume.

A number of the essays in this rather large book are concerned with even later Browning—the late poet as he influenced the next generation. This is familiar territory by now and there is not much new here, though editor Perosa's summary (Italian) essay (pp. 21–35) is gracious and comprehensive; Robert Langbaum's essay (pp. 37–55) rightly insists on Hardy's special relation to Browning and offers excellent, well-focused, examples to supplement James Richardson's good book on the subject. I especially enjoyed Peter Porter's wide-ranging essay on Browning's style (pp. 1–19); as a writer himself, he seems to me somewhat unique in this familiar project of stating Browning's modernity in balancing Whiggish history of Browning's anticipations with a sense of what is antithetical to many twentieth-century writers in Browning: Browning's bookishness even in his most vital characters and the sense of being in an "auditorium" of the poet's mind. Porter eloquently insists on the centrality of Browning's poetry of tone and voice to modern and post-modern poetry, yet also insists on a fundamental shift from the public voice and full articulation of the Victorian: "Our contemporaries feel that including so much detail, and often in stagy language, as Browning can do, is otiose." A rare appreciation of Browning by a contemporary writer to place in the line of Chesterton or Pound—once the typos galore (which the author was given no opportunity to correct!) have been taken out.

Finally, I should call attention to some interesting essays, non-conformist to the themes of the conference, on general issues in Browning. Ian Jack (pp. 125–135) most interestingly invites us into the workshop of the Oxford Browning to consider, with him, the importance of one reader's response to the poet's work: Elizabeth Barrett's comments on poems toward *Dramatic Romances and Lyrics* sent her in manuscript. He calls attention to important, hitherto mainly unpublished comments on "The Flight of the Duchess." It is a pleasure to see Jack thoughtfully and carefully teasing out of this intertext of poets the points that are useful to our understanding of the text: another example of his important decision to bring whatever contextual information he can find, with his own reasoned explanation of its significance, before readers of his text. Jack, who has written a good book on poets and their audience keeps perhaps too clear of the recent critical hubbub, and recent books by Erickson, Woolford, and Latané, on Browning and his readers. My own contribution (pp. 165–177) perhaps errs on the other side, as a too abstract statement of the theoretical problems of reading the reader in the dramatic monologues and the equal difficulty of ignoring the proliferation of readings and readers generated by these poems. I hope my final account of a reading of reading "The Bishop Orders His Tomb" brings these speculations down to practice and also suggests how productive it can be to approach the monologues aware of a problem of reading and also of a tradition of many readings already inscribed in the history of our criticism. Isobel Armstrong's essay on "The Problem of Representation in *The Ring and the Book*" (pp. 205–232) is especially wide-ranging, in ways that I found exciting. Her essay negotiates, on the whole very successfully, the difficult passage from ideas of political representation to aesthetic ones, primarily by using Foucault's notion of a broader breakdown in authority as an overarching concept. Representation, in the philosophical as well as political world, emerges as a concept that creates/registers the problematization of knowledge, art, and politics. Reading the Rome's opinion books, Pompilia, and the lawyers by the light of Arnold, Bagehot, and Mill on the problems of representation in democracy, Armstrong interestingly highlights the ways in which speakers' conceptions of their ways of speaking (aesthetics) are linked to social or political positions—for instance the highly formalized and manipulative use of language as art by the lawyers, whose legal "fictions" are arbitrarily made real by the law's ability to empower and enforce them as realities. I can't fully state here Armstrong's complex arguments—which also give some sense of not entirely overcoming the large gaps she attempts to bridge between different types of discourse, gaps which are not adequately bridged biographically by brief, if interesting references to Browning's connections to Congregationalist radical political positions in the 1860s.

The final turn to Habermas in order to oppose Foucault's pessimism about an endless repetition in the modern world of the "antithesis between the subject-centered universe and its negation" by a communality available to the reader who sees the limits of each particular monologue in Browning's poem and mediates between them (as Armstrong's own reading attempts to do) is similarly suggestive and highly interesting but not entirely developed.

There was an equally lavish academic tribute to Browning in that other great Abbey and resting place of his mortal remains, one he never knew, the Armstrong Browning Library in Waco, Texas. The Armstrong Browning Library hosted a large conference and presented an exhibition on "The Development of the Poet's Mind" that later toured at the Morgan Library in New York. This conference also brought together scholars from many continents, many critical platelets, and a good mixture of established names (Park Honan, Robert Langbaum, Clyde de L. Ryals, and others) with younger Browning critics and scholars. Many of the essays may be appearing in future volumes of *Studies in Browning and His Circle;* anyone wanting a more immediate experience of the observation can order up tapes of any or all papers (or your reporter's summary, which I won't, therefore, rehearse here). The highlight was perhaps a discussion following Ryals's paper in which he, Warwick Slinn, and Herbert Tucker (and others I may have forgotten) engaged in a game of house to distinguish contemporary critical approaches to Browning: If you knocked at Browning's door, who would reply? Answers: no one; someone else; a different Robert Browning; yourself, dear knocker. (Prizes will be given for readers' other correct answers.) In New York, another city in which Browning never slept, CUNY and the Browning Institute sponsored another commemorative activity, a joint conference on Browning and Hopkins, with papers on Browning by Gibson, David Latané, Ryals, and this reviewer, under Ian Jack's moderation. In Washington, a special MLA session organized by Debnam Chappell featured papers by Joseph Dupras, Ashton Nichols, and Clyde Ryals.

Two other full volumes devoted to centenary essays were mentioned last year but deserve the additional space available this year. A special issue of *Aumla* entitled *Browning Centenary Essays* and edited by Simon Petch and Warwick Slinn (71:1–181), reminds us (like the Venetian volume) by its quality that we are not alone in the new world order of English studies. It is an impressive volume that deserves to be ordered by your libraries if they don't take the series (the Australasian *PMLA*)—which they also should. The volume includes important individual essays but is also impressive for the level of discourse of the whole, which is anything but antipodal or removed from the contemporary critical scene. One essay, by Hilary Fraser on historiography (pp. 13–29), alone suffers from a failure on the international network: it seems to be unaware of Gibson's prior book on the subject, though even here its topic, Browning's affinities with the "resurrectionist" history of Michelet, is a fresh one, not treated at all in Gibson. Virtually all of the essays are well in touch with the debates of the 1980s in literary theory and criticism, more so than many published on these shores or in these pages. In line with this focus, Warwick Slinn's own essay, offered as a wrap-up (pp. 161–181), both surveys Browning's reception through the case of "Bishop Blougram's Apology" and suggests some of the critical issues that preoccupy contemporary criticism and this volume alike. Following the concerns of his own book and fine articles, he foregrounds the pattern in the critical carpet as "the problematics of the subject": in what ways can we talk of character in monologues in a time when character, the subject, is increasingly theorized as a verbal construct. Slinn interestingly approaches a somewhat different question from that behind his earlier work, which was, in effect, how do we read Browning's characters from (our own) post-structuralist point of view (if that is our view). Here he faces the historical issue. How should we describe Browning's implicit philosophical stance in his character-making? His answer is brief and schematic, as my summary must be. To him, Browning does not work in the dualist world of empiricism/idealism that recent historians have described but is always already dealing with a continuum of difference, as in Derridean thinking. Browning is, in Slinn's view of Hegel, in which Hegel approaches Nietzsche and Derrida, like Hegel himself rather than a dualist Hegelian. This is interesting but obviously needs a fuller and systematic explication, including a necessarily controversial reading of the "true" Hegel.

Other essays find less controversial philosophical analogues for Browning's version of the subject. Lisa O'Connor's study of Guido's second monologue (pp. 139–158), uses Nietzsche's idea of both self and social institutions as constructions of metaphor in order to plot carefully Guido's failed strategy in his second monologue: he uncovers (deconstructs) the metaphors that create society and the Church and then constructs a new, verbally puissant, self to set himself free from his judges, only to find his language is not after all powerful to control the outside reality of his coming execution—hence his desperate leap at words of authority, even to the name of the dead Pompilia herself. This good essay nonetheless creates the reader as a more essentialized subject than our Guido, able to see the difference between language and reality and their ironic interplay (back to mimesis) and able to see what Guido can't, the way in which his discourse empowers Pompilia against himself all along (an author-subject's message directly to his reader-subject about his character?). Rosemary Huisman's article (pp. 64–87) is a linguistic rather than philosophical approach to the problem of the subject in the dramatic monologue. Using Halliday's structures, she provides a fairly precise set of re-definitions of the relations of author, text, speaker, listener, and reader so familiar to Browning students. The implied author is "speaking subject"; we readers are the "spoken subject"; between one and the other is the "subject of speech," all that goes on in the text. The definitions allow her to suggest why we feel an especial link between author and ourselves as readers while we both stand in parallel relations to the subject of speech, speaker and listener in the monologue, which we hold at a distance. Better knowledge of reader-response approaches to Browning would have made Huisman perhaps less ready to assume easy agreement between poet and reader; the dramatic monologue, as we all know in the variety of interpretations we find on the critical table already, releases a great deal of new creative energy in the reader. As a way of defining the waxing and waning of subjectivity this approach is rather limited, a set of definitions of what we already know and a reading of poems that looks mainly, though interestingly, at variations in grammar in verbs.

David Lawton makes an attempt to define "Browning's Narrators" (pp. 88–105) in a more traditional (and sometimes too breezy or ponderous) critical voice and approach that makes it clear that there is more than one critical school down under, as in the U.S. or Britain. Far more than Huisman, he sees Browning as the tyrant controller of his monologue worlds, the "single face behind his masks" who exercises authority over his hermetic text and his enthralled readers. This is such a different view from the predominant one of the past decade and more, where our focus has been on the openness and deferral of closure in Browning (as in Tucker's work) and on the freedom of the reader (as in Latané, John Woolford, or my work)—and is therefore at least refreshing and interesting—that one wishes it had been better demonstrated. Instead Lawton gives us a different interesting surprise: a very good reading of "Childe Roland" as the one exception, a poem in which Browning confronts and admits his own unauthorial unoriginality. As in Harold Bloom's well-known reading, the poem is about the relations to past literature, what Lawton calls a dream intertext comparable to "Kubla Khan." Childe Roland/Browning finds his way as the failure to escape the literary past, especially the Roland of *Orlando Furioso,* the other Childe, and the abdicating but mad king, Lear: a fun reading, that leaves me ready to look for other intertextual approaches to other monologues which would, in the aggregate, undo Lawton's own assertions about the authoritarian norm in Browning. Proverbial wisdom to the contrary, you can't use an exception to prove a thesis about the rule.

Penelope Gay's article (pp. 47–63) makes the kinder feminist reading of Browning's poems on desire and women, one put forward a few years ago by U. C. Knoepflmacher (*VP* 22:139–159), namely that Browning's monologues provide a critique of Victorian patriarchal ideas and structures. (The harsher position was well presented by Nina Auerbach in the same issue; Ann Brady's *Pompilia,* noticed two years ago, was sympathetic to what she considers Browning's anti-patriarchal presentation of women, though I found her own readings marred by excessive idealization of Browning's heroine and her rescuer.) Gay's readings of monologues on gender and sexual issues are sensitive and compelling; the structures of her description of the age and its mind are too binary, feminist/patriarchal, passion fulfilled/passion repressed by society. Her own paper shows that Victorians were not as monolithic in their views as her premises assume. "Mid-Victorian" sexuality as she correctly finds it in Browning's women also contradicts her premises: passion unfulfilled and passion fulfilled both kill. If Freud hadn't existed to suggest that desire is not simply controlled from the outside like a spigot turned on or off by society, the nineteenth century eventually would have had to invent him.

One other article in this thought-provoking collection deserves particular mention and recommendation, co-editor Simon Petch's own "Browning's Roman Lawyers" (pp. 109–138), a splendid combination of a deconstructive approach to the lawyers' language in *The Ring and the Book* and a carefully researched look at the special discourse of legal language, generally, in the documents, and in the poem itself. Petch gives the best explanation I have seen for Browning's insistence on including those prickly, barely digestible monologues. Petch sees Browning centrally concerned not with the play of subjectivity against argument (the gourmandizing man and the aggrandizing advocate) but with the impersonal institutional quality of legal language that totally writes the subject lawyer in tune with the case. As Isobel Armstrong has also argued recently (in the *Browning E Venezia* volume, citing this article), the lawyers' language is not a quest for truth in itself but an ultimate kind of non-referential discourse in which all language is shaped by the competitive game of the law itself. In detail Petch is most interesting in showing the ways in which legal "semantic appropriation" works to shift normal references and values following the demands of the case, even "to redistribute roles according to the needs of the argument, and to rewrite the past according to the needs of the present." It may give even seasoned deconstructionists pause to see that they have fallen into the hands of the law, the most "written" convention of language (and deconstruction has presented a powerful redescription of the law to the legal world itself). Far from arguing that Browning succumbed to such a relativist legal version of truth, Petch suggests that he everywhere opposes a poetic truth to a legal. But the lawyers are central because he opposes their law within the legal structure he found in his documents, a competition of truth-claiming voices. The greater truth, the "supreme fiction" of both poetry and the law, is to be clutched from the very maw of the legal language in which it is being ground, not invented elsewhere: a noteworthy article in an interesting volume.

Victorian Poetry also had a centennial issue on Browning (27:1–170), a book-length performance edited by Thomas J. Collins. Last year I had space to review only the interesting central articles on contemporary critical issues and *The Ring and the Book* by Slinn and David Shaw. On the good eighteenth-century principle of declare your interest I note that I was on the Board genially gathered by Collins for the issue and even appear, as decade's work reviewer, in its pages. So I had better establish my credibility by beginning with the negative before I look at some of the other essays. Drew's work, reviewed below, makes a general point that Browning criticism has tended to remain among Browning enthusiasts/experts and not to enter much into the writing of general critics (Harold Bloom's interest in Browning would be the exception recently). This centennial issue, which might have hoped to place Browning in a larger evaluative context after 100 years, is not an exception. One would have liked to see names like Richard Altick (who does concern himself with Browning), J. H. Buckley, J. Hillis Miller, Christopher Ricks, or one of our many feminist general critics, or even a debate between Bloom himself and Helen Vendler on Browning's value and importance. Instead we have the usual suspects primarily focused on making sense of Browning without much concern with his place in a canon.

The strength of the volume, for I do believe it is worthy of the occasion if not a major event in the 100 year critical history, is rather in the area where I have been finding Browning studies strong over the past decade: as in the *Aumla* volume, there is a persistent and highly intelligent attempt to relate traditional views of Browning to the broadest theoretical issues that have been rousing our profession. This is true in those lead essays by two of our finest Victorian philosophical critics, Shaw and Slinn, which, with many gems of incisive thinking that we expect from these critics, nonetheless suffer from almost too much polemical assertion without the beef of criticism. The other articles as a group nicely balance theoretical concerns with new readings of Browning. They are, like those in the Australasian volume, finally more memorable as a group that maintains a high standard for current approaches to Browning than as major new contributions on their particular subjects. Indeed there is a remarkable coherence in the kinds of questions asked by the contributors.

The first three articles find different ways and different specific subjects to focus on the issue raised also in Lawton's article in *Aumla,* namely the question of authority (and of course its relations to the author) in Browning. This concern with the continuing power of the poet is altogether relevant in a man whose works have lasted 100 years beyond the usual length of a person's authority and seem headed for another 100.

Daniel Karlin, in an article on "Browning, Elizabeth Barrett, and 'Mesmerism'" (pp. 65–77), moves from interesting contextual material on the Brownings and Dr. John Elliotson's well-publicized sessions in hypnotism to a more general exploration of their discomfort with the kind of personal control of another they saw in the practice. The especially interesting point is that Barrett nonetheless ascribed such powers to Robert and his work and Karlin rather agrees with her and implicitly with Lawton's point, that even the dramatic monologue presents one person (author) controlling another (speaker). Karlin rightly sees Browning's poem on the subject restating some of the biographic concerns with mesmerism and also inscribing in its form its control. Even the reader cannot tell its relation to Gothic nor go beyond the text to know the outcome of the speaker's control over his subject-listener. Amen, except that the control is balanced by the way in which the poem both allows and provokes the reader to move to complicated judgment—for instance, what kind of possession is this that recalls Lovelace's triumph more than Byron's triumphs?

David G. Riede's essay on "Genre and Poetic Authority in *Pippa Passes*" (pp. 49–64) echoes Karlin's concerns with our uncertainty over even the genre of "Mesmerism" in his fuller and more critically complicated look at Browning's little epic of dramatic monologues and lyric interludes. Following the work of David Latané, which he knows, and John Woolford's, which he evidently hadn't seen, Riede looks at Browning's play with genre in the 1830s as partly a problem of authority: *Sordello* is written with lecture stick in hand even as the author tries to disembarrass himself of an authoritarian role; the dramas were criticized for the author's totalitarian control of all the characters. As in both Shaw and Slinn's readings of Browning's greater poem, Riede finds Browning pulling down (deconstructing) any assertions that are made by an apparently authoritative voice, most especially Pippa's own central lyric statements. Pippa doesn't control the egocentric and individual responses of her hearers, though she does affect them in ways consistent with their preoccupations; Browning shows us characters, in turn, trying to play tyrant or puppet-master with other characters. The central puppet figure is Pippa herself; but here, too, Browning deconstructs his own instrumental approach to her by calling into question such puppetry throughout. As in Woolford's view, Riede sees this as implicitly a political notion in poetry, what he calls an "experiment in republican genre" during a politically troubled period. The approach to the poem is not that new, but the conceptualization and specific readings make this a useful essay.

Finally, Rowena Fowler raises a more specific issue of authority, that of the tyranny of the male gaze, in a candid look at "Browning's Nudes" (pp. 29–47). The article brings together a good deal of information on Browning's references to nudes and raises the interesting question of power in the (usually male) vision of (usually female) nudes. I found the article confusing in certain respects: it adopts "the feminist perspective" but doesn't define this; sometimes the view seems to be that all erotic representation of women is a tyranny, which is one, but only one, feminist view and easily leads to the political tyranny of a new purity crusade, which would wish to put an end to articles like this one, with its lascivious illustrations of

Watts, Etty, Powers, and Ingres; it also isn't clear whether Browning is an exploiter of the naked feminine or a sympathizer. Here we need more awareness of possible changes in attitude from young to old Browning; his involvement in Pen's nude work, which is discussed but not properly illustrated, was coincident with a climate among serious writers that attacked excessive concerns for purity, just as earlier Victorian writers were sometimes sympathetic to the efforts to move away from the excesses of the Regency period.

Like Lawton's, these explorations of authority generally fail to look at the full arc of the complicated rhetoric of the dramatic monologue, the author's control/release of the reader. With a nice coherence, the volume includes three essays that concern themselves precisely with this issue. An article on *The Ring and the Book,* by Vivienne Rundle (pp. 99–114), examines the case of the second Guido speech as a way of looking generally at the reader in the poem. Like David Shaw in the same issue, she likes to empower her contemporary critical horizon by reading it back into Browning—"once again, Browning anticipates the turns of modern critical theory"—here both Hillis Miller's idea of the ethical moment in literature (when the reader is forced to judge) and the general concern with reader-response in the last decade. Of course, both issues have a long history; Browning does seem to have an eye on the reader, that British Public he has failed to please, and ethical judgment of literature is a modern revival, not an attempt at a new thing for our time. Rundle draws on Seymour Chatman's distinction between discourse (shaping approach) and story (events), rather as Slinn does implicitly, to suggest that Browning foregrounds—makes his stories about—interpretive stances rather than the events of tales. In this she sees a space opened up for the reader to exercise active involvement in the text. As a speaker most self-conscious about his rhetorical aim, Guido forces the reader to judge not just his actions but his way of presenting his tale. His shifting appeals to a general audience and then to a specific one in the poem force the reader to oscillate between entry into the poem as listener and exit to a removed overhearer's position. Such shifting perspectives force the reader to take an active role in judging Guido and, ultimately, in judging the differing discourses of the different books. The model for an active reader seemed to me persuasive; by contrast, the "ethical moment" remains more of a slogan than a critical tool. Ethical judgment is one of many reader responses; if we wish to we may privilege it without necessarily finding it inscribed into the text more than another kind of judgment.

Joseph A. Dupras' contribution comes the closest to being a lively new reading of a Browning poem, a look at "Reader-Auditor" coordination in the late poem "A Forgiveness" (pp. 135–150). Within work on readers he also offers a fruitful, relatively unexplored approach, focus on the conflict between our reading of the poem as text and our awareness of the oral performance that the listener in the poem experiences. This is another form of oscillation forced on the reader; and its effect, as in Rundle's conception, is also to sharpen the reader's perception and to force a more active response. As the violent, cuckolded husband speaks threateningly to the monk, we not only have to decide, as the monk does, whether he speaks as a prelude to revenge but also whether the monk experiences the same meanings we do. The form of the poem, from quotation marks to the heroic couplet verses, forces us to realize our divergences from the listener as we strive to imagine the different experience he has in hearing the monologue. Like Rundle's, this approach describes a model for reading Browning that authorizes a large area of freedom in his dramatic monologues and suggests why the poems themselves are so exciting to read—even after 100 years or 100 reads.

Finally, Yopie Prins's article on the much abused Browning version of Aeschylus' *Agamemnon* (pp. 151–170) makes a case for the apparent schoolboy literalism not being a mere perversity in Browning. Very much in the same way as Dupras, she sees Browning deliberately creating a tension between textual reading and voiced reciting as a way of forcing the reader into action. Here the effect, defined from no less fashionable a writer than Walter Benjamin, is alienation from our own language. Despite the pedigree of the theory, I'm not sure I can subscribe to it in the form Prins uses it, for it seems to give us the experience of another English speaker trying to read Greek

(Browning, for instance) rather than an equivalent to the experience of the Greek reader. As a definition of the aim of translation it conflicts with Prins's second point, which I can agree with up to a point, that Browning sympathized and aligned himself with the Aeschylean tradition of difficult poetry and wrote something rather like it in his own English poems, which would imply that the standard is accommodation to English, not alienation. Yet even here, as Honan demonstrated a long time ago, the astonishing variety of Browning's styles makes any generalizations about his style suspect. Reuben Brower's essay on the translation and his conclusion—which Prins cites—that "Browning was never more Browning than when as here he was being intensely 'Greek,'" were probably the only observations on Browning by a fine general critic who nonetheless shared F. R. Leavis' low estimation of Browning. Still, Prins's intelligent essay, like Browning's deliberately difficult translation, has the effect of making us think again about translation, especially about the relation of reader to translator, and it does so brightly and interestingly.

Appropriately to the centenary, Philip Drew published a useful review of criticism covering the entire century and some of the reviews during Browning's lifetime: *An Annotated Critical Bibliography of Robert Browning* (1990) in the Harvester Wheatsheaf series. Drew offers his work engagingly and modestly as an aid to future students; as a selective and briefly annotated list of works on Browning it fills a need that has been growing more obvious each year that William Clyde DeVane's *Handbook* (1955) and Honan's essay in *Victorian Poets: A Guide to Research* (1968) mellow and age in our scholarly caves.

Drew's summaries are particularly strong in the central areas where his own work has been so useful over many years: general evaluations of Browning's poetry and critical approaches to individual poems. Students will find the poem-by-poem lists especially helpful for stating major critical issues succinctly and for offering a workable number of important articles and sections from books. Drew restates some of the fears, traditional in the oddly self-conscious and insecure world of Browning studies, that Browning criticism may be an enthusiastic backwater of criticism, and he finds the run of articles, generally not included here, "pedestrian and ill-written." Yet he is also surprised, even a little pleased, to find how much has been written since the early 1970s on individual poems. His summaries are especially good on the later poems, long a barren terrain but now showing at least signs of critical life—a subject he elaborates on in the *Browning E Venezia* volume. Drew has a good eye as well for the summary that performs the traditional critical function as he sees it, "to estimate his [the poet's] artistic strengths and weaknesses convincingly for our time." He raises interestingly the issue of Browning's relative lack of place in general critical studies of English or even Victorian literature and calls attention well to critics such as Bloom who have given Browning the major location in their schemes that he deserves. He also tries to note Browning's position in the twentieth-century literary scene, though here he seems weak both in articles on Browning and moderns, such as George Bornstein and Loy Martin's work on Browning and Pound, and in general awareness of Browning's importance for contemporary writers, including our most recent laureate, Robert Lowell. Here one problem is that Leavis is given far too much credit for centrality in the critical discourse of our century; Drew ought to be more impressed by Bloom's high estimate of Browning as an indication of where Browning stands in contemporary notions of the tradition. He is also relatively weaker in identifying and describing more recent critical trends, where his discomfort makes for awkwardness. He is, indeed, not above roaring at "recent developments in literary theory," apparently meaning the general trends in critical self-consciousness of the past fifteen years too easily labeled post-structuralist. But this is keystone-cop conservatism: all the ringleaders—Tucker, Slinn, Ryals, Martin—receive warm salutations from this constable, as they indeed generally deserve, and warnings about a dangerous gang called deconstructionists. Only Christine Froula's (good) article on *Sordello* and modernist poetics comes in for some specific criticism for its approach. But if Drew appreciates intelligent criticism despite his prejudices against new-fangledness in theory, he fails to label and interpret it properly for tomorrow's students. Listings under "subjects" are the traditional ones, religion, music, and so forth: certainly valuable. Missing are feminist approaches, reader response, even genre (and also Donald Hair's fine book on the subject). Existentialism is allowed in under religion and philosophy, but nothing since; a student might receive the general impression that deconstruction was indeed some kind of extension of existentialist criticism. A particular problem was the decision to stop entries at the end of 1986, leaving out a number of interesting works such as Gibson's and Latané's and pre-aging the list as a whole. Such dates should be spelled out in the title so that future students don't regularly blot out three years of work—creating a kind of Bermuda Triangle of Browning scholarship. In any event, my late colleague William E. Buckler's book on *The Ring and the Book* (1985) qualifies by date and should be here.

There is an even more damaging omission in the summary of research materials, the wonderful omnium-gatherum of Browning manuscripts and books, *The Browning Collections: A Reconstruction* (1984), edited by Philip Kelley and Betty A. Coley, the most important bibliographical reference work on primary sources. Otherwise these summaries are most helpful, though they generally lack the focus on topics (say in Browning's biography) or on critical problems (as in the long and heated debate over Browning's text) that we are given in Drew's summaries of criticism. Certainly it is because of his generally judicious selection of works on Browning's individual poems that we will be most grateful that Drew took on this hard labor. The work of the 1990s is likely to be more sophisticated in its awareness of its critical approach; but we will not go beyond the need to engage with the ever provocative verbal mazes of Browning's individual poems; Drew's legacy here should promote the kinds of honest confrontations with the complexity of Browning's art that his own substantial contributions to Browning criticism have offered.

The poet who I fancy stirring in his place in the Abbey to find out how his works are doing may very well doze again, muttering, as he falls asleep for another hundred years, the words of his deathbed reception of reviews of *Asolando*: "How gratifying." A poet so often frustrated by lack of interest in his work in his lifetime might well be pleased with so much intelligent attention, in so many lands, focused on his work one hundred years after his death in Venice's cold Ca' Rezzonico.

Robert Browning: Year's Work, 1991-1992

The serious Browning student hardly needs reminding that the last decade and more has been a banner time for what used to be considered hard facts or positivistic scholarship, the preparation of Browning's texts. There have been—count them—three major scholarly editions of Browning out or in the works: the completed Pettigrew/Collins Penguin edition, now widely used in universities and about to have a full new Browning concordance keyed to its text. Then there is the grand old cause of the Ohio Browning, by no means dead, as I will indicate below (nor was Eric Griffiths' metaphor for it in his *TLS* review, November 22, 1991—a Dracula of an edition, bad but not killable—fair; not Dracula but something of a Phoenix in its new appearance after an early death). Then there is the excellent Oxford edition under the general, highly competent editorship of Ian Jack, a fourth volume of which is reviewed below. One is tempted to wonder whether the Browning world has again become a backwater in which hard work substitutes for current, cutting-edge thinking. But this would be just the wrong thing to say, because textual criticism, our higher criticism, has become once again a site of major controversy and interesting thinking that feeds every aspect of critical discussion. And to prove it we now have the most controversial recasting of Browning's text, a further full edition of the poems in the Longman annotated English poets series prepared by two entirely level-headed and fully qualified Browning critics in London, John Woolford and Daniel Karlin. Given the amount of earthquaking generated in earlier days by the question of whether copytext should be Browning's 1889 text, as in Ohio, or the 1888 (first ten volumes augmented by records of corrections that Browning planned)/1889 (the rest) as in Oxford and Penguin, the Longman decision to use Browning's first published text should be registering way up on the Richter scale of scholarly perturbation. Of course, you won't find the argument in any of the three competing editions, because they all began with the traditional premise that the author's last intentions should determine the accepted text for posterity: their business was only to work out in detail what those intentions were. Ohio came closest to anticipating the current opening up of the issue when they spoke, to our then amazement, of the text as a continually innovating medium. If they created a last-intentions, deathbed text, they also created a system of variorum readings that came as close as technology of those dark ages would allow to the hypermedia kit for creating one's own text at any stage in its development that new higher critics such as Jerome McGann are now fiercely developing.

Browning has been a central figure in one recent book directly discussing the nature of nineteenth-century publishing and the question of appropriate copytext. This is Allan Dooley's *Author and Printer in Victorian England* (1992) and I am sure he would not only not mind but much applaud my setting his argument up against the principles of the Longman edition, which are at least implicitly his target (Dooley has long been a member of the Phoenix rescue team at Ohio). I have neither the special knowledge nor the space to review Dooley's main work here, which is a splendidly detailed summary of what is now known of the physical business of printing in the nineteenth century, with special attention to the ways in which a fast-developing technology offered new ways of authorial control and also new possibilities of textual disintegration. His final chapter turns however to what he grants is finally an issue of ideology (or opinion), not of the facts of publishing: the current controversy over choice of copytext. Dooley characterizes both advocates of first (Longman) and last intentions (our other three editions) as ideologues, abstractly privileging original inspiration (texts only degenerate from their original inspired purity when handled by an editing author) or the author's ownership of a text until death does them part (the authority of a last will and text-meant). Such a familiar strategy naturally opens to his own natured, non-ideological ideology, and this he offers as the ideal of the author's "best and most successful effort to make the work come out right. "Granting that sometimes authors create a different text, so that there are indeed two versions, he defines a "normal" revised text as an attempt at perfecting an original intention by rhetorical changes. We have then only to decide which text best embodies the author's textual quest for his best self.

The metaphysics masking as common sense here is a little heady and not a little Arnoldian and as an argument it is clearly constructive, attempting to define some true text out of the deconstructive welter of possible texts exposed by the current rethinking of textual criticism. It does, however, embody some common sense that can be applied to Browning by directing us to the nature of his particular emendations. One can argue, as Dooley does explicitly and Oxford does by providing both versions, that the common reader will wish to consider the quite different early and late versions of *Pauline* as marking major shifts in author's inspiration. One can also argue that with most of Browning's work there does seem to be a general intention in his changes of only breathing, shining, and seeking to mend rather than making new. Even where he began major changes in point of view, as in the Christianizing of *Paracelsus* in 1849, later revisions seem to bring him closer to first intentions. Right up to the final collected edition (and beyond) we find Browning mainly concerned with better word choice, clarification for the reader, more effective phrasing. So if we are looking to canonize a text for that authority-seeking and not too curious reader, the common reader, we may well rest with the texts we all know, polished in turn by our three editorial enterprises, which have produced in the main identical texts. Certainly the common reader will also wish to have *Pippa Passes* with the excellent additions, familiar and important parts of the long received text, that he or she could only find in the small-print textual notes in the Longman edition; or, to take an egregious case, who would want to teach a class on a poem entitled "The Tomb at St. Praxed's" and find that old Gandolf "came me in" on the matter of the "shrewd snatch of the corner south" when we all know he "cozened" him— "Shrewd was that snatch from out the corner South." No, for this purpose, these new-fangled texts simply won't do. The common reader—who, I also fear, will never see this review—is hereby warned that these texts are pernicious and full of poison. And woe betide the unsuspecting graduate student who takes out this authoritative looking complete works, skips over the introduction, and begins to write an analytical paper!

But—imagine a graduate seminar on Browning, or a biographer or critic at work in the study, and the case is very different. We may want to know the early, inspired if not fully polished poet; or, as Karlin and Woolford argue, if we want to study the reception of the text and its historic relations with its culture and society, we will probably begin with the text in the form in which it first struck Browning's contemporaries. Some day a hypertext on our screen will allow us to press a button or tweak a mouse and move a text forward through all its emendations from manuscript to deathbed; in the meantime genetic work will simply be much easier if we start with the first text and piece out the changes (most often additions) rather than try to read Ohio in reverse. This is another very big textual project, and Griffiths and others have remarked that it is a shame Oxford and Longman could not be put at a round table (after all it was an Arthurian, Victorian idea before business took it up) and brought into a single project. But the idea makes no sense because this is fundamentally a different project; the two cannot be squared with all the best will in the world. The unconscionable waste of effort and library money, which very well could have been spared by some round-tabling, must be blamed not on this new generation of Browning scholars with new ideas of this time but on the elders who quarreled so mightily while producing, from the large view, three versions of the same textual project, all of which would have been strengthened by amalgamation. (But maybe without the spur of competition, as Mrs. Thatcher might remark, they would all be sitting around the boardroom planning the third volume and watching the meter run on grant money.)

What would also have been unacceptable would have been an expensive new edition based merely on the gimmick of first text. I was absolutely delighted to find that this Woolford and

Karlin edition is an extraordinarily well presented and learned text, one that well compares with the fullest and best annotated text so far, the Oxford one. Of course last come is best served and these editors stand on the shoulders of three giant editions. But the text has particular virtues as well as the thoroughness of clean-up position. They are especially in evidence in volume I, where the editors, generally persuasively, provide a tremendous apparatus of intertextual readings in classical, Renaissance, and especially romantic predecessors. They need not, and do not argue that Browning necessarily read all the works they find paralleling his text; what they do particularly well is restore the complex world of discourse about the poet, poetry, and society out of which the enormously intellectual *Sordello* developed. Annotation for *Sordello,* most of it highly pertinent, runs about one and a half pages for each half page of text. The text graphically shows, as the good annotation of Oxford also did, that Browning was very much in touch with the current of ideas of his time: no mere autodidact piecing together odd bits of learning without an idea in his dad's library. The extensive headnotes, again like Oxford but with even greater detail, provide full post-DeVanian summaries of what is known of the composition, dating, publication, sources and influences, and critical reception of the text. Summaries of Browning's revisions complement textual notes on the emendations in later publications, including the important manuscript revisions of *Sordello* now at Syracuse (also presented, less fully, in Oxford).

I found the apparatus of commentary and annotation, though equally thorough and authoritative, less innovative for the great sets of dramatic monologues originally published as *Dramatic Lyrics* and *Dramatic Romances and Lyrics* in *Bells and Pomegranates*. Although they provide a useful appendix on the publication plans for the series, the editors do not address the issues of the creation of Browning's distinctive mode of writing with the fullness that they bring to his relation to romanticism. Indeed, their chronological approach gives them no special place to proclaim the development of Browning's mature work on the themes of history, love, power, gender, and the rest that also clearly connect Browning to his age as much as to romantic thought on poetry. Not that such issues are not noted as they come up; but the contextual annotation is not nearly so full; perhaps that is asking, indeed, too much: a text whose annotation serves as a running intellectual biography of an age! But there is much overlap with Oxford—for instance, the useful recording of virtually all of Elizabeth Barrett's comments on the later volume of monologues.

I think a number of scholars will share my discomfort with the strict application of the Longman principle of publishing poems in the order of composition. Given the nature of the texts—first published versions—it might have been more consistent to keep series of poems together as first published. Instead you will confront an order never seen before, always based on dating, which makes hash of the distinctive orderings of dramatic monologues so much a part of Browning's first publication of these works. Those two wonderful volumes can indeed be read as tentatives toward poetic sequences, with many well-known diptychs and even triptychs, now alas dispersed or reversed. So just when we thought we could enjoy the pristine experience of these marvelous moments of new creation we are given an omelet; I for one may head for the Xerox room and cut and paste—really a very big job. A further problem is that the datings are for the most part anything but firm. I don't fault the editors on their chronologies, which are based on as good evidence as is available. But this is usually really very weak, as they often candidly admit, and could easily be upset by future discoveries. I would have much preferred a boldly indicated system of conjectural dates of composition, the present good arguments for them, but order as published. It is an irony that the other three editions all violated their own belief in authors' last rights with these famous collections by assembling a text that never was: latest revisions in Browning's early volume ordering. Now we have the first texts in conjectural diachronic ordering: logical to the Longman system but not to our scholarly needs.

I also was bothered by what seemed an inconsistent approach to titles; as far as I could see, some poems were given, as they should be, original titles with the canonical ones in brackets while others were simply given the canonical titles—

especially where a joint title (Camp and Cloister) was eliminated by the diasporic chronological rigor. By contrast, the overall chronological approach, into which fugitives have been dropped, makes this the most effective presentation of Browning's rather many uncollected works. I have already found their placement most useful in examining, for instance, the degree to which there are elements of the dramatic monologue in Browning's works of the 1830s. Yes, one could do this with other editions, where the fugitives are assembled somewhere, but the continuous read is a great help. There is even one new fugitive, an epigram by Goethe published only as prose in the letters. Emendations also offer a problem as an editor preparing an error-free text might be led to start following the poet's later changes too fully, on the assumption that he knew an error when he saw one, thus subverting the project; the approach has been conservative.

Suspension of these reviews last year kept me from seasonable notice of important installments in the two other Browning works in progress. The fourth volume of the Oxford *Poetical Works,* edited by Ian Jack, general editor of the project, Rowena Fowler, and Margaret Smith, covers much the same material as the second volume of Longman. Jack's is a complete edition, unlike Longman, and did include the plays intended for the stage (also not in Pettigrew/Collins but in Ohio). Longman has only *Luria* and *A Soul's Tragedy,* which appear also in this Oxford volume along with *Dramatic Romances and Lyrics* and the later *Christmas-Eve and Easter-Day.* I have already testified in earlier surveys (indeed testify on the dust jacket) to the excellent text produced in Oxford from Browning's last supervised edition with judicious editorial corrections. This is indeed essentially a purified version of the canonical texts we all know, as are Pettigrew/Collins and Ohio. In addition, the editing is based on full reference to the Brownings' correspondence, manuscripts, proof sheets, and corrected copies of various sorts, and provides authoritative information about the publishing history and revisions. The detailed knowledge of revisions gives us a glimpse at the complicated reality beneath Dooley's ideal of a polishing author. The editors note Browning corrected ("improved") a number of the dramatic monologues in his *Selections* of 1872, 1880, and 1884 but, as these volumes were not used for corrections for the 1888–1889 *Poetical Works* the corrections did not follow into the line of descent of the final edition used by our three canonical modern editions. What should the editor following the perfecting author to his best text do? Presumably use these; but Oxford never accepted Dooley's principles and let the (lazy or absent-minded) poet of 1888 have the last word on simpler principles of last intentions.

Oxford also continues the full and sensible annotation, among Browning editions especially good at helping the reader through difficult places. Elizabeth Barrett's observations, on which Jack has written interestingly, are given throughout and also summarized in head notes: an interesting intertextual tale. Also, as in Longman and in the distinguished earlier Oxford volumes, headnotes present helpful summaries of information on the poems of the sort we used to have to go to DeVane for, including even some critical opinion of the moderate, historically informed sort. A comparison with Longman, or with the new improved Ohio edition that covers these poems, or even the more succinct Pettigrew/Collins reveals of course a great deal of overlap in basic information. Five pages of scrupulous addenda for volumes 1–3 also suggest that there is no end in sight to additional relevant information. We have all learned a great deal out of the controversial competition of these no longer discreet and self-effacing higher critics. We may also come to regret not so much all this tetraplication of effort now as the damp our plethora of editions will place on anyone's proposals for a new edition in 2020.

The Ohio project of the *Complete Works* is not dead, though the volumes after the editors' period of self-examination and renewal began half way through the poems Oxford just covered, with the new, much improved edition picking up in volume 5 at *A Soul's Tragedy*. But the proof of their phoenixing is clear especially in the completion with the third volume of the first full modern edition of Browning's epic poem, edited by Roma A. King (volume 7) and King and Susan Crowl (volumes 8–9). I already reviewed volume 7 here favorably in the review of works in 1986 and, more briefly, volume 8 four years ago. The three volumes are generally all that the original Ohio was not, trustworthy, competent, useful. The edition gives us *The Ring and the Book* from the second, corrected, 1889 impression of *The Poetical Works*. Because Richard Altick's text in Penguin was based on the original, 1868–1869, volumes, we thus have a ready choice between author's first and last text. Browning made fewer important changes in this relatively late poem than he did in his earlier ones, but he returned to the text a number of times to polish and correct it. One of the weaknesses of the original Ohio was the failure to master all the historical evidence on Browning's publishing practices and various editions (some of it, it should be said, not then readily available). In less substantial ways the problem still affects this text. Michael Meredith (*SBHC* 15:41–50) has clarified a continuing confusion about Browning's 1872 reissue of the poem, which includes two states of volumes 1 and 2, some merely 1868 with a new title and others, also with the 1872 title, not actually printed until 1882 and 1883, but then embodying corrections as a true new edition. These versions are not distinguished by Ohio but they apparently had the good fortune to use the corrected volumes 1 and 2 in their variants. In addition, Meredith has clarified their confusion over corrected sheets of volumes 1, 3, and 4 in Beinecke, Yale. These have in fact independent corrections that Browning prepared but never used, and Meredith is doubtless correct to argue that they deserve a place in the history of the author's polishing intentions. In other respects the text is carefully and well prepared. The Ohio editors have become increasingly skillful in making emendations where they detect printers' and other errors that Browning failed to catch. (They found 16 in volume 7; 22, and 28 respectively in volumes 8 and 9.) Ohio has the advantage of offering their famous kit of all the variants, here most interesting for the manuscript and proof readings that allow us to chart the final progress of the epic in the making. I have found the text itself quite error free in my check of a few passages.

Volume 7 provided a map and essay-length accounts of Browning's sources, the composition of the poem, and the history of publication, as well as some meganotes on central issues such as the ring or Molinists. Doubtless Oxford—as

Meredith is already doing—will give a somewhat richer history of Browning's composition, based on full study of the letters: as noted above, an especial strength in their edition. The editor/editors of Ohio's text also provide little introductory material on the critical issues raised by the text over 120 years of reception, another point where Oxford and also Longman can be expected to be strong.

But the annotation itself in Ohio is a great achievement for which we have reason to be most grateful; indeed, the three volumes together have received a book's worth of closely packed annotation—over 200 pages in all. Like volume 7, 8 and 9 are especially rich in Biblical identifications. En masse, they show us how very much this work was written, consciously or unconsciously, as a kind of progress of the sacred text in the secular world: everyone—the Pope, Caponsacchi, and Pompilia, of course, but also even Guido and those lawyers—quotes and alludes to scripture endlessly, as these useful notes massively show. A poem about the use and misuse of words seems to set up a kind of running model in the apparent loss/possible potency of God's word in the world as it is misused or repristinated by different speakers. Remarkably few identifications of allusions to other writers, except Homer, Euripides, and a few other classics, and occasionally a Donne or Shakespeare: not a failure of the editors, I think, but a sign of Browning's unwillingness to work in another English writer's language and style (Longman looked for broader parallels of ideas and may find more to say of a broader context for this epic as they did for Browning's other epic of Italy). In volume 9 the editors deserve special kudos for untangling a triple Biblical reference and unfolding two triple word plays by Bottini on one page (p. 295) of notes. Occasional critical pointers were helpful, for instance the ambivalence toward Pompilia revealed deep in Bottini's allusions or the places where Browning betrays his identification with the Pope by anachronisms—an unattractive reality of the text to the recent critical tendency, on the whole I think correct, to unseat the Pope as privileged speaker. There were not enough notes that explained the legal and historical issues being raised by the text and, as in the general materials, little sense of critical issues and cruxes—which the scholar is left to work up on her or his own. And, yes, still a little excess and pedantry in notes that are in any case generally not as pithy as those by Altick (or Pettigrew in the two-volume Penguin). We are told that Augustine was "an" early Church father, given a long note on galleys and galley slaves, and twice given the gratuitous information that the mark of Cain, which Browning uses in its proverbial sense, was originally given by God as a mark to protect him. One of the few explanations of a difficult concept, that of "missing the mediated word," of Book 12—"Art can tell the truth even without words, i.e. through painting and music"—seems unfortunate. It might lead a young mind to drop English and go over to the Music or Fine Arts Departments—which Browning surely didn't intend! But these are small points in a most helpful labor of love of Browning—that acknowledges the abundant spadework of earlier editors and handbook writers on which it builds while it gives us a full new and authoritative guide to the text. All serious students of the poem will wish to have it handy. The books are beautifully printed, with no double columns or run-over lines and lots of space for notes. Alas, the price is commensurately high ($150 for the set, though we have all seen worse; indeed the Oxford 4th volumes is an outrageous $135 by itself).

With all these important editions of the last few years to review, I have only space for brief mention of a few other of the many works on Browning that have been coming in. Philip Kelley, now ably assisted by Scott Lewis after the unfortunate demise of the excellent editor Ronald Hudson, has brought the massive and elegant Wedgestone Press edition of *The Brownings' Correspondence* up to July 1845; as McDonald's might say, almost 2000 letters published so far and more at work every minute. This beautifully illustrated book, doubtless the last of the great nineteenth-century editions of letters, remains, as earlier volumes were, largely a treasure of Elizabeth Barrett scholarship, her Clarissa outweighing his Lovelace by a very high proportion. But here at last the twain are coming together. The editors rightly record their debt to the lifework of Elvan Kintner in editing these letters for Harvard, as well as Daniel Karlin's fine study. But it is interesting also to be able to read the letters not all by themselves, as they rested so long in Elizabeth Barrett's little leather case, but as part of a record showing both word and love-struck poets also much in touch with other people and other events. There are also quite a few new letters from Robert to other correspondents and, in this generous and not highly priced work, the great bonus of reprints of reviews of the Brownings' works. In this last area of scholarship, I merely notice the major, very useful study of Browning's reception through *The Ring and the Book,* both in reviews and in other records by his contemporaries, Gertrude Reese Hudson's *Browning's Literary Life* (1992)—which I review elsewhere [next entry] in any case.

Along with such an outpouring of textual scholarship on Browning, I should also note Michael Millgate's chapter on Browning and his son in *Testamentary Acts* (1992), a work of seasoned and impeccable scholarship by a major biographer and editor. Millgate does not attempt to uncover new material but he does read the record of scholarship on Browning's declining years and the heritage passed on by him to son Pen and, alas, from him, who left no effective will, to the Sotheby block, with shrewdness. The topic of his book, which includes essays as well on Tennyson, James, and Hardy, is the biographical record of significant literary legacies: who managed major authors' personal and literary estates and how did these constructions of endings also construct literary reputations. He makes interesting points about Browning's special closeness with Alexandra Orr, and might have brought out further the implications of her differences from Pen after Browning's death as they revealed conflicting authorized versions. A major issue seems to have been Browning's health, Browning, family, and most friends insisting on the vigor of his non-decline, with the last day in Rezzonico merely a dramatic curtain to an entirely robust performance. Millgate is fair to Pen's most difficult role in life, son who could never please his nonetheless indulgent father, then lonely keeper of what Lilian Whiting called the "very Valhalla of the wedded poets." He rightly praises Pen's gentlemanly ungreediness in managing his parents' valuable remains and his independence in resolving to release the love letters and to work with Hall Griffin toward a serious biographical record. I would only have wished that there would have been more wide-reaching observations on the various ways in which Browning's reputation was formed in his testamentary process: here Millgate seems perhaps too wedded to his own biographical approach and the result is we lack a full approach to this important moment of reception.

Finally, a useful specialized study, also factual and biographical in direction, was published by Nachum Schoffman: *There is No Truer Truth: The Musical Aspect of Browning's Poetry* (1991). I confess I feared to find it another summary of Browning's technical barbarities and gaffes, which have had a long prehistory in other such studies. Who said (lately, or even early other than the boasty poet himself) that Browning was more than an inspired amateur at music, though the inspiration itself is a great one in the history of writing about music? But I found this thoughtful book made just this point, admitting soberly Browning's occasional mistakes—that the "mode Palestrina" is nowhere to be found in the history of music or that "diminished sixths" also exist only in Browning—but also crediting Browning with a very high level of competence in music, whatever his errors in detail. He rightly stresses Browning's unique position among poets (though his follower in deliberately unmusical verses, Hardy, perhaps belongs here too) as a person trained to think about music as a professional musician does, competent in notation, performance, musical history, harmony, and even some composition. Schoffman's applications to the poems, despite occasional broader allusions to Pater on music, are mainly technical, but they show helpfully how Browning actually thinks of music, or uses metaphors or allusions to music, as a professional musician would. The curious for such things will find here a spiritedly argued identification of Galuppi's toccata—which he certainly proves existed as a form for the composer, a kind of lighter, more spontaneous sonata (he notes that Galuppi played, however, a harpsichord, not a clavichord, which would not have been loud enough with all those young lovers sighing and intriguing). Of course, such specialized criticism can err in generosity, as Schoffman's predecessors have often erred in sniveling carpings. When he compares the parleying with Avison to famous Beethoven's famous Ninth, because it breaks into song as the symphony breaks into words, he loses me. But this is a useful, well-tempered latest word on a subject often idiotically treated by the small and arrogantly unaesthetic.

As so often in these summaries, I now find only a last breath (not quite gasp despite all this textual reviewing) to give to the work most of us think about more, criticism. Joseph Bristow has published a bright and lively book, *Robert Browning* (1991), in the Macmillan's New Readings series introducing the advanced student (or retooling New Critic?) to more recent approaches to Browning. This he does usefully in this pedagogical work by displaying various critical approaches, from Tucker's deconstruction to more recent feminist or social discourse approaches, at work on reading the dramatic monologues. Again I must refer the reader who wants to know more to the longer review [next entry]. A similar updating of Browning criticism is provided in a more familiar format by editor Mary Ellis Gibson in *Critical Essays on Robert Browning* (1992) in the Hall series (a kind of New Theory update of the New Critical collections of essays in series such as Maynard Mack's Twentieth Century Views). Gibson has rounded up us usual suspects and mainly reprints works I have already acknowledged—and for the most part praised—in prior reviews; and she adds a helpful introductory essay; in fairness I would add that I would have included something from her important work on Browning and history to round out the selection of works from the last fifteen years of newer criticism. Like Bristow's, this selection clearly fills a need to allow current graduate students a chance to see more theoretical considerations in operation—breaking the tendency to move from pure theory courses in which they try to puzzle out Derrida or Lacan to the same old New Critical readings in period courses. Most helpful.

Finally, two critical works deserve individual citation. Warwick Slinn, with Tucker one of the important philosophical critics of Browning who offered interesting and provoking deconstructions of character and identity in Browning in an earlier work, concludes his new *The Discourse of Self in Victo-*

rian Poetry (1991) with two chapters on *The Ring and the Book*. The first, on language and truth, was already noticed favorably in the review of *Victorian Poetry's* centenary issue of Browning in which a large section appeared. The second is on the politics of self. Slinn here applies a more rigorous deconstructive approach to character-creation in the dramatic monologue than he had in his earlier work. Using social discourse theory, especially that originating in feminist theory in the case of Guido, Slinn demonstrates the necessary production of binary oppositions in the post-Romantic discourse embodied in Browning's speaking subjects. Subject (speaker) seeks to affirm itself and the universal validity of its speech but can only do so by reaching out for others within its discourse: either for the social discourse already established in society (Guido wishes to make himself the voice of traditional patriarchal societal power) or for an inner representation and incorporation of someone else (some other) either by identification with that other or by difference from the other (Caponsacchi and Pompilia both attempt to affirm their truth as a higher one by identifying with each other as a source of saintly rectitude—a marriage worthy of being made in heaven). I doubtless simplify a subtle and probing argument, but the conclusion is that all characters are necessarily divided in their discourse from the very origin of that speaking. Slinn shows that all such structures are indeed subject to deconstruction, which is exactly where Browning's larger plan, in which all human truth is finally limited—relative—kicks in. Slinn seems nonetheless bothered (as deconstruction has been bothered since the publicity over de Man's early politics) by his own stress on discourse-chopping in a tale of such obvious violence and apparently black and white social issues. He should not be. The politics of institutional or personal empowerment of individual self-assertion goes to the heart of moral issues, as Browning knew. Guido uses a discourse of patriarchy to try to make his brutality seem just. His notorious deconstructive skepticism about institutions, which makes him in this an attractive villain with whom Browning, who shows us a world of decadent discourse emanating from decadent institutions, can partly identify, is not the problem. The problem is his commitment, which Slinn unmasks so well, to making himself apparently invincibly strong and right by in fact subordinating Pompilia to his will: a deadly power-driven binary opposition crying out for skeptical deconstructive undoing. Deconstructing our empowerment in self-representation by appropriation of society's ideology or of other people is the beginning of the moral, and politically moral, life. Slinn might take the nature of the monologue further; despite talk of drama and the theater of the poem, he pays no attention to the binary structure built into the form itself, where a speaker is empowered by apparently subduing an other as listener—who actually lurks ready, as the end of the second Guido shows when Guido realizes he hasn't persuaded his listeners, to subvert all the power of his discourse.

Let me end by giving a little piece of equal time to masculinist studies of Browning after a decade in which both feminist study and, more emphatically, study of Mrs. Browning has made tremendous gains on the men's club and romantic pedestal approach to the Brownings. Herbert Sussman's "Robert Browning's 'Fra Lippo Lippi' and the Problematic of a Male Poetic" (*VS* 35:185–200) explores the dangerous fault line that Victorian poets experienced between society's construction of the manly, entrepreneurial male and the sensitive, female-gendered Romantic artist. The sexually aggressive "male" Lippo is also liberated by his identification with the new male commerce of art. Yet he demonstrates an underlying repressed desire for a world of men in his emphatically homosocial sharing of his sexuality with those not very effective and manly keepers of the watch and even a repressed fear of women that comes out in subversive imagery, as in references to John the Baptist and Herodias. Indeed we have in that apparently so healthy Lippo the emergence of Freud's most common form of degradation in at least his own bourgeois society: an artist painting angels to get money to spend his nights with whores: not such a pretty psychic picture after all but maybe no worse than the similar degradation in Andrea's marriage. So guys, you thought masculinist studies was all Peter Pan and romp-rites in the woods? No madmen in our attics? (With this review I have decided to come out of this particular closet scholarship, *Victorian Poetry*'s yearly reviewer in the attic, and let someone else review yearly work on the dainty ventriloquial buck of Camberwell; I've appreciated your complicity, my fit audience.)

Reviews

Robert Browning, by Joseph Bristow. New York: St. Martin's Press, 1991. xi, 178 pp.

Robert Browning's Literary Life: From First Work to Masterpiece, by Gertrude Reese Hudson. Austin: Eakin Press, 1993. xxi, 638 pp.

These are both interesting works on Robert Browning, but extremely different in subject and approach as well as size. Bristow offers a general introduction to Browning and an approach to reading him in certain contemporary modes; Hudson presents an enormous and very carefully researched history of Browning's career, with special focus on his reception up to *The Ring and the Book.*

Bristow's book, which appears in St. Martin's New Readings series, could be described, with every positive implication, as a high-level piece of pedagogical writing. My colleagues tell me they agree with my sense that we currently need approaches that introduce graduate students to major critical positions of the past twenty years of upheaval in literary study in ways that allow them to see how readings of particular authors and texts have been affected. Too often theory is read in a vacuum and then, when students turn to readings, they return to well-traveled roads—those many New Critical readings enshrined in collections such as the ones Maynard Mack used to edit in the Twentieth Century Views series. One approach has been to renew this tradition by offering an updated, post-New Critical collection of essays inspired by more recent theoretical viewpoints, as indeed Mary Ellis Gibson has recently done for Browning in her *Critical Essays on Robert Browning* in the G. K. Hall series.

Bristow takes another approach which may be even more helpful to the beginning graduate student or serious undergraduate. He offers a brief introductory work that is written in his voice but freely summarizes and borrows from recent work that he esteems. Rather than get into the often-tedious business of summarizing positions, as in a review, he presents different approaches as readings of well-known dramatic monologues. Such apparently humble borrowing actually brings a special excitement to the text and seems indeed especially well-adapted to the usual problem of multiple interpretations in Browning's monologues. Rather than try, once more, to nail down the exact position we should take toward Browning's so richly over-written Duke, Bristow is able to give us a panoply of differing interpretations. Such an approach actually frees him into dialogic critical activity, still a rare thing for all our admiration of Mikhail Bakhtin in theory: Bristow can be playful, can turn on his last position, can cancel or add readings because he speaks not merely for one critic at one moment of time but for recent critical thinking. Nor is this merely a matter of parroting others' particular readings. For instance, his reading of "Love Among the Ruins" is an especially precise work of deconstructive criticism, where the poem's creation of an antinomy between positive nature and corrupt society is interrogated at the end: is the lover's "extinguishing" passion so free from the destructive forces of the apparently different warlike society of the past?

Bristow's work is agile and exciting and should quickly take new readers into major issues in major dramatic monologues and even provide a healthy workout for those up on these issues. This is not a research work and makes no attempt to offer a new handbook of all-you-need-to-know on these works, but it does attempt two chapters defining the issues in Browning's self-conscious, ironic writing and rehearsing some of the critical approaches to dramatic monologues. I think it does its work well. Of course, Bristow also is a soloist, an author, as well as an orchestra leader, and his work does put forward an identifiable set of positions. He works hard to re-render Browning especially in the terms of contemporary social discourse theory (New Historicism). Browning is here defined as the "bourgeois liberal" who attempts to create a liberal subject free and independent of social or political constraints and turned inward, in its freedom, toward psychological exploration. This in itself is obvious, boring, or both; but Bristow gives it force by organizing much of his study around the interplay between such a self-conscious subject and two supra-individual situations, that of history and of love.

The study of history in Browning is less thorough and less aware of historiographical issues than Gibson's own book-length work on the subject (*History and the Prism of Art: Browning's Poetic Experiments,* 1987), but Bristow does take on here a number of major Browning monologues. He wishes to wrap a larger providentialism around Browning's many individual constructions of historical moments but runs into the problem, so familiar in Browning criticism, of building a larger system connecting poems on the quicksand of shifting individual readings of these so-mobile poems. His chapter on Browning's lovers is especially good—one wishes he had even expanded this subject into a monograph. The readings bluntly admit sexual language and desire to these poems, which is still an important achievement in our criticism of Victorian poetry; and they interestingly see Browning causing his subjects to face the limits of their self-understanding discourse as it faces the contradictions and non-discursive realities of gender and sex. A useful, not unthoughtful book.

If Bristow is tentative and playful, Hudson is somber and everywhere attempting definitiveness. This is a rather heavy read, replete with a full set of biographic details and notes for the part of Browning's life directly associated with his career (falling in love is, for instance, not considered part of this career record though Elizabeth Barrett's opinions on his works are). That is alright; we have all had enough romantic Browning biography and the Brownings themselves much preferred gossip about literary affairs than more talk about their own memorable affair. The research is, as far as this reviewer's eye can tell, an eye which was made glassy once by similar work, entirely professional, obviously the result of a major longtime project in Browning's letters. The only notable weakness is the failure to update letters and citations with *The Brownings's Correspondence* for the period in which they are available—an indication that this work has indeed been a long time in the works. Hudson has edited Browning letters herself and has generally known where to find the information she seeks. The book might have been as useful—which is very useful indeed—if it had left details about other career issues to the biographers and concentrated entirely on what is, in any case, its main focus, the reception of Browning's work.

Hudson has read through all the reviews, has a good sense of the weight and position of individual newspapers, weeklies, or reviews, and provides detailed summaries of what in fact was said about Browning's work. She also has compiled, through hard work in the indices of biographies and works of Browning's contemporaries, at least a cross-section of what she calls non-professional judgment, mainly what other writers wrote candidly about the publications. Although there have been a good number of individual studies of reception of particular publication and some surveys of large periods (for example, those by Lounsbury and Duckworth), this more comprehensive and systematic study allows Hudson to provide authoritative judgments where we have still been most often relying on literary anecdotes. She is especially helpful in settling the dust around issues raised by the poet himself, for instance the claim that only John Forster's review rescued *Paracelsus* from contempt. By the same token, the sheer bulk of commentary surveyed for a work such as *Men and Women* tends properly to interfere with critics' wishes to pass simple judgment on the reception: many individuals, in reviews or privately, saw the virtues of this wonderful classic production even as others seemed entirely blind or antagonistic. Hudson rightly sees in these reviews an increasing tendency to look for major work from Browning even when reviewers' difficulties in reading Browning's so-original work lead them to complain of obscurity or metrical harshness.

Hudson's book is an important research tool; despite its rather traditional format and language, it is in fact the latest thing: a full study of a major poet's reception. If Hudson does not build much of a structure of meaning on that information, no theory of bourgeois ideology or shifting discourses of cultural construction in an increasingly self-creating literary culture (I write parody without irony, since this is not just what

Bristow does but what I and most of us do nowadays), she certainly provides an accurate and full record on which such work, and newer-fangled literary approaches of the future, can be built. Indeed, if she had pulled together more fully in her final chapter the detailed conclusions she reached about the kinds of critical statements issued in different decades, she would have effectively outlined a history of changing critical discourse. Still, these are two useful works in quite different ways.

Browning: Living, Hating, Loving; or Uneven Developments: Theory in the Browning Boondocks

The Life of Robert Browning, by Clyde de L. Ryals. Oxford: Blackwell, 1993. xi, 291 pp.
Browning's Hatreds, by Daniel Karlin. Oxford: Clarendon, 1993. vii, 272 pp.
The Infinite Passion of Finite Hearts: Robert Browning and Failure in Love, by Pratul Pathak. New York: Peter Lang, 1992. vii, 208 pp.

Like most areas of study in the boondocks of literature, out where the shy and dangerous major texts of major authors still wait the traditional hunters' chary skills, the Robert Browning scholarly world has been unevenly ravaged—and now and then ravished—by those intrusive newfangled forces of theory, with their highly organized crews of deconstructive tractors and their prefab range of new interpretive buildings. Theory may not be declared dead—along, we may guess with other threats to the traditional environment—but it has cut important, often wide swathes into old boys' close reading way of looking at Browning, which was by and large to sit around the potbellied stove of his dramatic monologues spitting at them from different points of view: the Duke, is he a cad or an elegant card shark? the Countess, is she the fair maidenhood they liked to think they would fight for or is she one of those lying women? The discussion could go on and on because the author liked to set such fellahs just these kinds of posers. But we had some excellent new work by Herbert Tucker and Warwick Slinn bringing the radical cuts of deconstruction into the discussion; and the general approach was continued by Clyde Ryals as a look at German-style Romantic irony in the early Browning. We have had very useful rethinking of Browning's art along the lines of reader theory, especially by David E. Latané, Jr. with associated work by Dorothy Mermin, Lee Erickson, John Woolford, and myself. There has been a parallel upheaval in Browning texts, with Woolford and Daniel Karlin following hard on fine editions by Pettigrew and Collins (completed), by Ohio (now revived and much improved), and by Ian Jack (in progress and masterly traditional scholarship), with a radical choice of first published work as copytext for their Longman Browning (also in progress). New Historicism, Foucauldian, and Marxist criticism have had less full developments here, though Loy D. Martin's interesting kaleidoscopic study of Browning is thoughtful in some of these areas. The reader wishing a quick update on new approaches to Browning could perhaps best look at Mary Ellis Gibson's collection of contemporary essays in the G. K. Hall series; Gibson has also done important, separate work on rethinking Browning's relation to history.

Well may the old timers and young bucks of the Browning world ask: what next? Post-theory? more theory? shut your eyes to the big problems and do New Historicism in the dark, where any connections between the historical record and the textual product seem to be worth a playful bit of local interweaving—"blind and green they grope/Among the honey-meal." Of the books here under review, the one in the most apparently traditional critical genre, Clyde de L. Ryals's biography of Browning in the new Blackwell Critical Biography series (certainly a post-theory kind of project to answer the stream of new theory titles from Routledge that keep spilling out at us) is surprisingly best at accommodating the new terrain excavated by theory in Browning studies to his particular project. In this, his work leans strongly toward the critical side of the series title. And this is probably fortunate given the many assets of the author as critic of Browning. He is a rather rare creature who straddles the worlds of both older and newer scholarship. Thoroughly versed in the older issues in Browning and in traditional historical and editorial work, Ryals also not only hails from theorytown (a thorn in the heart of good-old-boy land) but carries the right cards in Browning studies, especially in his work on becoming. His quite full and myriad discussions of individual works by Browning go over familiar ground, both biographical background and diverse critical perspectives on the speaker, that make them both useful introductions for harried graduate students (or hurried professors whose minds are not those steel traps so prized by good-old boys) and suitable updates of the aging but still unretired DeVane *Handbook*. (Indeed, my only lament might be that Ryals did not take on the task of updating all the scholarship on the poems by a new handbook since this is mainly what his work will be useful for; but a reliable critical biography can serve many of the same uses.)

In addition, Ryals strikes me as very good in bringing more recent critical moves into his takes on the poems, especially good in doing so in an easy way that suggests that theory, far from being killed, has been finally accepted as not such a threatening neighbor. His own interest in Browning as a poet of a philosophical becoming, making his work and himself anew as he rises to new (and sometimes self-ironic heights), is a useful and repeated general way of interpreting Browning's career moves. It allows Ryals to move easily from the apparently so different work of Browning's first decade to the classic phase of the dramatic monologues of 1840–1870 in a seamless and fluid manner. The generic turns are seen as a part of a larger struggle by the nineteenth-century poet to develop upon his own personal insights, layer on layer, rather than on the firmer ground of traditional truths. Browning's central, brilliant move to presenting an entire world of others doing the same thing is thus seen as just that, a move within Browning's poetry based on his own experience, rather than a sudden new departure on a new agenda. By the same token, Browning's often ignored or deplored career in the last very active years of his four-score is slipped into without a lament or a border crossing; the interesting set that follow rather closely on *The Ring and the Book, Balaustion's Adventure, Red Cotton Night-Cap Country, Fifine at the Fair, The Inn Album,* and yes even *Aristophanes' Apology* (though one may still have one's doubts), are seen as natural outgrowths of the hermeneutic and generic issues raised in the famous epic—which is in its own way a restless turning away from monologues and back to the greater ambitions of *Sordello*. In this enterprise of seeing the entire Browning steadily and whole, Ryals has perfect credentials, having previously written full-length books seizing capably both the thorny ends of Browning's career. I would have welcomed more use of Tucker and Slinn's not so different if more deconstructive takes on Browning's career (to keep becoming is after all necessarily to resist closure and to see each new attempt at self-making as ultimately only a fictive rendering of an apparent reality, a fable of an endlessly deferred search for identity that is always already lost in differences that crop up like hydra heads when on attempts to find a firm base for the self—as Browning had found so early in his *Pauline:* that single autobiographical attempt, as Ryals rightly remarks, that is at the same time the first of the endless series of men and women failing while trying to ground their selves firmly). Such a perspective would help rein in, as well, Ryals's tendency to fall back into a version, if an updated one, of the Browning philosophy. He does speak of such a thing in his too lengthy summary (pp. 242–245) of Browning's belief in endless *Bildung*—though characteristically this Browning Society-esque homily is based on an interesting read of the poem "Development" as just that, an Englishing of the tradition of *Bildung*. (Similarly I was troubled by a bland use of the "becoming" formula to represent David and "Saul" when there his "philosophy" receives such authoritative typological affirmation.)

Ryals is especially good in using easily the work done on the rhetorical nature (rhetoric here used as poems as systems of communication with readers, not de Manian blowing trope-fuses) of Browning's work. Building on Latané's good work on Browning's relation to his readers in *Sordello*, he keeps gently pointing us to Browning's showman's pointer stick as indication that we are always in the theater of the poet maker-see. His observations on Browning's hermeneutics behind the theological poems (e.g., "A Death in the Desert") and more broadly in the more self-conscious work from the *The Ring and the Book* are especially good in seeing Browning facing intellectually and formally a world in which the poet cannot communicate important truths, only vigorously encourage the reader to generate from the text readings helpful to his/her own soul-building under modern conditions of ignorance about ultimates. *The Ring and the Book* is not, he insists, a relativist book in the sense that it argues all readings of life or literature are equally valuable (or valueless); it is a poem that leaves us to stretch our hermeneutic muscles (Hermen the mice of interpretation) and learn to find our truths in a world without established grounds of truth. Here another major contemporary writer on Browning, David Shaw, has been helpful.

I have to say that contemporary forms of social criticism are not well represented here. Ryals sees Browning as mainly a quietist in politics, which I think is a misreading of a liberal of his age. John Woolford's useful ideas of Browning's liberal political and religious strategy with his readers (which recalls Fish's Milton) could be helpful here as could a broader biographical look at Browning's milieu as a socio-economic fact, a place where base-superstructure thinking is helpful. And New Historicism does have something important here to offer in its general suspicion of the power-place of literary texts. Robert Viscusi has opened up the idea of Browning's liberalism as also a form of consuming imperialism, that odd web that leads from democratic Britain to imperial Britain in such a short time (and Browning, self-proclaimed liberal, would join the many Victorian liberal intellectuals who opposed Gladstone on Home Rule). More specific connections to his age would also have been easily available in the archives of reviews of Browning, which could have been more fully used. So, here are uneven developments of our contemporary ideologies into the lasting web of biographical-critical commentary, but certainly Ryals's is the book one now wishes to recommend to graduate students looking for an introduction to Browning and his work. I note only an occasional embarrassing awkwardness when Browning is made too directly to speak our speak, as when the young Browning, fresh from resigning his place at The London University, is made to voice his plans in a language he could only have had from reading Ryals's earlier book on becoming or where Browning, who obviously shared the idea, is given a post-Saussurean view of language as generative, "signs that allow man to gain a larger grasp on himself and thus grow in understanding beyond present verbal constructs," or where Sebald realizes after hearing Pippa's song that the "self in modern times is unstable" or, worse, where Guido is presented as a deconstructionist (bad men, including Guido and Hitler, are vulgar rhetoricians who push whatever buttons they hope will work, not vulgar deconstructionists).

As a biography, which is clearly not Ryals's main sense of his aim, this is passable and current at best. It makes no attempt at full-scale biographical research in primary documents. Because of the quality of the overall vision of Browning and his work and the updating of a few issues, and also because of its succinctness (all this and the life too in 250 pages) this rather than other modern summary biographies by Donald Thomas or Roy Gridley is nonetheless likely to be the most used reference biography, as, say, Griffin and Minchin's biography was for many years, for an indefinite period. While Park Honan and William Irvine's large combined work (1974 but much of Irvine's half dating from a good deal earlier), along with Mazzie Ward's two-volume work, remain necessary for details (to which may be added Roy Gridley on Browning in France, Daniel Karlin on the courtship, excellent recent studies of Elizabeth Barrett on their lives together, my own work on the early world and life, and of course the massive record being provided by Philip Kelley and his associates in the Browning letters), Ryals has done an acceptable and accurate job of updating the life (indeed the only error I detected was not on the life but the work, letting stand Lippo's view of "Hulking Tom" Masaccio as his successor and Ryals doubtless knew that, only forgot to say so for the beginning student). Yet there is little sense of Browning as a living person of the sort readers of biography naturally clamor for. And if this can lead to too much Stracheyan sensationalism in psychological wool-gathering, there is a legitimate need to allow the subject to live the ups and downs of life that we all know from our own lives or reading in Browning. Did he ever get angry, especially as a young man on the make sweeping away as best he could Wordsworth and other competitors? as a much laughed at writer of the most glorious failure to communicate of the nineteenth century? as one of the two greatest poets of the age who generally received harsh reviews and much worse royalty statements? You bet, and Ryals notes it was hard but it doesn't really convince like life. Did he have strong feelings about his grandfather, the ambitious man who was willing to violate the conscience of Browning's father to get him ahead? about the next tyrant, director Macready? about that icon of a patriarch Mr. Barrett of Wimpole Street? Yes, yes, Ryals answers, I mentioned all those events; but one feels Browning the man is too much of an icon, a great author of the great poems whose explication so many years later is a sign that it was generally a happy and triumphal progress. And of course there are women, those creatures masculinist studies now agree with feminist studies in indicating men have ambivalent feelings toward. Granted Betty Miller damned Browning too easily for loving his mother (shades of the double-bind, boy who loves/boy who doesn't love his mother, of *A Portrait of the Artist*). But Elizabeth was older, from a higher class, and then proceeded during their lifetimes to outclass Browning tremendously as a public poet; and the honeymoon was after all soon over for them, as for all, if not for adoring readers of the Browning romance. And, as I will note again in reviewing books below much concerned with Browning on love and hate, there were major problems, not just Elizabeth's successful authorship and failing health but a number of conflicts that did not go away. Yes, Ryals knows all this too, but it too seems soft-pedaled; Clarissa proves right, good manners can prevail. But the psychic cost needs to be more deeply explored, as Nina Auerbach challenged Browning scholarship to explore it some years ago in speaking of *The Ring and the Book* as the poem where the poet finally got even (yes, to be fair, Ryals knows that too, and cites it in a note).

And of course relations go on after even the separation of death; and Ryals, who presents the new evidence in the work of Virginia Surtees suggesting that the handsome, clever, rich, and aristocratic Lady Louisa Ashburton may have proposed to a somewhat passive and embarrassed poet, nonetheless distorts the tale by not indicating Browning's complex reactions, which are quite evident in the dark mood poems preoccupied with infidelity and lust that follow the episode. Even on the new evidence, which I have argued is not conclusive, it is clear Browning was not decisive, waited to decide, talked to others about it, perhaps was tempted. Tempted to replace Elizabeth in his heart: no, never: that was buried in Florence with her. But we make an icon of the man whom James found so divided between worldly self and private poet if we don't see other temptations deeply troubling Browning in this exceptionally well-heeled and well-endowed woman—the answer to his Don Juanish yearnings for both distinction (of the money and class sort that James reminds us is always in the British mind of his age) and passion in a far bolder type than even upper-class, sensual Elizabeth had offered. Am I making up a twentieth-century Browning? Read *Fifine* if you haven't, with its phallic symbols that Browning calls phallic symbols, its spark between a prostitute and her lover in the dark, its very guilty resolution in the "Epilogue" (that Ryals surprisingly tends to repress as biographical) to keep a lonely house and wait for the celestial Porphyria, blessed madame Elizabeth, to reenter his life and warm it once again).

All this is perhaps unfair, as the aim here is clearly getting the facts out and then focusing on the works; but the approach misses the value of biography, an area where theory has hardly dared to tread: if we have a vital view of the person behind the so aggressively maintained mask, we can't thereby necessarily predict the nature of the poem, as reductive biographical readings so often attempt and as Ryals rightly avoids doing; but we can bring to the poems fuller expectations, a more open mind about what they are doing, about the possible areas of interpretation we can explore without fearing we are merely importing our own concerns irrelevantly. The liberal hermeneutics of reading that Ryals finds in Browning can be applied even to the special science of biography with the following credo: never to distort a fact in the interest of an interpretation of a life, but also never to fail to explore a possibility of human diversity opened up by the facts.

Let me end these remarks on a most important new diachronic summary of Browning's poetic career by noting again its excellences as a running interpretation of Browning's poems. One quickly comes to trust the author and his judgments, to feel that the summaries are just and the criticisms sensible. If Ryals clearly values Browning highly and encourages us to reach for interesting poems beyond the usual suspects, he also knows where to stop, as with *Jocoseria,* which he rates low indeed. His thorough knowledge makes this work a joy as a place where you can find the quotes you need: Browning on Tennyson, Arnold, or Rossetti; the moderns as well as Robert Lowell on Browning—a nice way to end a book celebrating Browning's survival as a poet still becoming new in our newer horizons and beyond our new horizons.

Neither of the two other books under review attempts to summarize the work of criticism of the past twenty years; each instead explores a new realm, defined in general terms topically though in each case raising, or reraising, central issues of interpreting Browning. Both look in fact at rather similar topics: Daniel Karlin's at hate in Browning, Pratul Pathak's at love. Technically of course antipodal feelings, but even before deconstruction put all such opposites under potential erasure/reversal, we knew, as Mr. Bumble in his happy pre-textual view of things would say, *from experience* about the common linkage of the two master emotions.

Daniel Karlin's very useful and critically important work, with co-editor John Woolford, on the new Longman edition of Browning gives him unique qualities when he turns to a critical study of an aspect of Browning's huge poetic output. The edition has stirred waves as the fullest attempt in the world of Browning scholarship to call into question the old truisms about textual editing based on author's last intentions.[1] In the course of this work, in which the editors have offered a Browning of first published intentions, they have also been led to a rather fine work of editing that stresses more than earlier such work the genesis of Browning's poetry and mind

---

[1]For an interesting discussion of the more general debate on this issue in nineteenth-century texts, see Judith Kennedy, ed., *Victorian Authors and their Works: Revision Motivations and Modes* (Athens: Ohio Univ. Press, 1991) and her review essay on the issue in *VLC,* 21.

in his reading and *Ausbildung*. Karlin's study, a first critical study of the poetry to set beside his fine reading of the Browning-Elizabeth Barrett courtship correspondence is called bluntly, *Browning's Hatreds*. It is particularly rich in thick new information about the background, literary echoes and intertexts, as well as intertexts among Browning's own poems. His exceptional knowledge of poems great and obscure allows Karlin to move easily around a much wider canon of Browning works than is usually the wont in critical studies—and in this his work sits nicely in review next to Ryals's own broad command of Browning's entire career. "Ixion," "Of Pacchiarotto and How He Worked in Distemper," "The Heretic's Tragedy" (the first from the normally canonical major volumes of dramatic monologues in this list), "Mr. Sludge the Medium" (another barely read work from the major phase), *Luria and a Soul's Tragedy, Aristophanes' Apology,* among others, are given rather lengthy critical attention. The old poet, who can not be thought to appreciate being cast aside for his more youthful self by Karlin and Woolford's critical methods, would have at least been sincerely gratified by the appearance of a second work in the same year that takes so seriously so much of his oeuvre that modern critical comment has tended to pass over in silence or with a scoff at prose Brownings. *Aristophanes' Apology* (one of Ryals's neglected masterpieces, as well) indeed gets an entire chapter; and there are substantial discussions of parts of those two dragons at the gate of Browning's work, *Paracelsus* and *Sordello,* this rightly seen as a clear source to locate Browning's usually obscured set of ideas, that, along with the love letters Karlin knows and uses so well, as the best source—other than his one more direct but as enigmatic attempt to define subjective and objective poets in his prose essay on Shelley—of Browning's elusive poetics.

The result is a work for the already deeply initiated in Browning, who are ready to read the poetry as a whole rather than an anthology selection of great dramatic monologues. One can even prescribe: take one dose of Ryals as a general cure followed by daily dosings in each of Karlin's more detailed chapters washed down with readings in the more obscure Browning. May the patient survive the treatment! He should know that he is in the hands of doctors without borders to their enthusiasm for Browning's entire work; and here doctors may disagree—indeed this humble practitioner might wish the patient not accustomed to Browning's full complexity a return to simpler regimes of the canonical dramatic monologues, as our next book under review offers.

Karlin's apparently so unBrowningesque theme, not love but hate, may perhaps be easily understood as the naturally perverse binary occupation of someone who has done so much work (albeit work that properly restores the intellectual credentials to the twice-told tale) on the Brownings' love story. His project certainly attempts to unsettle our thinking about the usual themes of Browning, optimism, openness, sympathy, understanding of others, which have persisted in more sophisticated accounts of his work as a poetry of experience (Langbaum), of dis-closure and re-beginnings (Tucker), or becoming (Ryals). After all, all these terms, despite the suspiciously French sound of Tucker's, would have positive, life-affirming resonances to that great wielder of Browning against the forces of modern anarchy, his early biographer G. K. Chesterton. If Tennyson has been made more palatable to moderns and postmoderns by biographers stressing the black blood, madness, and social dis-ease behind his laureate affirmation, Browning has been allowed to hold onto his, well, Browningesque affirmativeness/amativeness.

Going beyond the usual canon here is helpful in destabilizing this image. As anyone who has done so has found, Browning has a great number of queer corners that show another side and, as Karlin's study rightly realizes, these are not quirks, closet or privy selves, or bounding Mr. Hydes kept pretty much at bay. Rather, they seem intrinsic to *all* he has to say. This is most apparent in certain passionate obsessions which seem to activate another side of Browning and which perhaps embarrassed him to some extent: the bitter quarrel with Lady Ashburton (his feeling in which Ryals, as I have noted, rather soft-pedals), the dislike for Mrs. Eckley, for George Sand, for Alfred Austin, for Napoleon III, for the American Medium Daniel Home, for Edward FitzGerald. Personal dislikes moved Browning strongly and intruded into his attempts at otherwise impersonal poems as strongly as his love for Elizabeth did—the last four hates producing memorable odd places in Browning's poetics. With Karlin's interesting examinations of most of these, often as in the chapter on Home, "Sludgehood," with excellent contextual discussion (he leaves off "Prince Hohenstiel-Schwangau" though one would think it both adequately full of hate and off the cannon), we are easily led to see that this passionate man, so passionate indeed about avoiding the appearance of personal passion in his verse ("so many utterances of so many imaginary persons, not mine" sounds spit out at us or his would be biographical critics) was a good hater and a good lover.

Karlin's overall game is to show that the two indeed very much go together. This is essentially a reading of poems of love and hate, not a biographical study. But I think it is worth saying at first that he seems not adequately to see how fundamentally the salient biographical cases demonstrate this point. Home, Napoleon III, George Sand, Mrs. Eckley, and finally, the doubly posthumous slur on Elizabeth by the happily dead author of *The Rubáiyát* (twice happily dead that Robert could not lay hands on him as he felt he had on his dead wife's memory), all grew out of a turbulence created by love under stress. Browning's possessive love of his wife (possessive *and* humbling, what the therapists now like to call co-dependency) turned into tremendous anxiety and ultimately very perceptible motions of repulsion or hate when he felt himself unable to protect her from dangers real or imagined—or in the case of FitzGerald's brutal hit from beyond the grave (thanking God Elizabeth was dead) absolutely irremediable and thus absolutely torturing. This process is rather clearly unclear at the heart of Browning's own hating, a jealous conversion of love to one into hate to another that probably hurt him most, his protectee next, and did little harm to the rather blackguardly persons Browning took on.

I think this leaves Karlin a problem that he never quite directly addresses. If the issue is, as the title suggests, Browning's (own) hatreds, then we expect the analysis of poems to be a deconstruction of the man equal to a kind of debunking (as in

Betty Miller's different attempt to find a neurotic, passive, and dependent figure behind the usual virile one). But Karlin, having missed the chance to see what especially tripped off Browning's personal hatreds, is too good a reader of the mostly impersonal poems to find in them a place where genial surface lifts to reveal the wolf teeth of the author behind. Sometimes, indeed, too good, as where his interesting look at *The Ring and the Book* focuses on Guido but doesn't hear the personal involvement in Caponsacchi's healthy hate for Guido that seems a vehicle for Browning's protective male feminism, perhaps a place where some of his resentment of the man who most hurt his wife but of whom he could not speak directly without hurting her more, that archetype of patriarchy Mr. Barrett, might escape in form hidden even to himself. For surely we cannot not hear parallels between the poet's famous rescue and that of his priest; nor, as Nina Auerbach or Adrienne Munich would not fail to point out, should we pretend not to see the male weakness, making itself strong by finding maidens to rescue, remaking upper-class, successful Elizabeth into the Pippa/Pompilia figure threatened with poverty and prostitution on all sides, hidden in the Perseus figure.

Instead Karlin more usually is forced back into an exploration of Browning's moral world, that world in which villains and good haters are given as vigorous, or more so, a say as Pippas and Pompilias. These are of course familiar projects and Karlin reviews the balances of evil and good well in poems such as *Pippa* itself, "Count Gismond," "My Last Duchess," and of course "Porphyria's Lover," sometimes with a wealth of editor-like information that seems perhaps a justification for going over familiar ground. Among the interesting essay-like subjects taken up in this gourmet guide to the hating Browning there is the very useful analysis of Browning's psychology, seen as a Cartesian search for a few first principles rather than a Freudian search for origins (though he admits this is an eighteenth-century heritage in Browning and in later chapters sees hate become dialectically transformed), a chapter on Browning's awareness, as a notoriously unpopular poet, of being hated (though the clustering of responses throughout a lifetime in a brief chapter somewhat overstates the appearance of suffering just as Ryals understated it by touching on it only now and then; a juster sense of Browning's reviews and his response to them is given in Gertrude Reese Hudson's massive recent study of his reception up to *The Ring and the Book*), and the chapter on sexual desire and hatred, which allows revisits to those familiar poems of apparent "madhouse" possessiveness and violence with an acute sense of Browning's sexual psychology of pathological behavior.

I was troubled by a kind of coyness when Karlin attempted, as he does a number of times very well, to go beyond his elegant descriptions of Browning's moral world of good, bad, and mixed characters to show deeper marriages of good and evil. When Auerbach speaks of *The Ring and the Book* as the murder poem for Elizabeth, we know the shocking rhetoric comes from a critical tradition, namely feminist, that has attempted to decenter lovey-dovey notions of happy marriages within bourgeois patriarchal structures, even those made in poetic heavens. But when Karlin upsets binaries of love and hate, the word deconstruct rarely enters his text, certainly not as a critical idea with a history and a family of arguments; yet this apparent innocence is then violated by theoretically unclarified uses of words such as "doubleness," "radical and irreconcilable opposites." We are told that "binary categories of human understanding collapse" (not in Derrida but in *Sordello*) and yield a "condition in which contraries are reconciled and the very principle of division is abolished" and that (in "Love Among the Ruins," not de Man) "the extinction of sight and speech means the extinction of personality, of selfhood, of the capacity to discern and express *difference*" (sic—italics but not with an a). Such coyness about Continental critical theory seems to me a real difficulty in a work that also doesn't even mention theory-inspired critical studies of recent eminence such as Tucker's, Slinn's, Ryals's, or Shaw's—all Anglophone: two American, one New Zealander, and a Canadian (Shaw and Ryals's work on the later poems are in the bibliography). And of course the effect of such too much critical gentility, even in the more repressive atmosphere of current British academic politics, is to weaken the value of these central moments of deeper study of love-hate in Browning by not pursuing them as more than fleeting *aperçus*. It seems to say to the reader that anyone could do that modish criticism but even then there would be some stooping. But indeed the work is not done, only hinted at; the lamp that is so brightly lit over Browning's minor poems and background seems to have remained dark over Derrida, de Man, Tucker, and so much more, including Foucauldian and New Historical work that feeds on exfoliating binaries at delicious ease. Where Ryals strengthens his own positions by relating them consciously to others current in the past two decades, Karlin seems almost to accept rules of criticism that tie his hands from putting in the best fight possible.

The case, I take it, is a classic binary, as Karlin seems always about to say, especially in the chapter on "Love's Double Face": the West puts love (is best) first and stigmatizes hate as a place mastered by the greater light that is love and that puts hate in its place. Manichaeanism, as Karlin notes, always threatens to substitute a dialogue of love versus hate; yet as Browning the orthodox says, or has his more orthodox wife say, "Love is all and Death [hate too, may we presume?] is naught." That is, Platonic tradition at its best has negatives such as death or hate as merely the deprivation of love, a complete construction that even obliterates its opposite. The deconstruction as I take it places love as in fact a special case, hate an example of the reversed norm: not as a thing in itself but as typical of intense human feelings, hate, jealousy, anxiety, and the rest of that broad stormy sisterhood that makes the rainbow of human feeling. So love, as your analyst says, is an emotion too, perhaps a rationalization of merely more complicated feelings, not a word that can suppress the variety of experience in its metaphysical and logocentric construction above the flux of difference (and differing feelings) that is reality. Hate, that we hate to admit, at least suggests more genuine feelings coming out in honesty. (Ouch, we begin to see why the construction was so reassuring: God was in his heaven, all was right, if not with the rest of the world, then with our sense of our own good and loving attitudes and motivations—scratch our rugged scars and find an innocent Pippa underneath!)

No wonder, as Karlin well shows, the Browning characters of energy are so often also those who acknowledge their negative feelings, at least sufficiently to express them; no wonder the good often seem so pale, having to construct away so much various feeling. The best parts of this study go right to this point, showing for instance why the pathological lover resents Porphyria's hypocritical love that masks her social and emotional power over him (God have helped Elizabeth if she had refused her poorer lover from the suburbs!), why Guido gains rhetorical power as he unmasks the wolf and lets it speak (the ancient rhetoricians, enemies of the constructive tradition of love in Plato, as Brian Vickers has reminded us, always insisted that persuasion had to be based on articulation of real feelings), why we prefer Ottima's passionate love and hate to Sebald's inarticulate oppression, first by Ottima, then by Pippa's appeal to conventional morality of love. He doesn't well see another mask of hate, the hegemonic impulse that spoke Englishmen so easily in that country's great century and that hates with a smile of ease and superiority. The politics of "The Englishman in Italy" have been seen, like the politics of Lord Byron's polyamorous activities in Greece, as more than merely personal and romantic. He comes closer with Guido, where he does see the Nietzschean reverse *ressentiment* of the old great against the vulgar modern tide as a form of hating that gets progressively revealed for what it is.

Karlin writes very well, knows a great deal, has much detail and specific research to offer and creates a number of elegant topics that reorganize traditional gatherings of Browning's poems. His subject should keep provoking rethinking of Browning and his poems. If other readers end up quarreling with part of it as I have, it will be an indication that they have also found it challenging in an important way.

Karlin's rather abstract look at often recondite poems on the intricacies of love and hate is quite different from that work that appears at first blush so topically similar, Pratul Pathak's *The Infinite Passion of Finite Hearts: Robert Browning and the Failure in Love*. Pathak's analyses focus on well-known oft-spoken-over poems and they are not particularly subtle; nor do they offer themselves as particularly new. Pathak's critical voice is modest, that of an inquirer sifting carefully through established critics on dramatic monologues on love relations, which he considers spaciously in diachronic order. In some sense this Peter Lang book thus still smells of the dissertation not too far behind it; it could have been presented in a more vivid, tightly argued, and critically decisive way, as Karlin's work is. This said, it has old-fashioned virtues of saying what it means and of sticking to its guns which give it a different kind of value from Karlin's more exhibitionistic work. Pathak has decided—as most of us have come to by inspired genius or by the repeated knocks of life's hard lessons—that relations are based on communication. If not, consult your local marriage counselor or shrink—indeed, if not, you will find that you will! While Karlin can suggest that the sense of neglect that drives the wife of Browning's gothic tale of a husband's revenge, "A Forgiveness," into a fatal liaison would have been more usefully referred out to a professional, Pathak brings such counsel with him into critical discussion. And sometimes it sounds silly enough! I had many a pleasant chuckle over the attribution of "problems in communication" to such classic cases of more than Hollywood marital failure as Porphyria and her lover, the Duke and his dear Duchess, Andrea and his lovely Lucrezia ("Lucrezia, before you go out, we need to talk about my failure to satisfy you through my artistic self-involvement and guilt obsession and also, dear, about your acting out.") But what am I—are you—laughing about? The failures may be colossal, but isn't that why these poems are so representative, such tropes for all our colossal failures to communicate. What is this detached laughter in my study but just the intellectualizing distance that I could pay good money to learn to avoid in Dr. Umlaut's office? and he may get me yet. So let's get serious about their lives, if not our own (today).

A surprising contrast with Karlin is that this collection of formal readings actually delves more usefully than the book of our expert (since Elvan Kintner's tragically early death) on the subject into the love relation of the Brownings themselves. Chronological readings allow Pathak to draw out a shadowy but useful allegory of Browning's life in his work—not as foolish biographical details in the work but as an emerging awareness of the difficulties of communication between humans that Browning's frequent poems on love (perhaps necessarily) unveil. Early poems show youthful monsters of egotism being put in their places in extraordinary and extravagant representations.

But if here the possibilities of learning to communicate seem only to be inflected from author to reader over Porphyria's head or behind the Duke's so self-dramatizing back, poems of *Men and Women* and later do seem to thematize exactly issues of difficulty of communication. More than Karlin (in *this* book), Pathak is sensitive to the very real ambivalence in the Brownings' relations from the start and to the increasing pressures from disagreements (as over spiritualism or Napoleon III) in the 1850s; more than Ryals, he brings them as forces into his readings of the works. The formal reading has little of Karlin's quickness and flashes of new connections, nor the philosophical assurance of Ryals; but we are forced, as in the good reading of the familiar and wonderful monologue, "Two in the Campagna," to think clearly over some issues that more subtle tropic analysis may evade: is that a failed relation (failed communication again) being hidden in a rationalization by the speaker about those very problems of communication (the counselors must have many such fools wise only to their own failures)? is he using the idea of ideal communication to avoid real communication?—and here Pathak might look more fully at the nature of the dramatic monologue's punishing lack of any effective dramatic governor, of the sort we have in a dialogue with another subjectivity, a lack that encourages such egocentric failures—as indeed real life doubtless offers at least middle-class Western humans more spaces for self-delusion than for interaction and possible growth. (The "dramas" of our modern lives, as most modern dramatists acknowledge, are more often solipsistic soul searchings or monologues on the therapist's couch than interpersonal events.)

If the rhetorical playfulness of the earlier love poems keeps calling attention to the humorless thematic nature of this criticism, the poems of *Dramatis Personae,* recognizably mature work of a matured experience of life, rather suggest its strength: here the poet who had lost the love of his life, once to the intrusions of daily little tragedies of miscommunication, then to death itself, looks much more earnestly at Pathak's own topic, now usually from the point of view of loss—"estrangement, infidelity, impending death and the missed moment due to lack of striving or . . . cowardice." The readings rarely offer much that is new, though "Too Late" as a drowning in drink may be the unfortunate exception (the speaker drinks a glass of wine to Edith's memory at the end; it is also a bit too much to speak of her as a woman with a speech impediment); yet it is helpful to think about these poems and the tale of "why the couple couldn't get along better" in the novel in *The Ring and the Book* as a mature cycle on love's frequent limits or terrible misbeddings—a prelude to the repeated themes of Browning's great successor as Victorian poet of love, Hardy.

Pathak too readily swallows whole Betty Miller's debunking Freudian read of Browning as the eminent Victorian as pathological mother's boy. But again more than Karlin, whom he cites as expert in this area, he usefully leverages biographical speculation into new possibility for criticism. His conclusion, a part greater than the whole of often mediocre readings that it summarizes, sees Browning as author on love preoccupied with monstrosities of lovers ingesting each other whole, the fantasy of total possession; or with using uninterrupted language to live out human relation in mere fantasy or self-rationalizing ways. This Freud-like, as opposed to Freudian, Browning takes those monologues of lovers' casuistry not as fanciful *jeux d'esprit*—embarrassments in the canon of dramatic monologues—but as serious cases of the typical failure that Browning's monologues demonstrate: to see beyond the necessarily false monologic vision of the self. Browning's array of miscommunicating lovers are thus not a group of pathetic cases sent off to therapy but representatives of the universal failure to connect displayed in the *comédie humaine* of Browning's great floor show of stand-up egos.

I wish I could recommend this book as highly as some of its thoughtful moments of reflection on its topic. Too often it shows not only weakness in responding to the power of imagination and form in the poems but also sloppiness in details

(Julia Wedgwood appears as Browning's new friend in the months after Elizabeth died), presentation (typos galore), inconsistencies (Browning is represented both as writing out of his conflicts with his wife and also, later, as needing to find failures in his writings to balance the perfection of his marital relation), and occasional bizarre interpretations that aren't even seen for what they are ("The Last Ride" is—not is a metaphor for—sexual intercourse; and having made this up Pathak proceeds to wonder how the woman could do such a thing!). I was bothered especially by a way of talking of love as will-to-power, presumably something males exercise over females except in aberrant cases like Lucrezia, and a readiness to expose female characters' problems as insecurity stemming from plainness (Countess Gismond, James Lee's Wife); one fears that compulsory communication may perhaps be only a concealed power offshoot of hegemonic compulsory heterosexuality. Having opened a window for seeing Browning's poems as about "communication problems" I have to close it by damning the good therapist and calling for more (critical) brain—"we have to realize that the Duke may have had problems in talking with his wife"; the end of "The Statue and the Bust" clarifies "the nature of the relationship as one built on imperfect understanding between the two principals"; we aim at understanding "the problems Andrea and Lucrezia have in communicating with each other"; "both Guido and the girl in 'The Laboratory' are victims of a breakdown in communication between the individuals involved in a relationship." Oh give me back the passionate, if doubtless miscommunicating, silences of "Love Among the Ruins," or *Last Tango in Paris*—or Caponsacchi taking in the full expressive meaning of Pompilia at the dark casement, lamp in her hand.

Index of Works by Browning

Note: For authors reviewed, see general Index, below.

"Abt Vogler," 108
Agamemnon of Aeschylus, The, 6
"Andrea del Sarto," 2, 108, 110, 173
"Apollo and the Fates," 141
Aristophanes' Apology, 9, 71, 139, 217, 224
Asolando, 62, 81, 110, 162, 171–172, 189

Balaustion's Adventure, 92–93, 164, 217
"Beatrice Signorini," 173
Bells and Pomegranates, 51, 97, 132, 195
"Bishop Blougram's Apology," 13, 44, 65, 114, 177
"Bishop Orders His Tomb at Saint Praxed's Church, The," 139, 162, 175
Blot in the 'Scutcheon, A, 6, 28, 57, 116, 151, 152, 154,
Brownings' Correspondence, The, 35, 59, 73, 77, 100, 150–151, 167, 201, 211
"By the Fire-Side," 108

"Caliban upon Setebos," 72, 94, 111, 141
"Childe Roland to the Dark Tower Came," 11, 13, 43, 86, 109–111, 137–138, 179
Christmas-Eve and Easter Day, 12, 13, 141, 197
"Classicality Applied to Tea-Dealing," 6
"Cleon," 2, 71, 108, 131
Colombe's Birthday, 6, 57, 152, 154
Complete Works of Robert Browning, The (Ohio edition), 5–10, 12–14, 31, 35, 37–39, 41, 45, 81, 97–98, 113, 149, 153–154, 156, 191, 198–200, 216
"Count Gismond," 65, 67, 227
Courtship Correspondence, The, 152
"Cristina," 17

"Dance of Death, The," 39, 73
"Death in the Desert, A," 11, 65, 218
"De Gustibus," 171
"Development," 171, 218
Dramatic Lyrics, 52, 113, 155, 195
Dramatic Romances and Lyrics, 52, 195, 197
Dramatis Personae, 135, 232
"Duty," 74

"Epilogue" [to *Fifine at the Fair*], 222
Essay on Chatterton, 6, 146
Essay on Debt, 6
Essay on Shelley, 6, 14, 22, 39, 50, 78, 88, 146
"Evelyn Hope," 17

Ferishtah's Fancies, 81
Fifine at the Fair, 19, 65, 84, 145, 163–164, 172, 217, 222
"First-Born of Egypt, The," 39, 73
"Flight of the Duchess, The," 174
"Forest Throught, A," 39
"Fra Lippo Lippi," 2, 13, 65, 206
"Fust and His Friends," 162

"Heretic's Tragedy, The," 224
"Home-Thoughts, from Abroad," 2
"How It Strikes a Contemporary," 63

"Impromptu on Hearing a Sermon, by the Rev. T. R.—Pronounced 'Heavy,'" 7
"In a Balcony," 84
"Inapphrehensiveness," 81
Incondita, 74
Inn Album, The, 67, 84, 217
"Introductory Essay": *See* Essay on Shelley
"Ivàn Ivànovitch," 104, 139
"Ixion," 224

"James Lee's Wife," 65
"Jochanan Hakkadosh," 66

INDEX OF WORKS BY BROWNING

Jocoseria, 223

"Karshish," 72, 141
King Victor and King Charles, 6, 116

"Laboratory, The," 234
"Last Poem," 5–6
"Last Ride Together, The," 17, 234
Letters, 21, 35, 100, 116, 150–151: *See also Brownings' Correspondence*
    to Count Amédée de Ripert-Monclar, 40, 78, 102, 116
    to Domett, 101
    early letters, 74, 77, 101
    early life, epistolary record, 78
    to Elizabeth Barrett, 77–78; love letters, 7, 21, 88–90, 101, 152, 224
    to Fanny Haworth, 78, 101
    to John Kenyon, 105
    to Katharine de Kay Bronson, 77, 79–80
    to Lady Louisa Ashburton, 165–166
    to W. C. Macready, 101
    to John Payne Collier, 102
    Ruskin letters, 146
    unpublished letters to James T. Fields, 21
Life of Strafford, 6
"Lines to the Memory of James Dow," 39
"Love Among the Ruins," 210, 228, 234
Luria, 6, 197, 224

Men and Women, 1, 2, 12, 13, 57, 64, 83, 97, 125, 135, 139, 212, 232
"Mesmerism," 93, 182–183
"Mr. Sludge, 'The Medium,'" 17, 63, 111, 224–225
"My Last Duchess," 2, 64, 70, 93, 141, 227

"Now," 81

"Of Pacchiarotto, and How He Worked in Distemper," 224
"One Word More," 66

"Pan and Luna," 124
Paracelsus, 2, 35–36, 38, 40–41, 43, 51, 78, 107, 109, 121, 132, 142, 155, 193
Parleyings With Certain People of Importance in Their Day, 212
Pauline, 2, 9, 11, 33, 35, 38–41, 51, 57, 62, 78, 98, 107, 109, 150, 155, 168, 193
"Pictor Ignotus," 2, 20, 108, 143
"Pied Piper of Hamelin, The," 162
Pippa Passes, 3, 10, 43, 48, 52, 116, 132, 155, 171, 183, 193
Plays of Robert Browning, the (Garland), 115, 154
Poetical Works of Robert Browning, The (Oxford), 5–7, 15, 35, 37–39, 41, 45, 73, 97, 115, 125, 154, 168, 191, 193–195, 197, 200
Poems, The (Penguin/Yale), 5–9, 11, 13–15, 31, 37–39, 41, 45, 73, 97, 99, 113, 153–154, 156, 191, 197, 201
Poems of Browning, The (Longman), 156, 192, 216
Poetical Works, The (1863), 12, 38, 63
Poetical Works, The (1865), 12, 36
Poetical Works, The (1868), 8, 9, 35, 82, 97, 199
Poetical Works, The (1888-89), 7, 9, 13, 37–38, 98, 153, 154, 191, 198
"Porphyria's Lover," 227
Prince Hohenstiel-Schwangau, Savior of Society, 10, 226
"Prologue" to *Asolando*, 172

Red Cotton Night-Cap Country; or Turf and Towers, 138, 164, 217
Return of the Druses, The, 6
Ring and the Book, The, 5, 8, 17, 45, 62, 67, 69, 77, 81, 83–84, 95, 97–100, 107, 109, 115, 118, 123–124, 130, 131, 133–135, 138, 147, 154, 156, 159–162, 175, 178, 180, 184, 188, 200, 202, 205–206, 217–219, 220–221, 227, 333

"Saul," 94, 141, 171, 218
"Sibrandus Schafnaburgensis," 79
"Sipping grog one day at sea," 6
Sordello, 2–3, 8, 9, 11–12, 28, 35–43, 47, 51, 52, 63, 78, 91, 98, 101, 102, 109, 118, 121, 128, 132, 136, 146, 183, 195, 218, 228
Soul's Tragedy, A, 6, 12, 152, 197–198, 224
"Statue and the Bust, The," 234
Strafford, 35-36, 75

"Thamuris Marching," 110
"Toccata of Galuppi's, A," 2
"Too Late," 233
Trifler, The: See Essay on Debt
"Two in the Campagna," 162

Index

Note: Index includes biographers, critics, and editors reviewed. For references to works by Browning see the separate Index of Works by Browning, above.

Abrams, Meyer, 18
Acton (Lord), 166
Aeschylus, 53, 79
Albrecht, Mary Louise, 43–44, 138
Allusions, use of, 10, 44, 72, 79
Altick, Richard, 5, 8, 97–100, 153, 199, 201
Anderson, Vincent, 111–112, 140
Armstrong Browning Library, 159, 176
Armstrong, Isobel, 175–176, 180
Arnold, Matthew, 71, 85, 136, 139, 175, 223
Ashburton, Lady Louisa, 163–166, 221
Asolo, 81
Auerbach, Nina, 69–70, 113, 126, 133, 134, 179, 221, 228
Austin, Alfred, 167, 225
Author intention, 20

Bagehot, Walter, 175
Baker, Lee, 106, 143
Bakhtin, Mikhail, 67, 132, 210
Balzac, Honoré de, 22, 64, 138
Barrett, Edward, 90, 133–134
Barrett, Elizabeth, 12, 33, 45, 63, 81, 87, 95, 106, 112-113, 125, 133, 135, 145, 164–165, 174, 182, 196, 198, 201-202, 211, 221–222, 226–228, 230
    Aurora Leigh, 113
    death of, 46–47, 63, 112
    letters, 7, 21, 77, 88–90, 101, 105, 115, 152, 224

Barrett-Browning family holdings, 31–32, 55–56
Beckett, Samuel, 20
Beinecke Library, 92, 116, 199
Belcher, Margaret, 43–44
Benjamin, Walter, 185
Benkhausen, 104
Berdoe, Edward, 111
Berens, Michael, 72, 141
Bergson, Henri, 108, 130
Bersani, Leo, 16, 130
Besier, Rudolf, 133
Bidney, Martin, 70, 138
Blalock, Susan, 67, 132
Bloom, Harold, 1, 11, 16, 46, 61, 84, 109–111, 137–139, 172, 179, 181, 187
Booth, Wayne, 119
Bornstein, George, 20, 92–93, 113, 152, 187
Brady, Ann, 94–95, 179
Brewer, William, 162
Bristow, Joseph, 204, 209–210, 213
Bronson, Katharine de Kay, 77, 80–81, 170
Brooks, Cleanth, 86
Brower, Reuben, 186
Browning, Eliabeth Barrett: *See* Barrett
Browning, Jane Smith, 28
Browning, Reuben, 29
Browning, Robert
    biography, 21–22, 30, 34, 41, 45–46, 80, 83, 97, 164, 203, 225
    childhood, 29, 161

and cousin Cyrus Mason, 27–30, 42, 152
and dark side of human nature, 23
death of, 56, 80, 127
early and middle periods, 15
and Elizabeth, 22, 54, 56, 63–64, 69, 90, 100, 103–104, 125, 133, 146, 150
foreign quotations and phrases, 40
French influence, 51, 104, 138, 148, 220
German influence, 51
and grandmother, 28
and incarnation, 140
Italian influence, 42, 46–50, 57, 61, 68, 104, 129, 138, 142, 148, 173
in London, 161
married life, 22
misogynist traditions, attack on, 94
philosophy of the imperfect, 1
philosophy of time, 108
possible love for Katharine de Kay Bronson, 80–81
and religion, 72–73
Russian influence, 104, 138, 139, 148
Shelley, influence of, 2
and son Pen, 32–34, 55, 57, 80, 81, 165, 170, 184
specialized vocabulary, 10
in Venice, 80, 171
and view of science, 107
Browning, Robert, W., 32–34, 55, 57, 80, 81, 165, 170, 184
Browning, Sarianna, 33, 57, 63, 80
Browning, William Shergold, 29
Browning Sr., Robert, 73, 145
Browning Society, The, 66, 107, 111–112, 135, 140, 169–170, 218
Buckler, William, 82–83, 85, 95, 129

Buckley, J.H. 181
Bullen, J.B., 173
Burckhardt, Jacob, 119, 173
Butts, William, 94, 147
Byron, George, Lord, 21, 79, 172, 182, 230

Caillois, 114
Calcraft, Mairi, 161, 167–168
Campbell, Dykes, 37, 153
Carlyle, Thomas, 34, 58, 68, 93, 106, 116, 118–119, 143–144
Cash, Johnny, 56
Cervantes, 43, 138
Chamberlin, The Lord, 36, 75, 153
Chappell, Debnam, 176
Charlton, James, 111
Chatman, Seymour, 184
Chaucer, 53
Chell, Samuel, 107–109, 130
Cheskin, Arnold, 66
Chesterton, G.K., 50, 128, 129, 174, 225
Cini Foundation, 169
Clough, Arthur Hugh, 65
Clubbe, John, 136
Coates, John, 43, 71, 138, 139
Coleridge, Samuel Taylor, 3
Coley, Betty, 31–32, 36, 54–56, 58, 73, 77, 150, 188
Collier, John Payne, 102
Collins, Thomas, 5, 24, 35–37, 39, 41, 115, 153, 154, 181, 216
Conrad, Joseph, 20, 23
Constance, 121
Cook, A.K., 99–100
Correspondence: *See Brownings' Correspondence* and Letters in Index of Works by Browning
Coulter, John, 104–105, 148
Crowder, Ashby Bland, 66–67, 112–113, 134, 155, 167, 168
Crowl, Susan, 167, 198
Curtis, Daniel Sargent, 80
Curtis, Ralph, 170

INDEX

da Caravaggio, Polidoro, 116
Dallas, E.S., 20
Dante, 162
Darwin, Charles, 85, 141
Davis, Kris, 123
Deconstruction, 3, 16–17, 47, 69, 83, 85, 91, 122, 123, 129–130, 132–134, 160, 180, 183, 210, 215, 218, 220
　signifiers, 3
　idea of the elusive self and, 19
　Nietzche's deconstructive formulas, 110
Dedalus, Stephen, 28
DeLaura, David, 136, 139, 146, 173
de Molina, Louis, 43
de Molinos, Miguel, 43
Denison, Edward, 103
Derrida, Jacques, 1, 3, 16, 46, 61, 123, 131, 177, 204, 228–229
DeVane, William Clyde, 11, 18, 40, 52, 103, 133, 137, 156, 186, 195, 198, 217
Dickens, Charles, 106, 169, 171
Dobell, 31, 55
Domett, Alfred, 35, 116
Donne, John, 33, 58, 120, 138, 200
Dooley, Allan C., 12, 43, 81, 97, 124, 147, 192–194, 197–198
Drew, Philip, 163, 173–174, 186–187
Dupras, Joseph A., 124, 137, 176
D'Urban, Fortia, 78

Editing, 8, 13, 79, 149
　by Browning, 36, 38, 82, 92
　of Browning letters: *See Brownings' Correspondence* in Index of Works by Browning
　of Browning poems and plays: *See* entries for individual works on Index of Works by Browning
　debate on 19th-century editing, 7, 168
Eliot, George, 169
Eliot, T.S., 20

Elliotson, John, 182
Erickson, Lee, 61–66, 69, 134–135, 136, 138, 175, 216
Euripides, 92
Everett, Glenn, 94, 141

Faulkner, William, 34, 58
Feminist issues, 69–70, 83, 115, 133–134, 138, 179, 183
Fields, James T., 21, 152
Finley, C. Stephen, 67
FitzGerald, Edward, 225
Flaubert, Gustave, 22, 138
Flower, Sarah, 73
Formalist criticism, 2–3
Forster, John, 6, 40, 75, 212
Foucault, Michel, 16, 175
Fowler, Rowena, 183
Fox, W.J., 20, 73–74
Fraistat, Neil, 113, 155
Fraser, Hilary, 177
Freud, Sigmund, 110–111, 123, 145, 206, 233
　and dreams, 85–86
Froula, Christine, 91, 136, 146, 187
Furnivall, F.J., 66

Gay, Penelope, 179
Gentileschi, Artemesia, 173
Gibson, Mary Ellis, 66, 82, 106, 117–121, 143, 144, 147, 176, 188, 204, 209, 211, 216
Gide, André, 20
Gilead, Sarah, 114
Girard, René, 84
Goethe, 68, 197
Goldfarb, Russell, 93, 137
Goslee, David, 162
Gridley, Roy, 22, 49, 50, 138, 148, 220
Griffin, Hall, 163, 202, 220
Griffith, Eric, 191

Haigwood, Laura, 125
Hair, Donald, 147
Hallam, Arthur, 20

Hardy, Thomas, 202, 203
Harvard College Library, 33
Hassett, Constance, 16, 18–19, 46–47, 51, 65, 87, 108, 131, 132, 140
Hegel, G.F., 161, 177–178
Hermeneutics, 2, 73, 141, 160, 168, 218
Herrnstein-Smith, Barbara, 1, 16, 46, 61
Hiemstra, Anne, 94
Hogg, James, 152
Hollander, John, 111
Home, Daniel, 225
Honan, Park, 15, 21, 38, 40, 147, 148, 149, 163, 166, 176, 186, 220
Horace, 79
Hošek, Chaviva, 92, 137
Hudson, Gertrude Reese, 202, 212, 228
Hudson, Ronald, 59, 73–74, 77, 79, 100, 103, 115, 150–151, 167, 211
Huisman, Rosemary, 178–179
Huizinga, 114
Humphrey, Rita, 79
Huntington Library, 12

Irvine, William, 21, 163, 164, 220
Isaiah, 13
Iser, Wolfgang, 121

Jack, Ian, 5, 11, 15, 21, 31, 35-39, 41, 73, 115, 116, 125, 152, 153, 155–156, 174, 176, 191, 216
James, Henry, 80, 83–85, 139, 170
Jameson, Anna, 36, 116, 173
Jauss, Hans Robert, 62, 121
Johnson, Samuel, 7
Jones, 108
Jonston, Arthur, 33
Joseph, Gerhard, 91
Joyce, James, 173

Karlin, Daniel, 88–90, 95, 101, 134, 146, 148, 152, 156, 173, 182–183, 191, 194, 201, 216, 220, 224–232
Karr, Jeff, 94, 141
Keats, John, 45, 70–71, 138
Kelley, Philip, 21, 31–32, 34–35, 54–56, 58–59, 73–74, 77, 79, 100, 102–103, 115, 150–151, 167, 188, 201, 211
Kendrick, Walter, 67
Kenyon, John, 73–74, 105–106, 149
King, Jr., Roma, 97–98, 100, 167, 198
Kintner, Elvan, 7, 21, 90, 134, 201, 231
Knickerbocker, 103
Knoepflmacher, U.C., 70–71, 134, 138, 179
Korg, Jacob 42–44, 47–50, 52, 61–62, 68, 93, 103, 129, 138, 148
Kristeva, Julia, 87, 132
Krynicky, Harry, 12
Kuhn, Thomas, 142

Lammers, John Hunter, 43, 72, 141
Landau, George, 94, 141
Landon, Laetitia Elizabeth, 102
Landor, W.S., 102
Langbaum, Robert, 64, 118, 135, 174
Lasner, Mark Samuels, 152
Latané Jr., David, 120–122, 125, 136, 175–176, 179, 183, 188, 216, 218
Lawton, David, 179, 182, 184
Leavis, F.R., 186
Leighton, Angela, 17
Letters: *See* Index of Works by Browning
Lewis, Scott, 201
Longman's Annotated English Poets Series, 156, 192, 216
Loucks, James, 162
Lowell, Robert, 187, 223

Macbeth, 13
Machen, Minnie, 99
Mack, Maynard, 204, 209

INDEX

Maclean, Kenneth, 125
Macready, W.C., 40, 57, 75, 101, 103, 116, 151
Maggs, 31, 55
Marks, Jeannette, 103
Martin, Loy D., 85–89, 95, 109, 119, 131, 138, 140, 143, 147, 187, 216
Martineau, Harriet, 102
Marx, Karl, 85, 142
Marxist criticism, 86, 143, 216
Mason, Cyrus, 27–30, 42, 152
Mason, Michael, 74–75
Maynard, John, 74, 120, 124, 125, 162, 175
McCusker, Jane A., 71–72, 139
McGann, Jerome, 192
Meckier, Jerome, 136
Meidl, Anneliese, 75
Melchiori, Barbara, 172
Melchiori, Giorgio, 171–173
Meredith, Michael, 57, 65, 79–82, 152, 153, 167, 199
Mermin, Dorothy, 23, 25, 65–66, 70, 136, 144, 145, 216
Michelet, Jules, 177
Mill, J.S., 35, 92, 175
Miller, Betty, 46, 110, 163, 221, 233
Miller, J. Hillis, 46, 111, 130, 181, 184
Miller, L.M., 93
Millgate, Michael, 202–203
Milnes, R.M., 102
Milton, John, 153
Minchin, H.C., 163, 165, 167, 220
Modernism, 92, 129
Monteiro, George, 93
Moore, Marianne, 49
Munich, Adrienne, 110, 113, 124, 133, 227
Myerson, George, 107, 142

New Criticism, 82, 86, 92, 114, 117, 118, 129, 131, 134, 135, 137–138, 204, 209
New Historicism, 117, 139, 210, 216, 219

Nichols, Ashton, 43, 176
Nietzsche, Friedrich, 110, 177–178
Norton, Charles Elliot, 33, 57

O'Connor, Lisa, 178
Orr, Alexandra, 163–164, 166, 202

Parker, 92, 137
Pathak, Pratul, 223, 230–234
Peckham, Morse, 8, 16, 37, 98, 143, 153
Penguin/Yale English Poets Series, 5, 31
Perosa, Sergio, 170
Petch, Simon, 159, 160, 177, 180–181
Peterson, Linda, 73, 94, 141
Peterson, William, 112, 135
Petronius, 162
Pettigrew, John, 5–7, 9–10, 13–14, 35–37, 39, 100, 115, 153, 201, 216
Poole, John, 116
Pope, Alexander, 79, 82–83
Porter, Peter, 174
Posnock, Ross, 83–85, 95, 139
Poston, Lawrence, 43, 142
Post-Modernism, 129, 133
Post-Reform Act politics, 78
Post-structuralism, 46–47
Potkay, Adam, 123, 130
Pottle, Frederick, 137
Pound, Ezra, 11, 28, 92–93, 125, 140, 144, 174
Poulet, Georges, 108, 130
Prins, Yopie, 185–186
Procter, B.W., 102
Pugin, A.W., 44
Purdy, Richard L., 116–117, 148, 151
Pynchon, Thomas, 20

Rader, Ralph, 66, 137, 147
Ranke, 118–119, 144
Raymond, Meredith, 105, 148
Raymond, William, 164
Reader-response criticism, 134
Ready, Thomas, 7

Reni, Guido, 173
Ricks, Christopher, 5, 7, 181
Ridenour, George, 113
Riede, David, 183
Riffaterre, 110
Righetti, Angelo, 172
Rio, Alexandre, 173
Ripert-Monclar, Amédée, 79, 102, 116, 148, 151
Rollins, Hyder, 21
Romanelli, Francesco, 173
Ross, Blair, 72, 141, 162
Rossetti, Dante Gabriel, 36
Rowe, M.W., 162
Rundle, Vivienne, 184–185
Ruskin, 136, 139, 146, 173
Ryals, Clyde de L., 42–43, 47, 50–52, 61, 109, 111, 119, 121, 131–132, 143, 146, 164, 176, 187, 215–221, 224, 228–229, 232
Rylands, John, 35

Sade, Marquis de, 22
Sand, George, 78, 225–226
Santayana, George, 108, 129, 130
Sargent, John Singer, 170
Satyricon, 162
Schoffman, Nachum, 203
Sexuality, 23, 70, 116, 145, 172, 206, 211, 234
   homosexuality, 85
   Oedipal conflict, 84
   and phallic symbols, 222
   private sexual life, myth of, 95
   sacrificing for art, 84
   sexual desire, 228
Shakespeare, William, 13, 53, 79, 125, 200
Shaviro, Steven, 111
Shaw, W. David, 1, 20, 46, 73, 109, 111, 130, 159–160, 181–182, 219, 228
Shelley, Percy Bysshe, 39–40, 58, 70, 79, 89, 91, 110, 131, 138–139, 146, 172, 224
   influence of, 2, 137–138
Shroyer, Richard J., 115, 154
Siegchrist, Mark, 14, 24, 138
Slinn, E. Warwick, 15–20, 46–47, 62, 65, 85, 87, 91, 108, 111, 122–123, 130–131, 159, 161, 176–177, 181–182, 184, 187, 204–206, 215, 218, 228
Smalley, Donald, 12
Smith, Margaret, 15, 31, 35–38, 73
Smith, William, 102
Smith, Elder, 7
Sotheby Browning sale, 56, 77, 150
   catalogue, 31–32, 34, 55, 116
Southwell, Samuel B., 145
Spiritualism, 13
Stendhal, 22, 138
Sterne, Laurence, 172–173
Surtees, Virginia, 165, 221
Sussman, Herbert, 206
Swinburne, Algernon Charles, 21, 34, 58, 70

Tebetts, Terrell, 72
Tennyson, Alfred, Lord 5–6, 13, 20–21, 58, 65, 71, 88, 92, 99, 102, 140, 202, 223, 225
Thatcher (Mrs.), 194
Thomas, Donald, 21–23, 148, 220
Treves, Frederick, 99
Trollope, Anthony, 169
Tucker, Jr., Herbert F., 1–3, 14, 16, 18, 42, 46–47, 51–52, 61, 85–87, 91–92, 108–109, 111, 118–119, 131–132, 136, 148, 176, 187, 215, 218, 228–229
Tulliver, Maggie, 27
Turgenev, Ivan, 104
Turner, Frank, 23, 71, 152
Turner, W. Craig, 27–30, 42
Tyler, Edward, 23, 144

Vendler, Helen, 181
Venice, 170

INDEX

Verbrugge, Rita Maria, 43
Vickers, Brian, 230
Virgil, 79
Viscusi, Robert, 68, 142, 219
Von Müller vs. Browning, 30

Waddington, Patrick, 103, 139, 148
Walker, William, 67, 134
Wanley, 162
Ward, Jonathan, 93, 140
Ward, Mazzie, 220
Wedgwood, Julia, 234
Wesley, John, 18
White, Hayden, 143
Whiting, Lilian, 202
Whyte, Lancelot, 145

Whitla, William, 164
Williams, Anne, 43
Wimsatt, William, 86
Woolford, John, 68, 135, 140, 142, 153, 156, 168, 172, 175, 179, 183, 191, 194, 216, 219, 223
Woolner, Thomas, 36
Wordsworth, Ann, 91, 111
Wordsworth, William, 33, 57, 98, 125, 220

Yates, A.W., 36, 38
Yeats, W.B., 20, 140

Zorzi, Rosella, 170–171